weekend language

PRESENTING
with **MORE STORIES** *and*
LESS POWERPOINT

ANDY CRAIG & DAVE YEWMAN

*For the leading providers of
mission-critical, best of breed, scalable,
seamless solutions that optimize, monetize
and operationalize robust businesses.*

CONTENTS

At 9:15 a.m. on a typical day of presentation coaching, we were seated in the conference room at a small but successful software company in Austin, Texas.

Our video camera was fixed on a company executive and our *venti* Americanos from Starbucks were piping hot.

In walked a member of the executive team who wanted to improve his presentation skills. Let's call him Jim. A whip-smart technologist, Jim's job was to make some pretty complex and abstract pricing software sound simple, meaningful, and, well, less boring.

After exchanging pleasantries with Jim, we turned on the video camera and said what we always say: "Shut the laptop, close PowerPoint, stand up, and give us the first ten minutes of your presentation. Just the words."

Jim dug his heels straight into the dirt. You see, he wanted to walk us through his thirty-minute PowerPoint presentation—the one he delivers around the world to customers, prospects, partners, and computer science students.

Against our better judgment and against precedent, we relented.

That thirty-minute presentation turned into forty-five minutes. With more than sixty PowerPoint slides on Jim's laptop, how could it not have gone long? Worse still, the slide tsunami drew out more than three hundred "um-ah" stammers. Three hundred! We counted with chicken scratches in our notebooks.

Driving home, we couldn't recall a single thing Jim said. But we couldn't get the three hundred "um-ahs" out of our minds. There's good reason for it.

In the 1970s, University of California at Los Angeles (UCLA) Professor Dr. Albert Mehrabian posed a question about the impact of body language and nonverbal communication: When we hear someone speak about feelings and attitudes, what do we believe most? Is it what they say, how they say it, or what we see?

The results were decisive. Ninety-three percent of what we believe has nothing to do with the words coming out of a speaker's mouth. Visuals accounted for 55 percent, vocals accounted for 38 percent, and verbal accounted for 7 percent. In Mehrabian's research people tended to believe the expression they saw, not the words spoken.

Decades later, this study is still used to illustrate the importance of factors other than words alone when trying to interpret meaning from a communicator, such as body language, facial expressions, hand gestures, and tone.

Does this mean you should mime your next stand-up presentation? Of course not. It means you need to focus even more on the words you're using.

What we've found time and again when training corporate executives for speeches is that if you get the verbal part right, the vocals and visuals of communication will follow. Said another way, the words—that smallest 7 percent in Mehrabian's study—are the trigger point, the driving force for every other aspect of a stand-up presentation.

And that's why this book focuses, first and foremost, on getting to the point, passing the "So what? Who cares?" test, and telling stories. If you master these concepts, you'll have much more performance energy, and your nonverbal and vocal communications will pop to your benefit.

So what?
Who cares?

After all, it's what happens when we're at our best as public speakers. And when is that? On the weekends.

Weekend Language

Think about it: on weekends, we're all great communicators because our default is storytelling. When we go to a party on Saturday night, we don't talk about how we optimized our calendar last Wednesday to monetize our mission-critical, best-of-breed, seamless-solution-provider business. (If you do, that's probably why you haven't been invited back to many parties).

Instead we tell a story about something that happened on Wednesday. On the weekends our speech is conversational, simple, clear, and interesting. We speak in examples, anecdotes, and analogies.

And what does our audience do with those stories? They engage. They ask questions. They laugh along. And then they walk across the room and say to their friends, neighbors, husbands, and wives, "Hey, you should hear what happened to Heidi last week. This is classic." That's the portable, sticky communication Chip and Dan Heath talked about in their bestseller, *Made to Stick.* Nothing "sticks" like a good story.

But then Monday morning hits. We step into the office and downshift into product feature lists and ten-point plans (that no one cares about) full of jargon, "high-level" terms, non-words, and nonsense.

And to punctuate this meaningless language, we beat the snot out of our audiences with 118-slide PowerPoint presentations chock-full of twelve bullet-pointed sentences per slide. Text is shrunk to ten-point fonts to make sure we can squeeze it all in. And if we're feeling particularly frisky, we might even zoom in some clip art. This approach is generally called "Show Up and Throw Up" and leads to "Death by PowerPoint"—that syndrome affecting audience members who have to sit through 118 slides without any discernible point; that speech where people walk outside and think, *"Well, that's an hour of my life that I'll never get back."*

Show Up & Throw Up *leads to* Death by PowerPoint.

Audience members typically don't remember anything from those types of presentations. But they do remember stories.

Stories are the superglue of verbal communication and a staple of weekend language. The Heaths call stories the stickiest, most memorable, most portable form of communication. It sounds simple because it is, but it's what separates meaningful, memorable communication from the pointless and forgettable PowerPoint-driven corporate blather we spew in the boardroom and during sales pitches Monday through Friday.

The approach and techniques found in this book are designed to help you replicate your existing strengths as a weekend storyteller so you can drag them into your weekday presentations to and conversations with customers, partners, employees, and investors.

In fact, we've put them to good use over the years as executive presentation and storytelling coaches at Google, adidas, Dell, Microsoft, Ingram Micro, OpenText, CA Technologies, Petrobras, Zurich Global Life Insurance, Bazaarvoice, Rackspace, Expedia, eHarmony, eBay, CBS, T-Mobile, Cook Medical, Sony, and many more.

In summary, our counsel at these top-flight companies boils down to one simple acronym:

We prescribe this approach daily to C-level executives, salespeople, marketers, developers, engineers, and human resources personnel. And while it's not rocket science, it makes them all better presenters. It did for Jim.

Ten days after his 300 "um-ah" disaster, Jim rocked our world with version two of his presentation. He had new confidence, a clear message, told stories with the necessary details, and spoke slide-free for ten minutes. But more important was what he didn't have. Those three hundred verbal tics were gone. And that's because he had focused on his words first—using weekend language to describe his weekday work.

S.T.O.R.Y. Methodology: Five Steps to Kick-Ass Presentations

1 **Suspend PowerPoint:** Oh, unclench your butt-cheeks; we're just asking you to ban it for the next thirty days, not forever. We wouldn't ask you to do it if it weren't absolutely necessary. It is. People who create their slides before developing their verbal narrative are just asking for trouble. The results are predictable: dense slides, low energy, "um-ah" verbal tics, and bored audiences. Basically, a lot of slide-heavy speeches mean forgettable presentations and a total waste of time. From this day forward, slides will be the last things you create, not the first. That'll mean fewer slides and less crap on each slide.

2 **Tell A Story:** Don Hewitt, the hard-charging founder of CBS's *60 Minutes*, once explained the secret to his show's success this way: "It's four little words: tell me a story. That's all we do, tell them a story." It sounds simple because it is. Clear, compelling, and memorable presenters tell stories. They illustrate the business value they provide through analogies, anecdotes, and examples. And a great story will deliver all the key messages you hope to get across without ever having to utter those boring, meaningless, all-about-you, mission-statement-like key messages you have written on a whiteboard back in your office or on a plaque in the lobby.

3 **Organize Your Narrative:** No offense, but your presentation's not about you. It's about your audience. You have something they want—products, services, information. But unless you communicate what's in it for them, you're dead in the water. What is your major message? If the audience spontaneously combusted after the first twenty seconds of your speech (go with it), what message would you have imparted? Does it pass the "So what? Who cares?" test? Can it overcome the built-in cynicism of your target audience (frequently coupled with the attention span of texting teens)?

4 **Remember Mehrabian:** When it comes to making an impact in a presentation, delivery can mean as much as content. The famous study by Dr. Albert Mehrabian shows that vocal and nonverbal communication can account for as much as 93 percent of message understanding in certain circumstances. Consider a presenter's vocal inflection. The strategic use of pauses. Body language. Verbal pacing. Hand gestures and eye contact. Where you, the presenter, stand in relation to the audience. Great presenters work to remove distractions while emphasizing authentic characteristics. Bad presenters ignore Mehrabian at their peril.

5 You Must Prepare: This really isn't complicated. You prepare, you get better. You don't, and you won't. You can't fake this; you can't wing it. Great presenters practice obsessively because it makes a difference. In the same way a software company might beta-test its software before taking it to market, you should beta-test your language—out loud—before using it with your internal and external audiences. But don't stop at practicing out loud; take the next step and videotape your run-through. In fact, record it and then watch it with a critical eye on your nonverbal behavior and a critical ear on the speed of your speech, the use of dramatic pauses, and the inflection in your words.

You know how some speakers at the beginning of a presentation will say something like, "If you remember nothing else, remember this" and then drop a big message on the audience? Well, here's our attempt at that in this book.

If you remember nothing else about communications from this book, remember this: good speakers tell great stories. Often they do nothing else. The best speeches are sometimes five or six stories linked by a common thread or theme.

People remember and repeat stories. In fact, if you tell more stories, use less PowerPoint slides, and practice out loud, you'll be the best speaker at your company.

So how exactly do you get to that place? Read on...

1
suspend
powerpoint

Want better presentations? Ban the use of PowerPoint over the next thirty days in your business, association, nonprofit, or school.

It'll be painful, but it will make everyone in your organization better presenters.

In his superb biography of Apple founder Steve Jobs, Walter Isaacson interviewed Jobs around forty times, often on long walks around his neighborhood. When it came to PowerPoint, Jobs was unequivocal, "I hate the way people use slide presentations instead of thinking... People who know what they're talking about don't need PowerPoint."

Without the crutch of PowerPoint, presenters will have to think through each point they're trying to make—the way they verbally illustrate it and the visuals they use to reinforce it.

If nothing else, it will serve as a needed breather for your audiences. And, boy, do they need a breather.

There are thirty million PowerPoint presentations delivered every single day around the world. A shocking abuse. What's worse is that the statistic is from a 2008 Microsoft report, and the abuse has only gotten worse since then.

Thirty million PowerPoints.

Every day.

And 90 percent of them suck.

The real issue we have with PowerPoint is not that presenters use it, but how they use it. And it's far too easy to blame Microsoft. As much as we respect the work of Yale Professor Edward Tufte, we differ on this point.

We've attended Tufte's one-day course, "Presenting Data and Information." It reinforced his reputation as a master of presenting data and analytics. But when the subject turned to PowerPoint, he went off. On Microsoft.

He placed the blame for bad PowerPoint presentations squarely on the shoulders of the Microsoft marketers who created ready-made PowerPoint templates. But, to us, that's like blaming AT&T because you drunk-dialed your ex at 3:00 a.m.

When we raised the issue during session "office hours," he shut us down, saying we were "arguing causality." We may spend the next ten years trying to decipher his point, but here's *our* point: no one—and we mean no one—puts a gun to your head and says you've got to manufacture slides with a dozen bullet-pointed sentences apiece on them. Or with spreadsheets on them. Or with the clouds, bubbles, and arrows that comprise high-tech flowcharts. Or the like.

Why do so many smart people deliver such stupid presentations?

That's lazy. That's bad communication. And that's your fault. Not Microsoft's. Yours.

Make Them Think, Not Work

Why do so many smart people deliver such stupid presentations?

Here's why: presentations in the corporate world are created backwards.

Tell us if what follows sounds familiar. You're assigned a date for a presentation to customers, partners, employees, analysts, industry peers—whomever. You probably follow one of three paths:

1 **You e-mail your marketing department** for a suitable PowerPoint presentation you can use with this group. After reviewing the slides, you think about how you're going to talk to each one.

2 **You search your company's network** for relevant decks you could smash together into a new presentation (the path our software exec, Jim, had initially taken). After the great mash-up, you think about the verbal connective tissue.

3 **You nobly set forth to create a set of slides** specifically for this particular audience. Only then do you consider what you're actually going to say.

All three paths are dead ends—roads to a presentation wasteland where audiences don't understand or care about what you're saying, and where none of what you say sticks after the fact.

That's because you prepared backwards.

And it really hurts you on presentation day, with content that isn't meaningful to the audience, presenters who aren't clear or compelling, and messages that aren't memorable when the audience walks out the door. It's not only the length and content of the presentation but also the delivery that suffers. Incoherent content is what draws out those "ums" and "ahs" and other distracting nonverbal tics.

The bad news is that the elimination of PowerPoint for thirty days will make your job of creating meaningful, memorable presentations much harder. You'll have to prepare more and prepare longer. The good news is on the day of the presentation, all that work will make it easier for your audience to understand your message.

That's a good thing. You can and should make your audience think about your point of view, what you do and how you do it, your products and services, or your approach to solving a problem. But don't ever make them work to figure out what it is you're trying to say. That's your job.

Think about how much work it takes the audience to decode the standard crappy slide deck. We often can't tell the difference between most PowerPoint slides and most Word documents. And while the PowerPoint might be easier for you to develop, it's a lot harder for your audience to understand.

At a certain point, your audience will stop working at it. Audiences today have the attention span of texting fifteen-year-olds so when you've prepped backward and you're not ready, your audience checks out.

That's when the prospect in the back row pulls out her iPhone and checks her e-mail. And it's all because you took the easy path, the lazy path, the wrong path.

Cringeworthy Abuses

1 Too much text
2 Uninspiring graphics
3 Ummmmm

The people at SlideRocket, ClearSlide's competing product to Microsoft PowerPoint, polled a thousand businesspeople in 2011. Thirty-two percent of respondents said they had fallen asleep in a recent presentation. According to the SlideRocket blog post, "too much text and uninspiring graphics topped the list" of cringeworthy abuses.

To avoid sitting through another PowerPoint presentation, they were willing to give up a wide variety of activities:

24%
WOULD GIVE
UP SEX
THAT EVENING

21%
SAID THEY'D
RATHER DO
THEIR TAXES

20%
WOULD PREFER
A VISIT TO THE
DENTIST

18%
WOULD VOLUNTEER
TO WORK ON
SATURDAY INSTEAD

24% of respondents said they would give up sex that evening! *(Does that tell you how much people hate bad PowerPoint presentations?)*

This is our audience. Your audience. And they're screaming for something different, so much so that they're willing to remain celibate and do their taxes on a weekend while having a root canal. Wow.

A Picture Is Worth a Thousand Words. Even in 6:40.

Presenters at the Technology, Entertainment, Design conference, or TED, typically get this right. They recognize that they, not the PowerPoint, are the presentation. They are comfortable with being in the spotlight on center stage. Most understand that a simple prop—like a human brain or a wheelbarrow full of sugar —is a much more engaging visual than a slide.

You are the presentation, not your slides.

But when they do employ PowerPoint or Apple's Keynote, they typically use pictures, a statistic, or one word to illustrate their verbal narratives. They keep it simple. Garr Reynolds, who writes a terrific blog we love, *Presentation Zen* (presentationzen.com), offers one practical application: use the three-second rule.

Good presentation designers try to keep their visuals so simple that the audience can absorb them in three seconds and then turn their attention back to the presenter for context or further meaning.

It reinforces the point we just made: you are the presentation, not your slides.

This evolution from slideware overload to imagery won't be easy. You can either take baby steps, or you can rip the Band-Aid right off.

After all, desperate times call for desperate measures. In this day of "Death by PowerPoint," it's time for something radical, something almost crazy, something that goes completely against the grain of corporate presentations: PechaKucha (pecha-kucha.org).

It's a Japanese term that means "chitchat" or "chatter." But what it could mean for your organization is a much more efficient use of your time.

It's not about the speaker. It's about the audience.

In February 2003, Astrid Klein and Mark Dytham, two architects based in Tokyo, had had enough of long-assed presentations with tons of text-littered slides, so they set out to create a new approach to presentations. What they dreamed up was sheer brilliance. PechaKucha is a technique that forces speakers to present in quick, efficient bursts of just six minutes and forty seconds.

The idea is helped by a feature in Microsoft's PowerPoint software that allows each slide to automatically advance—in PechaKucha's case, after twenty seconds. So each speaker at a PechaKucha event gets twenty slides, and each slide advances after twenty seconds on screen. So the total presentation time for a speaker is 6:40. And you're done.

Genius.

Now think about that approach for a minute. Think about all those seemingly endless corporate presentations you've endured over the years. Think about the bad slides. Think about the boring content. Now think about the wasted time and cost.

You don't need PowerPoint to deliver an effective presentation.

Dave Paradi, coauthor of *Guide to PowerPoint*, did. He estimated that those thirty million PowerPoint presentations made each day could add up to $252 million— or the estimated worth of 2008 and 2012 US Republican presidential hopeful Mitt Romney:

> *"If we assume some relatively conservative meeting parameters of four people per presentation, a half-hour presentation on average and the wasted time due to a poor presentation is one-quarter of the presentation time, we arrive at a waste of fifteen million person-hours per day. At an average salary of $35,000 per year for those attending the meeting, the cost of that wasted time is a staggering $252 million and change each day."*

All that money. All that time. All those slides.

What if you took the PechaKucha approach instead? Using that approach, twelve executives would all be done speaking in less than two hours.

The audiences would love it. The speakers might hate it (they'd feel like they needed more time; they'd feel "naked" without eighty-seven slides; they'd be intimidated).

But it's not about the speakers. It's about the audience.

PechaKucha has been described as "the love child of PowerPoint and Twitter," and what it takes aim at is the overall bloat, the intellectual laziness, the awful slides, and the lack of preparation that are all so rampant in the corporate world.

It's radical, almost crazy, and completely against the status quo of atypical corporate presentations.

But it could just be the best thing to ever happen to your organization's meeting and speaking culture.

The reality is you don't need PowerPoint to deliver an effective presentation. (That thud you just heard was a Microsoft PowerPoint product manager's jaw hitting the ground outside of Seattle.)

Really, it's completely legal to deliver a presentation without using PowerPoint. Honest, we looked it up. (We didn't look it up).

Bill Gates was one of the worst presenters in the corporate world for over thirty years. You know it. I know it. Chances are good that even he knew it.

It's no wonder. Just look at a few snapshots of the kind of PowerPoint slides he tried to present. Heck, even Presidents Clinton and Reagan—both legends for giving powerful, compelling speeches—would lose energy, authenticity, and interest trying to present slides like those.

But did you see Gates present at TED in February 2009? Among other things, he described how the costs associated with treating malaria crush the economies in the cities and countries where the disease is an epidemic. That is, of course, on top of the human toll.

To illustrate this point, he released a jarful of real, live mosquitos six minutes into his presentation. Mosquitos, of course, are well known for spreading malaria.

The audience gasped, and then laughed nervously. It's rumored that eBay founder Pierre Omidyar was so jarred by the stunt that he stood up from his front-row seat and walked to the back of the room. His Tweet validates the rumor:

@pierre
Pierre Omidyar

That's it, I'm not sitting up front anymore. #TED

4 Feb 09 via txt

Then, after a slight pause and with a big cheesy smile, Gates reassured his audience that those mosquitos were not infected. He had them—the audience, not the mosquitos—in the palm of his hand. It was more energy and enthusiasm than most audiences had ever seen from the Microsoft founder.

It would have been negligent—and possibly criminal—to deliver the point about malaria, mosquitos, and the need for vaccines with a PowerPoint full of bullets, bar charts, and technical bubbles. Gates did use PowerPoint slides that day, but the slide accompanying his mosquito stunt was a huge color photo of a mosquito landing on someone's arm. He adhered to Garr Reynolds' three-second rule.

In stark contrast to Gates, Glenn Bennett, the chief operating officer of adidas, is a terrific speaker. One day in 2004 we sat in a room with Glenn, who was getting ready to fly to China for one of his internal "town hall meetings" with his global operations team.

"I don't want to just show up with slides and do the 'blah, blah, blah,'" Glenn said, sitting at one end of a giant conference table. "That's what we always do, and people tune it out."

The content Glenn was preparing was essentially a call to action, a message to his team that the next six months were going to be tough sledding, and he needed them to knuckle down and execute.

But before that, Glenn needed to do his homework.

After some thought and some discussion, we filled several big Post-it Notes with potential talking points, and Glenn started to talk out a rough draft of his speech. We videotaped his ramblings, and a few minutes into his third or fourth time on camera, we found a simple message—and quickly figured out a simple delivery methodology.

Glenn was going to nix slides completely. Instead he'd have a flip chart in the room. When he opened his speech, he would walk up to the flip chart, draw a big circle in the middle, and write one or two words inside it—his major messages.

Then he'd walk into the audience—putting himself physically close to them in order to deliver the call to action. He needed them to be focused; he needed to look them in the eyes from close up—not from a podium on a stage—and he needed to hammer home a few key messages.

Ban projectors and laptops from staff meetings.

But imagine a few weeks after the speech. How would the audience members remember exactly what Glenn said? Would they know what to do, specifically what actions to take? Even rousing calls to action can be somewhat abstract (like the football coach who yells, "I want you to be the best you can be. All right, let's go!")

Abstraction is the enemy in communications. Great communicators break things down so there is absolutely no ambiguity about what they want the audience to do, think, or feel. So Glenn, who's almost obsessive about preparation and practice, is at the town hall meeting being held in China's Guangdong Province just north of Hong Kong. He's got the flip chart thing going and his speech is roughly thirty-five minutes old. Then he stops.

"Reach under your chairs," he told the operations team assembled in the room, "there's an envelope taped to the bottom. Open it."

You can imagine dozens of audience members ripping open envelopes. In the envelopes were laminated books containing specific targets, margins, and metrics for the team—all stuff that global operations geeks just love.

"These are your metrics," Glenn told the audience members. "And I'm coming back here in six months. We're going to sit in this room, and I'm going to hold each of you accountable for the things in this book."

Now could you do that? Could you ditch PowerPoint slides? Reduce your message so it fits inside a few circles drawn on a flip chart? Use something unexpected like the book taped under the chairs to hammer home the details?

Of course you could. You just need to do your homework.

YOUR HOMEWORK

Outlaw PowerPoint for thirty days. Company-wide. Oh, unclench your butt cheeks; we're not talking forever, just thirty days.

Force your employees to develop their narratives first. Turn that approach into muscle memory. Then, and only then, reintroduce PowerPoint as a "potential" tool they can use to visually illustrate their major messages.

How do you do that, exactly? Easy, you ban projectors and laptops from meetings; you encourage your staffers to come to meetings prepared to just speak rather than rely on a crutch called PowerPoint; you remove the norm that says a presenter has to have forty-eight slides to be considered properly prepared to speak.

If you have to present during this time, you figure out your key point and you build a speech around that single word or goal or phrase. You focus on your "talk track" and think specifically about what you want your audience to do after they finish listening to your presentation.

And you outlaw PowerPoint for thirty days. You can do it. **So that's your homework.**

Day 31: Three Bonus PowerPoint Tips

You've read this far and you deserve a reward. Here are three specific tips to employ if you decide to use PowerPoint slides after your thirty-day embargo:

1 **Use the B key.** Launch PowerPoint or Keynote and go into the presentation mode—where the slide fills your entire screen and that of the projector to which you're connected. Now hit the B key. What happened? Your screen went blank, didn't it? Now hit the B key again and it'll come back. Cool, huh?

It's amazing how many people aren't familiar with this one simple trick. If you're speaking and someone asks a question or you want to go off topic for a bit, just tap the B key, blank the screen, deal with the question or the topic, then tap the B key again and you're back in your flow.

2 **Hide busy slides.** It's often the case that your slide deck is also your handout for people who didn't attend your presentation—or perhaps it's going to be e-mailed to your entire company so there's a legitimate reason to have slides containing lots of information. Go into the "slide sorter" view in your slide deck and find a busy, detailed slide. Now right click with your computer's mouse. You'll see an option to "Hide Slide." Click on that and when you're in presentation mode the slide will not appear.

What this means is that you can include text-heavy slides in your deck but you don't have to use them when speaking. You can think of this as a way to build twenty good, clean, simple slides for presenting, and forty busy, detailed slides that are basically an appendix—necessary information but the kind of data dump that would put an audience to sleep in seconds.

3 **Use presenter mode.** Newer versions of PowerPoint and Keynote enable you to project one slide to an audience but also have a "cheat sheet" of sorts on your desktop. For example, take a peek at the following slide.

The big slide is the one that shows up on the projection screen—what the audience sees. The entirety is what you see on your computer. With just a quick glance at your laptop on the conference room table you can see the next slide and your core message for the slide currently projected, plus you have a clock so you can see how much time you have left.

These tips are incredibly useful and, again, you'd be amazed at how many people don't take advantage of them when presenting with slides.

2
tell a story

Comedian Dennis Miller once ranted, "As it turns out, adult life is just tall grade school."

Miller was highlighting our ageless tendencies toward immaturity, but we think it's a poetic verse that every corporate executive should have needlepointed on their office rugs before they're ever allowed to present again. Because when it comes to clear, compelling, and memorable presentations, sales pitches, technology demonstrations, or employee meetings, stories make all the difference.

If you think storytelling sounds too simplistic for the corporate world—that it's child's play—think again. Storytelling works, especially at work. And it's catching on with startups and grown-up companies all around the world. That was the case with one enormous technology company based just outside Seattle.

Early in 2007 the company recognized the need to pump up its storytelling capabilities across its ninety-thousand-person business. Since then, more than forty-five hundred of its marketers, salespeople, developers, and executives from around the world have taken a storytelling workshop based on the bestseller *Made to Stick*.

As one learning and development leader likes to say,

> *"Storytelling is a muscle. And it's one that we don't exercise nearly enough."*

It's important for all presenters to exercise that muscle more often because storytelling brings clarity to your company vision, your products and services, and your reason for being. That clarity is the first step of commerce.

And that's nothing to kid about.

Stories Deliver Messages

During one storytelling workshop, a software manager in the back of a large meeting room raised his hand. His question: "Why do we speak like idiots?"

After the laughter subsided, we told him what we tell everyone, "Not sure, but we appreciate you providing us with job security."

Truth is, your audience hates key message-speak.

Contemporary communication is filled with jargon, words that don't exist in any dictionary, and a common, almost tribal urge to try to communicate in a form of corporate Klingon. You know, that abstract, esoteric, and indecipherable language we think sounds smart and "high-level" but is really only understood by other Klingons.

It's the kind of nonsense most companies have written in their key message documents that get e-mailed to all employees for use in customer meetings, public presentations, and media interviews. And it makes everyone in the boardroom or the brainstorm feel really good.

The ability to tell a story fades away in business settings.

Problem is, it leaves your audience nauseated.

No one outside of your four walls cares about "leading providers of end-to-end, mission-critical, seamless, scalable solutions that optimize stuff."

Your audience cares about themselves. What do they get by working with you? How will it help their lives and businesses? Has anyone else benefited from what you do or how you do it?

The best way to answer these questions is through storytelling. And a great story will deliver all those key messages you want without sounding like key message-speak.

For example, in 2003, we ran a storytelling workshop for a Portland, Oregon-based janitorial services company.

It made liquid cleaners that schools, hospitals, and bus depots use to wash their floors and countertops. A team of about two hundred executives and salespeople spent hours talking about the company's "sustainable earth" products and sustainability emphasis in research and development. We couldn't have cared less. Frankly, it didn't mean anything to us. This was 2003, and sustainability wasn't a household word. Even today, we would have no idea how its "sustainability" efforts were any different from GE's or Dell's or one of its chief competitors because every company talks in glowing terms about its sustainability program.

(Note to self: If you're in a commodity industry and you're using commodity language such as "sustainability," then what makes you any different from anyone else? If that difference isn't abundantly clear to customers, then you are sentencing your salespeople to price-based competition.)

So we ran a contest in the room—giving each table of ten a half hour to come up with the single best story that illustrated the environmental safety and quality of its cleaning products.

The spokesperson for the second-to-last table said this:

> *"Before we take a new cleaning product to market, we take a goldfish and drop it in a bucket of that product. If the goldfish swims, we know those chemicals are safe enough to seep into the earth. In fact, you could drink a glass of it and be just fine. We've done it before.*
>
> *"However, if the goldfish dies, we know we've got a massive quality control issue on our hands, and we have to go back to the drawing board. That's what sustainability means to us."*

Shazam!

Now that's a concrete, vivid, and compelling illustration of an incredibly abstract concept such as sustainability. That's a memorable story. We literally don't remember anything else that was said that day, but we'll never forget the goldfish story.

And think of the visual you could use to support this story. It would be a mistake to use anything other than a goldfish in a fish bowl—or a picture of that—to visually illustrate it.

Good communication isn't rocket science. We're all natural storytellers but that ability often fades away when we are in business settings.

During one recent presentation coaching session at a web hosting and cloud services company, a skeptic challenged his colleague's attempt at storytelling for an internal audience.

> *"I totally see how this would work for external audiences. But I think it'd be awkward if you told a story like that at an internal meeting." Before we could chime in, two others jumped to the presenter's defense. "I disagree. It would really stand out," they countered. "It would be so different from the way we normally do it that it would be refreshing and more memorable."*

That's the point. As the Heaths tell us in *Made to Stick*, stories are passed down from generation to generation and are the oldest and stickiest forms of communication. Stories are the fundamental building blocks of effective communication.

We frankly can't understand why you wouldn't search for an appropriate story to include in your next presentation. And your next. And your next.

You'll have plenty of options when you do.

Examples

Examples are the lingua franca of presentations. They illustrate broad business strategies. Use them early and use them often.

When it comes to making people care, you have to get granular. It's not enough to say your company has saved its customers millions of dollars, even though it may be true. But if you say your company saved Acme Inc. $18 million in four years due entirely to your product, you will have their attention. When you have an audience whose attention span is measured in nanoseconds, you've got to be as concrete as possible.

Back in 2006, web content management company Vignette (now part of OpenText) was preparing for a road show. The once high-flying company was now trying to rebuild its post-bubble business and reputation. During prep sessions for customer, partner, media, and analyst presentations, company executives told us all about the scalability of its solutions.

Yawn.

Every software provider claims to have scalable software. You need to illustrate that scalability to rise above the messaging sameness, build credibility, and strike a connection with companies that might need scalability (if they can first figure out what the hell it means).

We threw down the challenge: "What's the best example of your software's scalability? Where was it? For whom? When was it? How scalable? Prove it."

One executive got medieval (a little *Pulp Fiction* homage for fans). Leo Brunnick, senior vice president of products and marketing, dispatched two marketers to check the case studies and call salespeople, account managers, and even customers. After weeks of research and hours of practice, Leo rocked this story:

"NASA is one of our clients that we've been working with for years. NASA had an opportunity to host the single largest online event in world history. They sent the 'Deep Impact Probe' into space to intentionally collide with a comet. They wanted to explore the comet and do some research. That's pretty cool stuff. And NASA said, 'Let's invite the world to come and watch.'

"You see, NASA has a business model that requires the support of the public. So by getting the support of the public, they get more funding. It's critical for them to inspire the public. So they said, 'World, come watch this project,' and the world came. On the morning of July 4, 2005, a quarter of a billion people simultaneously watched online while this NASA Deep Impact Probe collided with the comet. An absolutely huge event. It actually exceeded the largest online event before it, which was the inaugural Victoria's Secret fashion show, which a lot of people remember because it crashed the servers and took down the Internet while it was trying to go on.

"This was an even larger event that NASA was trying to serve. That many people. And the content: one billion images, one billion pages served up to the public during the event. And it didn't go down. You can just imagine if NASA were to invite the world to come watch, and out in the living room there's Grandpa with a little kid on his knee saying, 'Look, you're about to see something that no one's ever seen before,' and he gets a '404. Page Not Found' error because the site can't handle that traffic. That wouldn't be good for NASA. So it's at that moment when the business absolutely, fundamentally has to depend on the scale of our solutions."

He told that story in one minute thirty-six seconds. And while it's a nice short story, he didn't sacrifice the details, and it illustrates the heck out of that word "scalability."

Look at all we know about this project. All those nitty-gritty details. It's really tough to find the "gory" details, but don't settle for less. Don't settle for the abstract. Because for a message to be memorable, it needs concrete details.

Would you remember the company DriveSavers if we just told you that they can recover data from hard drives pretty well? Probably not. But what if we told you they pulled all the data off a PC that'd been in a 1,700-degree fire? Or that they'd saved twelve Simpsons' episodes—and probably producer Bill Oakley's job— by finding them on a crashed hard drive? Story details matter a great deal. Those details and that color also add credibility to your messages.

Concrete details add color and credibility to your messages.

Anecdotes

These anecdotes might be the most underused form of communication in corporate presentations—yet the most available. You talk to more customers, partners, developers, and market watchers in one week than we can fathom.

What did one of them say? Where were you? What happened? Who were the characters? Make us feel like we were there.

Anecdotes get a bad rap. Corporate executives tend to view them as irrelevant or childish. Same with stories, metaphors, and analogies—all the stuff of communications excellence. They toss them away and substitute corporate-speak full of jargon and acronyms.

It makes us crazy because anecdotes really work. Consider the following political example.

It was the last week of the 2012 US presidential campaign. In his closing pitch to voters—and a plea to continue working and calling to get out the vote on election day—President Barack Obama took an Iowa audience back in time to the 2007-2008 Democratic primary contest for the party nomination:

"It was early in the...primaries; we were still way down in the polls. And at the time I was still competing in South Carolina. It was one of the early primary states, and I really wanted the endorsement of the state representative down there. I'd met her at some function where nobody knew me, nobody could pronounce my name. They're wondering, 'What's he thinking?' So I asked her for an endorsement, and she said, 'I tell you what, Obama. I will give you my endorsement if you come to my hometown of Greenwood, South Carolina.' And I think I had a little bit of wine during dinner because right away I said, 'OK.' So it's about a month later, and I'm traveling back to South Carolina. We flew in late at night; we'd been campaigning nonstop. We land in South Carolina, at around midnight. We get to the hotel about one o'clock in the morning, and I am wiped out. I am exhausted. I'm dragging my bags to my room...and just as I'm about to walk into my room, one of my staff taps me on the shoulder and says, 'Excuse me, Senator. We're going to have to wake up and be on the road at 6:30 in the morning.' And I said, 'What?! Why?'

*Anecdotes
really work.*

'Well you made this promise to go to Greenwood, and it's several hours away.' I try to keep my promises so a few hours later I wake up, and I'm feeling terrible. I think a cold is coming on, and I open up the curtains to get some light to wake me up but it's pouring down rain...terrible storm. And I take a shower, get some coffee, and I open up the newspaper and there's a bad story about me in the New York Times. I was much more sensitive at that time to bad stories...I've become accustomed to these now. And finally I get dressed. I go downstairs. I'm walking out to the car, and my umbrella blows open, and I'm soaked. So by the time I'm in the car, I'm wet, and I'm mad, and I'm still kind of sleepy. It turns out that Greenwood is several hours away from everyplace else. So we drive, and we drive, and we drive. Finally we get to Greenwood...although you don't know you're in Greenwood right away because there are not a lot

*of tall buildings around. We pull up to a small field house.
And I walk in, I look around, and I don't hear a lot going on.
The state representative said she was going to organize a little
meeting for us, and we walk in and there were about twenty
people there. They're all kind of wet too, and they don't look
very excited to see me. But I'm running for president, and I
do what I'm supposed to do. I'm shaking hands, and saying,
'How do you do? Nice to meet you.'*

*'I'm making my way around the room and suddenly I hear this
voice cry out behind me, 'Fired up?' And I'm startled. I don't
know what's going on. But everybody in the room—this is a
small room—they act like this is normal. And when the voice
says, 'Fired up?' they say, 'Ready to go!' And so once again I
hear the voice, 'Fired up?' They say, 'Fired up!' It says, 'Ready
to go?' They say, 'Ready to go!'*

*'I look around. I turn behind me, and there's this small woman.
She's about sixty years old. It looks like she just came from
church...she's got a big church hat. And she's looking at me...
kind of peering at me. And she's grinning, smiling, looking
happy. Turns out she's a city councilwoman from Greenwood
who also moonlights as a private detective. I'm not making
this up; this is true. And it turns out she's famous throughout
the area. When she goes to football games, and when she goes
to rallies and goes to public events throughout the area, she
does this chant of hers. She does it wherever she goes. So for
the next few minutes she just keeps on saying it, 'Fired up?
Ready to go?' And I'm thinking...this woman is showing me
up. This is my meeting. I'm running for president, and she's
dominating the room. I look at my staff, and they just shrug
their shoulders. They don't know what to do. This goes on for
a few minutes.'*

*'Here's the thing, Iowa: after a few minutes, I'm feeling kind of
fired up. I'm feeling like I'm ready to go. So I start joining in
the chant; my staff starts joining in the chant. Suddenly I feel
pretty good. And we go on to talk about the lives of the people*

in the room...their families and their struggles, their hopes for their kids and grandkids. We drive out, and it's still raining but it doesn't seem so bad. For the rest of day, even after we left Greenwood, even though we still weren't getting any big crowds anyplace, even though people still couldn't pronounce my name, I felt good. And I'd see my staff, and I'd say, 'Are you fired up?' They'd say, 'We're fired up!' I'd say, 'Are you ready to go?' They'd say, 'We're ready to go.' We brought that to Iowa, and during rallies this became a chant. The woman, her name is Edith Childs, she became a celebrity. She was written up in the Wall Street Journal, and folks did news stories on her. This became one of the anthems of our campaign back in 2008.

'Now here's the end of the story. We knew we were coming back to Des Moines for the last campaign rally I'll ever do for me. We were getting kind of sentimental, so we called up Edith Childs. 'Why don't you come on up. We'll fly you up from South Carolina, and you can do this chant...one more time for good old sake.' It's like getting the band back together again. And you know what Edith said? She said, 'I'd love to see you, but I think we can still win North Carolina, so I'm taking a crew into North Carolina to knock on doors on election day. I don't have time just to be talking about it; I've got to knock on some doors. I've got to turn out the vote. I'm still fired up, but I've got work to do.'

'And that shows you what one voice can do. One voice can change a room. And if it can change a room, it can change a city. And if it can change a city, it can change a state. And if it can change a state, it can change a nation. And if it can change a nation, it can change the world. And Iowa, in 2008, your voice changed the world. And Edith Childs asked me to ask you if you're willing to stand with me tomorrow? If you're willing to take your friends and your neighbors and your coworkers to the polls tomorrow? If you're willing to make sure we finish what we started, she's pretty sure we'll win Iowa. She's pretty sure we'll win this election. She had just one question for you and that is: 'Are you fired up?!'"

Companies overlook the power of these kinds of anecdotes. For example, one of our clients makes athletic apparel that's really light—featherweight shoes, shorts, and shirts. As part of product testing, the company brings in small groups of athletes to get feedback.

Now a lot of companies use focus groups and most of them don't think about the compelling anecdotes that such groups can yield. When a high school basketball team came to look at the company's latest gear, one sixteen-year-old sophomore walked over to the table where shorts were laid out. He picked them up and was amazed by how light they were (roughly four ounces). He turned to the company sales rep and said, "These are the shit. Where do I buy these?"

Now the company could have talked forever about its manufacturing process and its choice of materials and stitching. But that single comment from a sixteen-year-old speaks volumes about how light its products are for playing hoops.

It's just one anecdote. But it works for us.

Analogies

We simply love analogies or metaphors. They lead to real light bulb moments of clarity and understanding. Done right, they give you a colorful, quotable, Tweetable, memorable nutshell description of your company, product, or service. Just ask Ginger Bunte, former CFO of Golfsmith.

Analogies are universal.

In 2003, Golfsmith was a company in transition. After a great deal of success in its first thirty-six years, a new management team set out on an aggressive plan to shift the company's identity and focus—internally and externally—from a golf club components cataloguer to a "leading multichannel golf retailer."

Like most companies, Golfsmith's clear and compelling narrative was there but buried in, and spread out among, the conversations of numerous company executives. This was a pretty scary realization for a company that was suddenly answering to bondholders and the SEC as a public debt company. So, we put the CEO, CFO, and fourteen other executives on camera to listen to their business goals and strategy, dig beneath the jargon (e.g., "multichannel retailer"), and uncover the colorful and compelling language that best described the new Golfsmith. The result was something special:

> *"We're a candy store for golfers. And we're expanding aggressively across the US with the goal of building The Home Depot, Best Buy, or Barnes & Noble of the $6 billion golf retail industry.*

> *"Our forty-six activity-based stores offer twenty-six million golfers the same kind of experience that Barnes & Noble has for book shoppers or Starbucks has for coffee drinkers. Golfsmith's stores are playgrounds where customers can take golf lessons from a PGA pro...learn to build their own golf clubs from scratch...get custom fitted with the latest technology...or use the newest club to launch monster drives on the eighteenth hole of Pebble Beach in our computerized golf simulators.*

> *"That's probably why our average customer spends forty-five minutes to an hour per visit in our stores, and why we sell more Callaway and Cleveland golf products than any retailer."*

The simple process resulted in a killer message for customers, investors, employees, business partners, and reporters. For example, here's how a few articles described the company after the new language had been implemented:

You know it's sticky messaging when it's repeated
almost verbatim by reporters. And "candy store for
golfers" became the opening sentence of the company's
first annual report.

We've been delivering storytelling workshops
based on Chip and Dan Heath's *Made to Stick* book for
several years. The Heaths call analogies "high-concept
pitches." What that means is taking something people
already know and essentially playing it forward. For
example, *"Die Hard* on a bus" is how the movie *Speed*
was pitched to Hollywood executives.

We were delivering a *Made to Stick* workshop at a
technology company's office in New Delhi a few years
back. Before the session, we'd been concerned that a lot
of our stories and information were American, and we
wondered aloud if they would translate while we were
several thousand miles away.

During the workshop we put "*Die Hard* on a bus" up on our slides and asked, "What movie is that?" Almost everyone in the room said *Speed* and smiled.

Turns out analogies are universal in scope.

The Backstory

Open any magazine or watch any news program on television and you're likely to see a backstory, usually something that helps develop the main story, like the Olympic skater who grew up poor but is poised to win gold. We love the stories behind the stories, but people don't tell them. Here are two old examples and one new one:

In 1856 a new dean named Henry Liddell arrived at Christ Church College at Oxford University in England. Liddell and his wife, Lorina, had three young daughters, and the family befriended a tall, gangly, twenty-four-year-old mathematics professor named Charles Dodgson.

When he was a small child, Dodgson caught a fever that left him deaf in one ear. At seventeen he suffered from whooping cough, which led to a weak chest, and he also stammered badly. After Liddell's arrival, Dodgson became especially close to the three girls, Edith, Lorina Charlotte, and Alice, and used to take them on rowing trips along the River Thames near Oxford.

It was on one of those rowboat trips on July 4, 1862, that Dodgson invented a story to tell the girls. In his diary, he remembered the day had a "cloudless blue above, the watery mirror below, the boat drifting idly on its way, the tinkle of the drops that fell from the oars..." After Dodgson told the story, one of the girls, Alice, begged him to write it down for her. After some delay, Dodgson eventually put pen to paper, and he gave a handwritten, illustrated book to Alice in November 1864.

The story was called "Alice's Adventures in

Wonderland," and Dodgson is far better known by his pen name, Lewis Carroll. The book became one of the most popular children's books in the world. Dodgson became so popular, in fact, that after reading Alice in Wonderland, Queen Victoria suggested that he dedicate his next book to her, which he did.

And that's the backstory of "Alice's Adventures in Wonderland."

Around the same time Charles Dodgson was writing stories for Alice and her sisters, a Swedish inventor was reading his own obituary in a French newspaper. And it wasn't a very kind obituary, saying, in part, *"Le marchand de la mort est mort"* ("The merchant of death is dead"). It also said, "Dr. Alfred Nobel, who became rich by finding ways to kill more people faster than ever before, died yesterday."

Now Nobel, the inventor of dynamite, was still very much alive. His brother, Ludvig, had died, and the newspaper had made a horrible mistake. So not only had he lost a brother, he now knew how he would be remembered. The premature obituary apparently had a huge impact on Nobel. And on November 27, 1895, Nobel in his last will and testament assigned the bulk of his considerable fortune to establishing five Nobel Prizes to be awarded annually in physics, chemistry, medicine, literature, and peace (economics was added in 1969). When Nobel did die, in 1896, he left a fortune of 33 million krona—or around $9 million—to endow the Nobel prizes.

Backstories are the color commentators of stories.

When Nobel invented dynamite, he naively thought it would be a force for peace, saying, "On the day that two army corps can mutually annihilate each other in a second, all civilized nations will surely recoil with horror and disband their troops." Nobel died around twenty years before World War I, which is probably just as well when you think about it.

And that's the backstory of the Nobel Prize.

People love the stories behind the stories.

Dodgson's ailments led to a classic children's story; Nobel almost choking on his espresso while reading his obituary led to the Nobel Prizes. Backstories add context and understanding. They're the color commentators of stories. They can be powerful and engaging—in literature and business.

One fall afternoon in Seattle, we were working with a senior executive at an enormous technology company; let's call him Tom. He's a great guy and a fabulous speaker, but it was early in the presentation coaching process, and Tom was busy and a bit distracted.

We were preparing to announce one of the company's brand-new products, a huge touch screen computer— something dozens of people can touch simultaneously to share photos or play games, and now something that several years later is the brains of numerous tablet computers.

"What is this?" we asked Tom gesturing to the coffee-table sized product sitting in front of him.

"It's a rich, seamless new computing paradigm," Tom replied on camera.

So do you understand what the product is from that explanation? Are you rushing out to plunk down dollars to buy one? A paradigm shift! Wow.

No, us neither.

But the throwaway backstory about the product was there all along; it was just hidden beneath all that corporate nonsense.

Turns out the product was developed by a couple of company engineers in one of their garages back in 2001. The engineers worked on other hardware during the day, but on evenings and weekends they tinkered with what became the huge touch screen.

The company has almost ninety thousand employees in more than 160 countries; it's the furthest thing from a startup, but the product was quite literally developed in a garage by two engineers who already had day jobs.

It gets even better. When it was time to show an early prototype to the CEO, the engineers drove to a nearby IKEA store and bought a wooden coffee table. Using a circular saw they cut a hole in the top of the table and built the first prototype by duct-taping a flat panel display to the coffee table, positioning five cameras underneath the display, and then, very cautiously, they drove the entire contraption to the CEO's office.

Personal stories are another way to light a torch under your audience.

The CEO, who's not easily impressed, loved the prototype and gave the two engineers $2 million to build a real prototype.

Now that's a true story. And yet a whip-smart guy like Tom was describing the product as a "rich, seamless new computing paradigm."

We know what you're thinking: a "new computing paradigm" is exactly what it is; it's a computer you can use without a mouse or keyboard. And until recently that was pretty unusual.

No argument from us regarding what it is, but a *big* argument, a huge angry screed, an impassioned rant from us about how we frame the touch screen computer story. It's not useful to use such dry, dispassionate, nonsensical language to describe something that's actually pretty cool. Especially with such a vivid, concrete, kick-ass story sitting right in front of you.

If you have a backstory, bring it to the forefront of your next presentation because people love the stories behind the stories—even those about "rich, seamless new computing paradigms."

Personal Stories

In 1997, poet and novelist George Dawes Green launched The Moth (themoth.org) from the living room of his New York apartment. The goal was to promote "the art and craft of storytelling" in our everyday lives. Years later, thousands of storytellers have shared their dramatic and emotional personal tales with audiences in cafes and clubs. As The Moth says, "audiences are drawn to stories like a moth to a flame."

Indeed, personal stories are another way to light a torch under your audience. Just ask Eric Hansen.

Eric sold Bazaarvoice's online software to insurance companies around the world. Among other things, that Austin-based company helps businesses develop ratings and reviews on their websites. While this is a natural fit for companies such as Best Buy or Home Depot who sell tangible products, it can be a much tougher sell for companies with abstract products such as life insurance. So Eric makes it personal.

> "The reason to use Bazaarvoice in your business is personal to your customers, and it's personal to me actually. My great grandfather, Maurice Smith, was a farmer in South Dakota during the Great Depression. He actually wasn't a very good farmer. He had trouble making a profit in that endeavor and out of pure necessity became a life insurance agent for Midland National Life Insurance.
>
> 'The way it worked in those days is that the home office would mail him a crate of applications. He'd load them into the back of his truck and hit the road. He'd drive off to the places he knew— the farms, feed lots, feed stores, and cafes in the surrounding area. He'd speak to the farmers personally about buying policies from him. He'd complete the applications, and he'd drive back home when they were all filled out. He'd mail them back to the home

office and wait for another crate of "empties" to come back his way. He was actually very successful at this and found that he could support his family this way. Like any successful salesperson he was looking to improve his performance. One day, as he was waiting for another crate of empties to arrive from the home office, his farm's pig had a litter of piglets. This gave him an idea for a promotion. He'd offer a free piglet with the sale of a life insurance policy. So he loaded the pigs into the back of his truck—along with blank policies—and took off on his sales route. To Maurice's surprise, he couldn't give away a single piglet. Farmers of the Great Depression viewed the piglets as an act of charity and were too proud to accept them. Maurice drove home with his crate of policies and all his piglets. If Maurice Smith had had the ability to simply ask his customers what was important to them, he would have known that the promotion was a bad idea."

Eric—whose only visual for this presentation is a picture of his great-grandfather in an insurance sales booth—then pivots to his core message, that that's one of the many things Bazaarvoice can do for an insurance company's business. Its service gives you the ability to truly know what your customers want because they're telling you all over the web—on your website, on Facebook, on Twitter, and more.

According to sources on the scene, Eric told this story to the executive team of one of the largest insurance companies in the world. After the meeting, the insurance executives were overheard recounting the "pig story." One brainstormed that Eric could have brought in a stuffed pink pig as his prop.

Who's presentation stood out? Eric's, or a competitor's with all those bullet-pointed slides? Who's message stuck with the audience? As you consider that, consider this: Eric got the sale.

Sanity Check

- Doing what Eric did does require a leap of faith—the courage to try something different.

- And that can be scary— you might fail; it could be uncomfortable; and it's far from the safe-but-boring slide tsunami.

- Do it anyway.

Evergreen Option: Imagine

One word has the ability to turn everyone into great storytellers.

The word is *imagine*.

Instead of tech company speakers burying audiences with text-heavy PowerPoint slides and an endless stream of jargon and acronyms (in a world where seemingly everything is "robust, scalable, integrated, best-of-breed, optimized, and monetized"), how about we tell stories that begin with the word *imagine*?

Imagine what might happen if, instead of enduring ninety minutes of indecipherable blather, an audience gets to hear a speaker tell great stories beginning with that single magic word.

This is more than a theoretical discussion. Recently we worked with a software company that's very involved with a prominent issue: keeping companies secure online. We asked several of their sales representatives what the company did. And we got a lot of nonsense in response. The company was a "leading solution provider" that offered "visibility into compliance" and had expertise in "configuration management."

Are you still awake?

Our heads were spinning. But after a little digging, a few pointed questions and some practice by the sales reps, a pretty decent story started to emerge. Try reading this out loud:

> *"Imagine you're the head of technology for Zappos.com, the online shoe retailer that just exposed the personal info of twenty-four million users to hackers (names, e-mails, addresses, and even encrypted passwords). Yikes! Well, our software prevents just that kind of intrusion. Essentially we help big companies—*

banks, hospitals, retailers—be more secure and save lots of money in the process, because they can make smarter decisions about how to set up their security systems. For example..."

Now even if you're not a technologist, you understand a few basic things about the company—and it all took less than thirty seconds. Perhaps you'll even continue listening. Now imagine what happens to your brain if a speaker starts with, "We're a leading solution provider that offers configuration management and visibility into compliance for corporations."

Uh, what happened? Did you just nod off too?

And the catalyst that sparks the revolution is one simple word:

imagine.

It's not just small technology companies that struggle with blandness. Here's how a massive non-tech company describes itself: "Our $22 billion company creates unique time to value through a comprehensive suite of innovative solutions that help clients within the Human Age."

Wow.

Curious? It's Manpower Group—they help people get jobs.

Manpower's pitiful pablum won a 2011 "Guff Award" from Lucy Kellaway, a writer at the *Financial Times* and now a personal hero of ours. You can read her hysterical column at http://tinyurl.com/WLguff.

It's simple. Good speakers tell stories. Stories stick like glue to the minds of audience members and can start with a single magic word that will help vaccinate you against jargon and the kind of nonsensical language that muddies contemporary communications.

Imagine that.

Imagine your presentation. Now imagine using a story that plugs directly into the major message you want to deliver and brings that message to life. This will take some work to get right.

You see, journalists have two jobs in a newsroom: reporting and writing. If, as a reporter, you interview ten sources who give you statistics, facts, quotes, personal experiences, and examples, then you have a lot of information from which to pull. It makes writing a lot easier. If, on the other hand, you're a lazy reporter and interview only one source with very little knowledge, writing becomes nearly impossible. The point is: do the reporting for your next presentation. Talk to people in your organization who know the details and have the knowledge.

Do the reporting.

To flesh out the details of his NASA example, Vignette's Leo Brunnick assigned two staffers to do some reporting. They read the NASA case study as a starting point; they interviewed the salesperson who sold the technology and services to NASA; they interviewed the account manager who worked directly with NASA on the Deep Impact Probe online event; they spoke with a customer at NASA to get the details right. Did this create more work? Absolutely. Did it make Vignette's presentations better? No question.

So think of your best story that illustrates your work or the point you're trying to make and go do the reporting to unpack the vivid details that make it concrete and memorable. Your presentation is all about saving money? You tell a story about an employee in your New York office who saved the company $45,000 a year by switching off twelve computer servers before he left work every night for a year. That story acts as a springboard into the broader message: saving money.

Without a great story, you might be a weekday communicator who needs to go fishing for some weekend language.

So that's your homework.

3
organize your narrative

"But don't you want to save the best for last?"

asked a confused C-level executive mid-session.

"Absolutely not,"

we replied.

"The best content you have always— always—goes first. Right up front."

There's a scientific method to this madness.

The first two minutes of any presentation are "cognitive hallowed ground." So says Dr. John Medina, a Seattle-based neurologist and author of *The Brain Rules*.

What he means is that in those first two minutes, your audience's eyes and ears are wide open. It's the point at which they actually care what you have to say. They're leaning forward and actively listening—neurologically "clicked in." They're a sponge for your major message. But there can be a massive drop-off after that.

The question is: What are you going to do with that first two minutes? Can you make the audience care? Think about it. If you lose the audience in those critical first two minutes, does it really matter what you say in the ensuing forty-five minutes? No. Because they're gone. Oh, they may physically stay in the room, but mentally they checked out when you didn't get right to the point, didn't make it about them, and ignored the neurology of the first two minutes.

So what? Who cares?

No offense, but again, it's not about you. It's about your audience. You have something they want—products, services, information. But unless you communicate what's in it for them, you're toast.

It's what we call the "So what? Who cares?" test. And it's just human nature. It's a test you apply several times a day when you're browsing the Internet, meeting with someone, or participating in a conference call.

If the audience spontaneously combusted after the first twenty seconds of your speech, what message would you have imparted? Would your audience care? Would it be about them or mean something to them? Or would it be all about you?

Your answer to that question is what's sometimes called your "elevator speech." In a crowded and confusing market like yours, you sometimes get only one shot at setting your company, agency, or association apart from the pack—whether in a sales meeting, on stage at an industry conference keynote, or on an elevator ride. And you typically get about thirty seconds to grab your audience's attention.

So, remember, when someone asks, "What do you do?" they really don't care what you do. What they're really asking is, "What can you do for me?"

With this in mind, your message better be drop-dead simple for your audience to understand and without the need for any translation. It better clearly define what makes you different. It better be framed and articulated in a way that makes it easy to deliver across your entire team—with consistency. And it had better mean something to every team member.

For example, Austin-based software company Zilliant was wrestling with its elevator speech in 2008. Industry jargon and insider language were robbing Zilliant's messages of clarity and differentiation. Its executives—including the fifteen we put on video camera—liked to talk all about how its software "optimizes pricing in a B2B competitive bid sales environment" and the like.

But every company in the price-optimization software market talks about how they optimize prices. This commodity language was selling Zilliant short and making its software look and sound just like its competitors'. And it certainly didn't highlight Zilliant's ability to pinpoint the exact price their customers should demand in every single sale.

Furthermore, the lack of a tight, customer-focused elevator speech had a stranglehold on Zilliant's executives when it came time to deliver a company presentation with impact—particularly in the opening.

That was the challenge confronting CEO Greg Peters.

"I'm not a company cheerleader," he said, in a matter-of-fact tone. "I feel my presentations are sometimes boring. And I don't particularly like public speaking. So you've got your work cut out for you."

That's how Peters greeted us in our first presentation prep session—three weeks before his keynote address to dozens of customers and prospects at Zilliant's inaugural customer conference.

After weeks of on-camera interviews and hours of presentation rehearsals, Zilliant's compelling, concise, consistent elevator speech became an asset to salespeople on customer calls and executives on the corporate stump:

"We take the guesswork out of pricing. That means we take that money your sales teams typically leave on the table in sales negotiations...and put it right back in your pocket as pure profit.

"For example, a $30 billion global energy management

Your message better be drop-dead simple.

company is adding $1 million a month in pure profit to its bottom line by using our software to determine the best prices for its products and services."

What followed were memorable analogies and customer examples that added clarity, credibility, and color. This—and a dedication to on-camera practice sessions—helped transform Peters into a comfortable and compelling storyteller who mixed analogies, examples, and anecdotes into his thirty-minute presentation.

So when Peters took the stage to address dozens of customers and prospects at Zilliant's inaugural customer conference, he did so with a clear headline, a memorable stunt, and a powerful first thirty seconds that sounded and looked like this:

Lights dim. The O'Jays' "For the Love of Money" booms in the room. Peters takes the stage with a duffel bag in hand. He unzips the bag and pours $7,000 dollars in cash onto a small table. He moves to center stage, flashes a wide smile, and exclaims: "The days of leaving money on the table are over...because we take the guesswork out of pricing."

With a clear headline, a memorable stunt, and a powerful first thirty seconds, Peters had his audience right where he wanted them.

He was in control; the audience was far from bored.

Not bad for a self-proclaimed "boring" speaker who hates public speaking.

In fact, audience members ranked Peters' presentation second highest of the three-day show. Second only to the professional, full-time guest speaker hired specifically for the conference. And many noted the "money drop" stunt.

What made Peters' narrative so effective was the translation, among other things. Rather than leading with what his company's technology was, he led with what it does. So in the future, try this: instead of telling your audience what your product, service, or technology is, start by telling them what it does for them. What do they get? We'll get to you and your services and technology eventually, but you can't start there.

Remember, it's not about you. It's about them. Once you nail that down, then—and only then—will you get permission to tell them how it works and what sorts of feeds and speeds it features. But you've got to start with them. If you don't, you might be burying what journalists call "the lede."

Journalism 101

We're both journalism wonks. What you learn the first day of journalism school is that reporters are in a constant search for the "lede," which is the first twenty-five words of the article or on-air story. It summarizes the article and includes only the most important elements of the subject matter. Basically, it tees up the rest of the story. (Side note, it's spelled "lede" to distinguish it from "lead" back in the days of lead type in newsrooms. I know, right?)

Looking back to Journalism 101, we recommend the "inverted pyramid." It's the format of every news story. The concept is simple: the best, sexiest, most important information is presented first. The meaning, the nutshell—the lede—goes up top, right below the headline in the fat part of the pyramid. From there, you build out the story.

It's too bad most executives never took Journalism 101, because far too few presenters get right to the point. It's like CNN's Richard Quest once said when asked about the first tip for a television story or a presentation, "You've got to grab 'em by the grapes."

In *The Brain Rules*, John Medina reminds us that all humans consume information the same way: meaning first, details second. So if you immediately unload all fifteen features of your cool new technology or your lifesaving drug, your audience won't be able to process the information. Because you haven't put it in context yet. You didn't give them the meaning first.

In 2007, a $30 billion IT distributor was struggling with a common communication challenge: how to unite ten different divisions and dozens of services under one core message. What's the umbrella message, the one thing all of those services and divisions mean for our customers, partners, and salespeople? In short, it was in search of its lede.

The company was suffering from what *Made to Stick* calls "featuritis," in that the messages were nothing more than a list of the company assets, offerings, and features. But none of them passed the "So what? Who cares?" test.

So we put the CEO and more than a dozen executives and salespeople on camera to dig beneath the features and the jargon and uncover a clear lede and the stories to illustrate it.

Today, the company describes its core message this way: "We're the ultimate IT matchmaker. We sit at the intersection of four thousand vendors, thirty thousand resellers, and hundreds of thousands of customers. And we help them make sense of all the technology options out there and put the right pieces together to grow their businesses. For example..."

And each of those ten divisions? We replaced the corporate-speak with storytelling—examples, analogies, and anecdotes—that brings the divisions and what they do to life while clearly describing the value of each.

Try grabbing a video camera and hunting for your company's lede. Once you find it, you've got to put the rest of your content in the right order so that it flows naturally and keeps your audience engaged.

World-renowned chef Jamie Oliver put the inverted pyramid into practice at his October 2010 TED Talk, "Teach Every Child about Food." He took the stage and said, "Sadly, in the next eighteen minutes when I do our chat, four Americans that are alive will be dead through the food that they eat."

Jamie used his shocking statistic right up front to grab his audience's attention and frame his narrative—even before he introduced himself. He clearly looked at everything he had in his arsenal and asked, "What's the most important thing I have to say?" Then he put that in the first seconds of his presentation.

Now that's a lede.

In early 2008 Ingram Micro North America President Keith Bradley was preparing remarks for 400 of his senior managers who were about to converge on the company's Southern California headquarters for a conference.

A few weeks before the event, we sat in a small meeting room and talked out the various things Keith wanted to tell his top managers. For many companies it's not often that 400 top executives come together in one place, so the temptation is to turn a fire hose of information on them—to make sure they don't miss anything and leave with their heads so full of data that they might just explode before they check in for their flights home. Add to that the harsh reality of a business operating in a tough economic climate—

Sanity Check

- Do my talking points pass the **"So what? Who Cares?"** Test?

- Do I have a clear, unmistakable headline?

- Is my story in plain English?

a period where grinding out the execution of a business plan was going to take guts, determination, and teamwork.

As we scribbled down various messages on the meeting room's whiteboard it became clear that fire hose of data could easily be unloaded on those 400 people.

But we couldn't find the lede.

Ingram is the world's largest technology distributor, a Fortune 100, $42 billion company with 17,000 employees in countries around the world that operates as a kind of middleman between 1,400 supplier companies and 185,000 partners who sell what they make. The company has more annual revenue than American Express, Comcast, and Coca-Cola, and runs a complicated operation, so there's typically a lot to talk about.

But when Keith stood up to practice delivering all that information out loud, things didn't quite fly right. His "talk track" wasn't bad, but it certainly wasn't good. After an hour or so, we did what consultants do: we suggested a coffee break. As we chatted with Keith, a genial Irishman, the subject of vacations came up and we asked Keith what he did last summer. He lit up.

He'd climbed Mount Kilimanjaro in Tanzania, a 19,341-foot dormant volcano that's Africa's tallest peak. He'd been dreaming of conquering Kilimanjaro since he was a kid in Ireland flying over it en route to a relative's home in Africa. He talked excitedly about the team of 36 people who'd helped him and three friends reach the summit. He talked about his fear of heights and how altitude sickness had struck the team on the morning they started their ascent to the summit at 1:00 a.m. He talked about being 150 feet from the very top of the mountain and thinking that he couldn't make it, that climbing into thin air had seemingly robbed his lungs of their ability to work. And finally he talked about stepping onto the summit having counted 347 steps to travel 150 feet up at a punishing 70 degree angle. He said he just focused on the "18 inches of dirt" in front of him, took 10 steps and then did it again.

Gone was the long, detailed boring list of stuff we'd written on the whiteboard as initial talking points; gone was Keith's flat delivery of that information (Keith's a good speaker, but a combination of Bill Clinton, Steve Jobs, and Zig Ziglar couldn't have delivered that long list of blah, blah, blah with emphasis and energy).

No, Keith's summer climb was a great story, full of passion and energy. As we slurped our coffee, it seemed obvious that these crystal-clear messages could easily be used for Keith's senior managers in a few weeks: a team that gritted its teeth and ground its way to the summit, a team that had support from 36 sherpas, a team that focused on the "18 inches of dirt" in front of it and just kept going.

Keith's communications director Jennifer Anaya was smiling at the end of the coffee break. She realized what Keith, perhaps inadvertently, had delivered: the core message for his management offsite meeting—his lede, something as simple as "18 inches of dirt."

The rest of our session was spent filling in the data points of Keith's climb and baking in segues to the state of Ingram Micro's North American business. As we unpacked the details, some fabulous anecdotes came to life.

At one point on the climb up Kilimanjaro, there was a pathway that had crumbled. Peeking over the edge of the pathway, Keith and his colleagues saw the 1,000-foot drop.

"What happens if we fall here?" Keith asked a sherpa.

"You're going to die," was the curt reply.

It can be scary to keep going, but it's essential—both in climbing and in business.

During the speech Keith used a few photos of his fellow

climbers, but no PowerPoint slides. He didn't need them. He knew the story, and he knew how to link it to the business and implore those 400 managers to keep focusing on that 18 inches of dirt before them and execute the business plan. As he talked about taking 347 steps over that last 150 feet to the summit, he pantomimed taking tiny steps and pausing—seemingly exhausted from the effort. In other words he knew his material so well that he was able to work on his stage presence— his performance. That's a level many presidents and CEOs never reach, but Keith did.

Keith was extremely diligent about practicing his speech. In fact, in the weeks leading up to the event, not only was he before our cameras several times, he was also on the elliptical machine at his health club with his speaking notes propped up before him. He was practicing out loud. The guy exercising next to him asked, "Who are you talking to?" "Oh, I'm practicing my speech," Keith replied.

It was at that point we knew Keith would conquer those 400 managers like he did Kilimanjaro. And he did. In fact, around Ingram Micro, it's still known as the "18 inches of dirt" speech.

Signposting

It's staggering to us how many speakers don't take advantage of a basic tool that audiences just love: signposting. When you're driving, you look at a signpost to see how far it is to the turnoff or the next city. It's nice to know how far you have to go, right? How long it's going to take to get home or to Aunt Betty's.

Think of it this way: when you write a long e-mail or Word document, you probably use bullet points to call the readers' eyes to two or three of your most important points.

It's the same principle for master speakers. Quite often they will use a signpost—a verbal bullet point—in their presentations. It might sound something like, "In the next ten minutes I want to tell you the secret of life." Now, if that's of interest to you as an audience member, you now know not only that you're going to be privy to a big secret, but also that you're going to be sitting there for ten minutes.

For example, after the money dump, the clear opening, and a short story, Zilliant's Greg Peters turned to his audience and said, "I'm going to talk about three things today: one, I'm going to talk about 'answers'...two, I'm going to talk about 'science'...and three, I'm going to talk about 'the future of pricing.'"

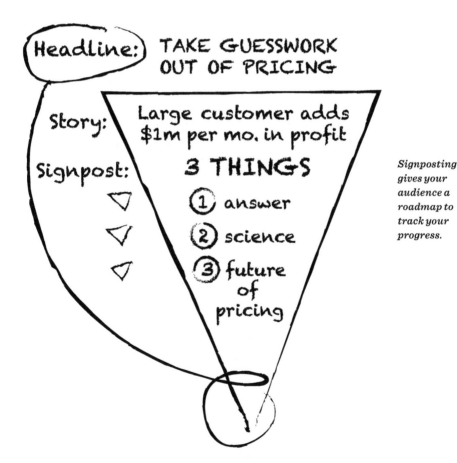

Signposting gives your audience a roadmap to track your progress.

That simple style gave his audience the roadmap for the next twenty-five minutes. With his effective signposting, they always knew where they were in the presentation, and Greg would help. Each time he got to the next section, he'd call it out. "Number two," he'd say with two fingers in the air, "let's talk about 'science.'"

Guy Kawasaki, author of *The Art of the Start*, often fashions his presentations as top ten lists. If his objective is for his audience to remember all ten things, then this approach will fail. Our brains simply are not wired to absorb and recall that much information in one sitting. However, he likes to say that he uses top ten lists so that "even if I suck, you can track my progress."

Think about it. If it's been fifteen minutes on the clock, and Kawasaki says, "Point six," then it's a pretty safe bet we'll only be here for fifteen more minutes. At that moment a collective exhale cascades across the room. We know where we are in the talk. Contrast that with the pinhead who was assigned thirty minutes for his presentation; he's just hit forty-five minutes on the timer, and he appears to have gotten a second wind. We have no idea where we are in his talk or when it will conclude. That's when we mentally check out and dive into our e-mails or leave the room entirely.

We've all had that kind of experience. At a college commencement, we were in the audience when the commencement speaker threw in a joke, "The last thing you need on the day of your college graduation is some old guy going on for hours and hours." And then he did just that. It made us want to stick forks in our own eyes (we resisted).

So tell the audience how long you're going to take. It's simple but effective. And here's the real secret to signposting. If you tell the audience your presentation is going to be forty-five minutes, you end in forty minutes and everyone thinks it's the best presentation of the day. Why?

Because you just gave them five minutes of their lives back.

Good speakers never go long. Never, never, never, never, never. Ever.

Never.

Clear versus Dumbing Down

Your message isn't a secret, is it? So don't hide it in your own clever version of corporate Klingon. No one—and we mean no one—outside of your building cares about your "optimized processes," "monetized solutions," or self-anointed "leading provider" status. Get to the heart of the matter with a description that anyone and everyone can understand.

Bono, U2 frontman and uber-ambassador to Africa, once was asked how he manages to hold his own in conversations with economists and heads of state when discussing debt relief and financial plans for Africa.

He replied, "If someone can't explain to me very quickly what this particular theory is, I'm not coming up to the conclusion that I'm stupid and they're smarter than me. I'm just saying, 'You're not very good at explaining...try it again.'"

That's sweet music to our ears. It reminds us that one's job as a communicator is to, well, communicate. Using jargon, fancy words, or contrived language is not the way to accomplish that goal. And don't come back at us with the "but everybody talks that way" excuse. That's a cop-out, and it's dangerous. If you're using the same words as everyone else, you're not differentiating yourself from the competition. You're just using commodity language to describe your commodity service.

Which brings us to two terms common in the business world that we absolutely despise: "dumbing it down" and "high level."

There's nothing dumb about making complex theory, technology, or business plans clear and simple to understand.

That actually takes a lot more work and intelligence to pull off.

Exhibit A: Richard Feynman.

Feynman, a professor at the California Institute of Technology (aka Caltech), was a physicist who did a lot of work in quantum electrodynamics, superfluidity, and particle physics. He won the 1965 Nobel Prize in physics and worked on the Manhattan Project with J. Robert Oppenheimer to develop the atomic bomb. He also pioneered the fields of quantum computing and the concept of nanotechnology.

He was one of the smartest men to walk this planet. Know what his nickname was? The Great Explainer. Not The Great Scientist or The Great Physicist.

No, it was The Great Explainer because he could take the most advanced theories in physics and have seventeen-year-old undergraduates leaning forward in their seats.

He had a guiding principle: "If a topic could not be explained in a freshman lecture it was not yet fully understood."

He was truly the Steve Jobs of his field and of his time. Someone who could make it so simple and clear. And no one ever accused him of dumbing down information or science.

A few months back, a friend told us Feynman used to say that truly smart people can break down complicated concepts into something more digestible. Our friend said he'd heard that even fellow Caltech professors would sometimes sit in on Feynman's lectures because he was so good at doing just that.

Get to the heart of the matter with a description that anyone and everyone can understand.

There's real value in being able to talk about such things in a way that mere mortals can understand, even those who have only a passing knowledge of quantum electrodynamics or liquid helium.

That's why Feynman was such a great example of

what we like to call "low-level language."

Frankly, most senior executives represent what could be called "anti-Feynmans." They tend to say things like, "Oh, I don't want to dumb it down" or "I want to keep it high level" because it's easier to use abstractions and jargon than it is to really, truly communicate and deliver a core message with conviction and credibility.

"Dumbing it down" usually means you don't want to do the work to make it simple and accessible for all of your audience. Like, say, using terms such as "quantum electrodynamics" without offering a clarification— a "what that means is" or an example. "Dumbing it down" is a term of arrogance and condescension to an audience that simply isn't as smart as the speaker or writer (like, maybe, Feynman's audiences).

The fix is simple: start with a clear, simple core message so you reach everyone in the audience. Then you can dive into complexity (remember Medina's "meaning before details").

Translate and illustrate high-level concepts for your audience.

And while we're on the subject, the phrase "high level" leaves us a little pissy too. It typically leads to abstract, esoteric, and indecipherable drivel. No one would expect an audience to get the "physics of the superfluidity of supercooled liquid helium" without a clear translation or good example. "High level" typically means the speaker or writer is communicating using industry-insider language that's extraordinarily difficult for the rest of us to understand.

Around ten years ago, we sat through an entire presentation on an arcane software protocol called "OFX." Befuddling. We had no clue what the acronym meant or what the protocol actually did, which was a big problem because we were charged with explaining it to the company's customers.

After the meeting we asked an experienced colleague what OFX stood for. She paused, sighed, and then said, "I have no idea. But they use it all the time." (We subsequently found out it stood for "Open Financial Exchange." Which makes as much sense today as it did ten years ago).

So consider this a plea for clarity, concreteness, and "low-level" communication. Translate the high-level concept into the meaning to the audience and illustrate it with stories and clear, concrete language that describes why your audience will care.

Be specific, be clear, and please, please, please make sure that you're speaking to everyone. If it's possible to explain quantum electrodynamics and the physics of the superfluidity of supercooled liquid helium in terms a college freshman could understand, there's hope for all of us.

We've found a few phrases that will help you get on the right path.

Magic Words

The following are a few key phrases that will reveal whether you're getting to the point and telling stories. If you hear these words come out of your mouth, you're probably on your way to good communication.

"Imagine" This is the most elegant word in a presenter's arsenal. "Imagine" immediately puts the audience in the position of, well, imagining. It's a perfect way to describe how your business vision or new product or service will play out in a customer's business or life. "Imagine you're the CIO of a major bank, or maybe an IT developer. You probably care about three big things..."

"What that means is" What that means to the listener or reader is critical. It's what they care most about. Translate it so they don't have to work to figure it out.

"For example" Some companies have thousands of customers and partners. Chances are, there's an example out there that best illustrates what you do or how you do it.

"Our customers tell us" No one cares about you; they care greatly, however, about what you can do for them. This simple phrase is a great way to overcome objections or biases that hinder your point of view.

"Think of it this way" Analogies are incredibly effective yet underused in the corporate world. This phrase will put you on the path to an analogy. It's also a useful way to reframe a negative.

"What makes us different" You're in a pitched battle with your top competitors. This is no time for ambiguity. What's the one thing you do that no one else can do? Call it out very clearly.

Let's use an example. Unless you have an advanced medical degree, you probably don't know what "ablating tumors with sub-millimeter accuracy" means.

It's what the Heath brothers in *Made to Stick* would call the "Curse of Knowledge." This curse often plagues medical professionals who know so much about treating cancerous tumors that they've forgotten they have to explain it to mere mortals like us.

Tell us if this sounds familiar: you walk into a cell phone store. There are shiny phones and predatory salesmen everywhere. You ask one simple question, the salesman's "Curse of Knowledge" kicks into high gear, and you immediately want to run from the store and gouge out your eyes (well, at least we do).

The jargon and acronyms seem endless: 3G, 4G, LTE. It's staggering and more than a little intimidating.

Incidentally, do you know what "LTE" actually means? It's in all the cell phone commercials, and people at our telecom clients toss the term around like it's the tech equivalent of FBI, which everyone knows means "Federal Bureau of Investigation."

So, do you know?

If not, here's the answer: LTE stands for "Long Term Evolution."

So now you know. But you probably still don't care. We sure don't.

That's the "Curse of Knowledge" at work.

Don't use confusing acronyms.

Made to Stick reminds us that we always need to be conscious of the curse. But the executives at one of our medical industry clients evidently hadn't read the book, because when we first asked them, "What does your company do?" as one they said, "We make a laser that ablates tumors with sub-millimeter accuracy."

"Oh," we responded. "That's nice." But we were crying on the inside, Feynman was spinning in his grave, and anyone who had to contend with such indecipherable nonsensical language would surely be ready to kill or seriously maim.

So what exactly does "ablating tumors with sub-millimeter accuracy" mean?

Let's back up quite a few steps.

Imagine you have a lung tumor, imagine it's pretty big, and imagine you're eighty-five years old. Your list of treatment options just got a lot shorter. You won't survive invasive cancer surgery, so what do you do?

That's where the laser can help. It's a massive robotic arm—sort of looks like a dentist's chair on steroids—but instead of a light on the arm, it has a laser beam.

That laser beam contains a dose of radiation that can be up to one hundred times higher than comparable treatment methods. And the reason it can shoot such high doses of radiation into your lung tumor is that it's incredibly accurate; the beam of radiation is about the width of a human hair, or as the executives like to say, it has "sub-millimeter accuracy."

It gets better. The laser is built on the same mechanics as a spot welding machine on an auto production line. So the laser beam is on a huge mechanical arm that can move it all around your lung tumor. In fact, your lung tumor can get blasted with high doses of radiation from one hundred or so different angles.

It gets better. Not only is there no cutting, no blood, and no physical knives, but you can also rest on the laser machine's bed in your street clothes, plugged into your iPod, jamming to your favorite tunes.

It gets even better. Chemotherapy kills a lot of cells, even good ones. The laser only zaps the bad ones, so there's no nausea and vomiting.

The company tells the story of an eighty-five-year-old patient whose cancer went into remission after just three forty-five-minute treatments.

"Ablating tumors with sub-millimeter accuracy?" Are you serious?

Here's how one of the company executives actually described the process (after a bit of prodding from us):

> *"Imagine you have a lung tumor, and your doctor tells you they're going to treat your tumor using surgery—what does that mean? It means they have to cut you from front to back, open you up, and take out part of your lung. Then you have to recover from that major surgery.*

> *"So that's your treatment option, and then the next day your doctor calls you and says, 'I have a new treatment for you. It's a laser. All you do is come in, lie down on a table for forty-five minutes a day for three days, and then you get up and walk away and you're done.' Which option would you choose?*

> *"The laser has the ability to treat cancerous tumors with sub-millimeter accuracy, which means it can attack and destroy a tumor within the width of a human hair—that's how accurate it is.*

> *"That's really important because it means the treatment won't kill or damage surrounding tissue—and that's one of the things that makes our laser different from the competition and different from the other treatments used today to treat cancer."*

Now you'll notice those last few paragraphs contain almost nothing about the company itself, and that's intentional. Audiences need narrative; problem is, most companies don't give it to them.

You'll also notice that the executive used the dreaded phrase "ablating tumors with sub-millimeter accuracy" but then immediately explained and clarified it (with some magic words).

Have empathy for your audience.

The magic words can translate almost any kind of nonsense into something that actually makes sense for audiences—that's why they're magical.

Now the laser isn't a miracle cure; the patients treated by it already have cancer and many of them die. But for patients without many options, for patients suffering from lung, brain, and prostate cancer, it can be a godsend, a lifesaver. And when you tell that story, you'll have the attention of most audiences—because it's about them, it's not about the technology that ablates those tumors with sub-millimeter accuracy.

And that can be magical.

Organizing your narrative might be the most challenging part of your presentation. After all, you know so much about your subject matter that you could talk for days. It's very difficult to determine the ordering of your information, though. What goes first? What goes second? Think about your presentation from the audience's perspective. Or as a good friend once said, "Have empathy for your audience." If you were sitting in the twentieth row at your presentation, what would you want to hear?

You can do this. All it takes is a little work. The worksheet on the next page can help you develop and organize your narrative. You don't have to match things up perfectly, but see if you can put a few notes or talking points in each box, and then use the completed document as a cheat sheet when you practice your speech.

First things first: what's your headline or your lede? Does it pass the "So What? Who Cares?" test your audience will apply? Here's a good exercise: if you were writing an article about your subject matter for the front page of tomorrow's *New York Times*, what would be your headline and first sentence? Would it be all about you and your company, or would it be about your audience? Or can you combine the two objectives?

Now take your stories and statistics from chapter 2's homework and organize them using this form. Where do your stories and statistics go in the flow of your narrative? Remember, you can begin the presentation with a story, or you can spread them out to illustrate important points.

Would signposts make it easier for your audience to follow along? You don't have to have three things. Heck, you might keep it really simple and talk about only one thing (that too is a sign post). This worksheet is just a tool to guide you in the process. It can serve as a valuable starting point to help you organize your narrative. Said another way, it'll ensure you don't use PowerPoint as your starting point.

So that's your homework.

Presentation Plan

HEADLINE

Clear, simple, conversational

SO WHAT? WHO CARES?

POINT 1	POINT 2	POINT 3
Illustration (story, statistics)	Illustration (story, statistics)	Illustration (story, statistics)

CONCLUSION

You can download the worksheet at ElevatorSpeech.com.

4
remember
mehrabian

Now that you've fine-tuned
your narrative—the verbal part of
your presentation—it's time
to revisit Professor Mehrabian
to make sure your vocals and visuals
(or nonverbal communication) enhance your story.
Far too often, they stand in the way of it.

You'll recall that Mehrabian's research revealed that vocal
and visuals can account for as much as 93 percent of your
audience's perception when you speak about your feelings
and attitudes.

Said another way, your audience puts a lot of weight
on the expression they see on your face, the pitch and tone
of your voice, the gestures you use, the speed at which you
speak, and the overall energy you display.

In the end, presentations are more than just words.
And when all three forms of communication work together,
the impact is profound.

Vocals

Vocals signal intent, telling your audience how you're
feeling at that moment.

Try this exercise to measure tone of voice: Say "good
morning" like that annoyingly perky colleague who loves
early-morning meetings. Now say "good morning" like the
red-faced boss who's angry that you're late for the meeting
with clients. Finally say "good morning" like you're the
nervous twenty-two-year-old intern who has to admit to
Jack Welch that he just clogged the toilet in Welch's private

executive bathroom. Hear the difference? It's the same two words each time, but the meaning is totally different. And it's all because of the way you said them. Because of the vocals.

There are really three elements to a good vocal cadence: pausing, pacing, and projection. Let's look at each one separately.

Pausing

Next time you see a comedian in person or on television, listen for the silence. If it's a good comedian, he or she will be silent on stage for several seconds in between jokes—hopefully as gales of laughter cascade throughout the room.

Do you ever remember being silent during a presentation for more than one or two seconds? Probably not, but there is tremendous power in pausing.

When President Obama was inaugurated on January 20, 2009, his opening words boomed out to hundreds of thousands of people on the National Mall in Washington, DC, and around the world. "My fellow citizens," one second, two, three, four, "I stand here today" one second, two, three, "humbled by the task before us," one second, two, three, "grateful for the trust you have bestowed," one second, two, three, "mindful of the sacrifices born by our ancestors."

There is tremendous power in pausing.

PAUSING, PACING, PROJECTION

Volume

-10-

-5-

-1-

punch

His pauses were enormous, separating his thoughts for the audience and—on that occasion, quite practically—giving the sound system time to broadcast his voice to a massive audience, some of whom were probably standing about a mile away. The pauses also successfully isolated the only three words in his opening sentence that mattered: humbled, grateful, and mindful. That's what he wanted citizens to absorb.

You can visualize good pausing as a series of peaks and valleys, like a rollercoaster ride. Master communicators hit a key point at the peak, and then use a pause (the valley) to let the message sink in. Or they'll pause for a few seconds in the run-up to a major point, cueing the importance by saying something like, "If you remember nothing else today when you get home, I want you to think about this..." (one, two, three, four) "pausing is a key skill in speaking well."

President Obama likes to pause right before a key word, which has his audience leaning forward as they await that next word. Others, like us, like to hit our point and then...pause...to let the audience marinate in that point. Either method can be effective. Both have audiences rocking forward and back like a cat with a ball of string.

Pauses give the audience time to digest what you've already said and time to prepare for what you're about to say.

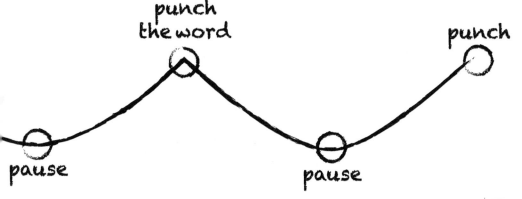

Vocal pacing is key because it leads to emphasis, intonation, and a conversational tone. When people aren't prepared for a speech, it's typically the vocal aspect that suffers the most. They rush through their remarks, which are devoid of any human expression, and they use "high level" language that is barely decipherable to the audience. Vocals then flatline and things go downhill very quickly, especially if the language is accompanied by a boatload of bad slides.

We've coached lots of people who combined flat delivery with lots of non-words. One useful exercise another coach we know showed us is to only speak when you're touching a piece of furniture. So you stand and start your presentation rehearsal while resting your hand on the back of a chair.

Across the room, maybe fifteen feet away is another chair. At some point you remove your hand from the first chair and stroll slowly over to the other chair, and you DON'T SAY A WORD until you touch the back of the second chair.

The whole exercise takes three seconds but, oh, it seems like a lifetime to people who typically rush through speeches or fill pauses with non-words like *um* or *ah*.

Pauses give the audience time to digest what you've already said, and time to prepare for what you're about to say. We sometimes forget that, but master communicators —and good comedians and presidents—know that pausing is a key element in effective speaking.

Another tip for people who can't pause: This Saturday morning, select an article from the newspaper. Read it once. Then read it again, and insert a circle every place you think it would be natural to pause when reading it aloud. Stand. Now read it out loud with an emphasis on those pause marks. Do this regularly and you'll start to build muscle memory around pauses.

Finally, set yourself up to succeed on presentation day. Never take the stage without a bottle of water. It allows you to manufacture pauses at predesignated points in your presentation with a simple drink from the bottle. You'll eliminate that nasty lip smack that some presenters get when nervous, and you'll also build a pause into the process.

Pacing

Picture this: you're in the boardroom with all the big cheeses from your company, or maybe a new business prospect or a grumpy client. Everyone settles in and the meeting begins. They all look at you and you start to speak.

At that point, adrenaline is coursing through your system. *Maybe this is what crack feels like,* you think. Perhaps you've had an extra cup of coffee or one of those disgusting-tasting energy drinks to make sure you're full of oomph; perhaps you've exercised that morning to keep your energy high, or maybe you're just naturally exuberant.

Whatever the reason, when you open your mouth to speak, the words come out faster than Jeff Gordon's car speeds around a NASCAR track during the Daytona 500. You barely take a breath as you speed through the presentation's key points and, possibly, PowerPoint slides. It seems like speed-reading, and it's like turning a fire hose on your audience from two feet away. Thirsty though they may be, a lot of water is going to go right by them and be wasted.

We've got to get cadence and pacing right. Pausing is part of it, but a conversational tone and the right language also help ensure comfortable pacing. And it's no surprise that rehearsing also helps a great deal.

An audience won't work to listen.

It's fun to watch great speakers use pacing. When they want to create dramatic tension, they'll often inch closer to the audience and lower their tone a little—almost a conspiratorial whisper to pass along a great nugget of information.

When they want to crank up the emphasis and energy a bit, they'll go loud and their verbal cadence could be visualized as huge mountaintops with deep valleys in between them. The pacing crests and then falls off for a second or two.

You may think that pausing and pacing seem almost trivial, but they are more important than you may think—to the audience's attention, to your ability to connect, and to message delivery. Which brings us to projection.

Projection

Dave's a loudmouth. He admits it. His wife knows it. And Andy suffers from it. So in a conference room or boardroom, Dave doesn't really need a microphone. But not everyone is a loudmouth; some people need amplifying. And when you're speaking, a key thing for the audience is this: they have to be able to hear you.

An audience won't work to listen. If they can't hear you, they'll quickly move on to texting, telephoning, talking to each other, or just eating their rubber-chicken lunch.

Tip: get out of your chair.

But if you combine great, deep pauses with comfortable verbal pacing and projection that's loud enough to reach the person in the back row (who is loudly slurping his iced tea), you'll have ticked another box in the progression to becoming a master communicator.

The key is to strike the right balance. Too soft and slow is agonizing. Too loud and fast is like listening to your teenager's favorite speed metal band. On a scale of one to ten, your audience will appreciate you if you hit volume six to seven for most of your presentation, and they'll really lean forward if you occasionally dial it up and down to keep them off balance.

You should be at your loudest at the very beginning of your presentation—when nerves have a Jedi-like stranglehold on your vocal chords and your diaphragm. Punch it out for the back seats in that critical opening two minutes.

Remote presentations are almost a no-win format, particularly a telephone conversation or a webcast. They automatically remove the visual of the presenter, one of the most dominant forms of communication (as you'll read shortly). Your audience can't see you. And you just know they're checking their e-mails, talking to colleagues, and only half listening to you. In this case, vocal communication takes on even more significance. It becomes more important for presenters to pause, change their volume, and add emphasis to certain words or statistics.

Here's a tip: get out of your chair. Get a headset on, and walk and talk. Gesture as if your audience is sitting right in front of you. You'll be more conversational. You'll have more performance energy. You'll have greater volume, since your diaphragm will be elongated, allowing increased airflow. Research also shows that we're more believable when we stand. So stand and punch it, even if your only audience is the cat.

Um, ah, right, so, you know

Michael Erard wrote *Um....: Slips, Stumbles, and Verbal Blunders and What They Mean.* He notes a fascinating exercise in the book. Researchers recorded nineteen hundred telephone conversations. Transcribed them into eighty thousand words. Twenty-five percent of those words were fillers: "um, ah, right, so, you know." Four percent alone were "um." The point is that it's natural and everyone does it, but it's necessary to curb once it becomes distracting. You can do two things to reduce or eliminate this pattern.

First, practice. Nine times out of ten, use of fillers indicates a lack of preparation. In your mind you're trying to recall which slide comes next or which sentence in your handwritten script comes next, but what you say while thinking is some version of "um, ah, right, so, you know."

The second is to retrain your muscle memory. This is a longer process for those serial language fillers. When you feel the urge to fill with "um," squeeze your throat muscles to stop the progression. This one might take a village, people. At the public speaking group Toastmasters, audience members clap their hands every time a speaker says "um." They snap their fingers when they hear "ah." They shake a can of pennies when they hear "you know." And so on. It's incredibly annoying and frustrating, but it makes the presenter aware of their annoying tic. Because most people don't realize they fill their sentences with so many fillers.

Left untreated, a pronounced tic can prevent you from getting your message across.

Does this really happen? As Sarah Palin might say, "You betcha." Here's one sad but true story with identifying elements removed to protect the guilty:

Several years ago, the entire senior management team of a multibillion-dollar software company gathered at a luxury resort for an offsite meeting. These kinds of retreats are common for managers, of course. During this particular offsite, the CEO had brought in an economist to speak to his senior executives, someone from an Ivy League institution, a deep thinker who could outline what the economic outlook could be in twelve to eighteen months—information that would be critical to the company's prospects and product lineup.

Let's call the economist Bob.

Unfortunately, two things combined to sabotage Bob's presentation. First, more than fifty executives sat in the meeting room with their laptop computers open, their eyes darting between him and their computers. The darkened room was lit by the low glow of their screens. Second, Bob possessed an undiagnosed and crippling "um" tic.

As the presentation started, Bob, possibly nervous at speaking to such tech industry bigwigs, stammered through his opening remarks before slides filled with dense economic data were projected onto a large screen.

A pronounced tic can prevent you from getting your message across.

Like Jim in our opening chapter, Bob peppered his remarks with "ums" and "ers" to the extent that the executives started to send each other text messages from their computers making fun of him. In fact, one attendee said the execs were betting on just how many non-words Bob would use during his presentation. One person was assigned to count the tics and meanwhile a mini Las Vegas blossomed in the room as the execs bet money.

"I had him down for two-fifty," said one exec who attended. "Others had three hundred, four hundred."

An hour later one senior manager had some extra spending money for his offsite evening activity.

The economist's message didn't get through.

If only Bob had practiced his remarks and asked someone to evaluate him before flying across the country to speak to the bigwigs.

We don't know for sure, but we're willing to bet that Bob wasn't invited back—and that to this day he remains blissfully unaware of his shortcomings when it comes to presenting effectively.

Visual

Presentations are a lot like show-and-tell in elementary school. And what your body language shows needs to be aligned with what you're telling your audience in words. If they contradict one another, your audience will believe what they see versus what they hear. That's where Mehrabian's research really comes into play—visuals accounting for 55 percent of the impact in some instances. Yet this is another area that the overwhelming majority of speakers ignore.

Eyes always, always, always beat ears when it comes to ingesting information. Oh sure, we listen with our ears, but have you ever seen someone give a speech when his zipper was open? Do you remember anything he said? Probably not. Have you ever seen someone use the "fig leaf" position when speaking? Hands crossed at the crotch. Awkward, right?

We're visual creatures.

Visuals account for 55 percent of the impact in some instances.

We're talking not only about the visuals for the speaker—what she wears, does he move around, are the gestures distracting, and so forth—but also the staging of the event. If speakers are trapped behind a podium with an attached microphone, it's tough to deliver a good speech.

While we're on the subject, let us say a word about something we absolutely, completely, and utterly hate: podiums. We're convinced they are the devil's furniture.

Some years ago we were tabbed as "difficult" by an event management company because we insisted that they move a podium occupying center stage in the room where we were scheduled to speak.

The conversation went something like this:

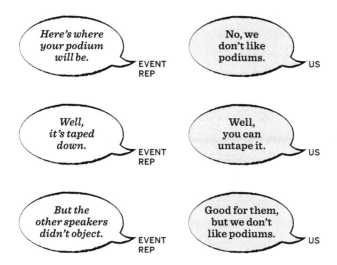

Eventually, after supervisors were called and feelings hurt, the podium was shifted to the side of the stage.

Podiums suck royally because 1) they put a big block of wood between you and your audience, 2) they encourage lazy presenters to read from scripts that rest on the podium, and 3) each of those things flatten vocal patterns, eliminate eye contact, and siphon the energy right out of the room.

Finally, a podium limits presenters' physical pacing—your movement on whatever stage you're using, whether it's a conference room or an actual conference stage with hundreds of people watching. Movement is a key element of an effective presentation, and its execution is a common source of uncertainty. Focus on movement with purpose.

Have you ever watched comedian Chris Rock? He is constantly in motion on stage, whipping his microphone cord aside as he paces frantically from side to side, telling jokes.

We can't all be Chris Rock, and frankly even trying to make a wisecrack can be the quickest way to kill a speech, but we can learn from how performers like Rock move.

"I think Eddie (Murphy) taught me this, early on," Rock told *Inside the Actor's Studio* host James Lipton some time ago. "It's just a little device. If you stand in one place, people can talk to their friends...but if you move they have to pay attention."

We coach speakers to move in a shallow semicircle facing the audience. Not only so they have to stay involved like Rock's audiences, but also because movement like that helps shake off adrenaline that's coursing through the body of every speaker ever (hint: if someone says they don't get nervous before a speech, that person is lying or clueless. Fear of public speaking is the #1 fear.)

Podiums are the devil's furniture.

When you don't walk comfortably from side to side, adrenaline will do funny things to your body, introducing a series of distracting "tics." Some speakers sway from side to side, as if bracing in a strong breeze; others will cross their legs at the ankles, seemingly indicating that they have to pee; others will do the side-to-side two-step (of your Uncle Maury after three gin and tonics at the last family wedding); others will take small steps toward and then away from the audience, giving the impression that the speaker is also a salsa dancer.

All of these tics are things unchanneled adrenaline can do to a body. A casual stroll from one side of the stage to the other (think Steve Jobs during his Macworld keynotes) will shake off the adrenaline and can also help you think as you walk and talk. Small pauses in that walk will make you appear thoughtful and perhaps even wise.

In other words, you need to calibrate your movements just like you calibrate your messages. Left untended, bad pacing can kill a speech, just as good pacing can enhance it.

We're admittedly stubborn about staging. Garr Reynolds of PresentationZen.com talks about "presenting naked," which means that there's nothing between you and the audience.

Nothing. Zip. Nada.

Especially not a podium. We hate those things.

Ready Stance

Without a podium to protect you, you'll need to consider your presence, and that starts with your stance. The key visual stance is what you might call "open." Think of it like you're about to give someone a big hug. Nothing is crossed, you're energetic, you're smiling, and your body language is completely open toward the audience. If you're in a big arena, you gesture above your shoulders.

If this seems a little like acting, it is. Actors often talk about "performance energy," and it's a similar thing for great speakers. By now, you already know that you can't just say the words; the next step is to completely own the material you're "performing" and command the room.

If that sounds like hard work, it is. But we didn't say this was going to be easy, did we? We said it's pretty straightforward.

Eye Contact

A lack of attention to your eye contact can cripple even the best presenter. A good rule of thumb for eye contact is to look at each member of your audience for one or two seconds as you talk. If you stare at an audience member for longer than two seconds, it can get awkward for the audience member. Think about it—when was the last time you stared into someone's eyes for, say, five or six seconds? Try it now. Stop reading and look at yourself in the mirror for five seconds or look at your spouse or dog for five seconds. It seems like an eternity, right? (Don't try this out on the guy sitting next to you on the train. You might start a fight).

Eye contact is a key part of body language.

Typically, when we stare at people for five seconds or longer, it's a prelude to a kiss or a fight. It's "animal kingdom" time when the dominant predator tries to establish, well, dominance.

You can't do that to your audience. For practice, in your next meeting count, *one Mississippi, two Mississippi,* in your head as you look at your colleagues or friends around a table. That's a socially acceptable amount of eye contact and something we do almost without thinking when we're in casual conversations.

Now try this in your next meeting: look at each person for a fraction of a second. Flit your eyes around that table like Richard Nixon at a press conference during Watergate; look at ten people in a second.

No matter what you're saying at that point, people will think you're lying. Such a frantic lack of eye contact makes audience members think the speaker is insincere.

Another common trait we see in our corporate clients is looking at inanimate objects when things get uncomfortable. For example, perhaps the company's quarterly earnings aren't good. We've seen CEOs stare mournfully at the conference table or podium while addressing shareholders or employees—or, more accurately, during rehearsals with empty chairs where reporters, shareholders, or employees will be during the actual presentation.

Astute observers will read your body language when you speak. Eye contact is a key part of that body language, and as with most nonverbal elements, done well it can help cement your message; done badly or neglected, it can cripple your message.

Gestures

Rule of thumb for gestures: the bigger the room, the bigger the gestures.

If you're presenting in a big conference room, on a stage, or in a hotel ballroom, it's really difficult to gesture too big. Try it, go into the biggest room at your office—or just your backyard at home or any park. Imagine an audience before you, and lift your hands above your head like you're boasting about catching an enormous fish. It might feel weird (okay, it will feel weird), but such large gestures can help reinforce your message.

A lot of speakers will gesture within themselves; that is, their arms and hands will only move around in the general area of their stomachs and waists. If they're sitting around a small conference table, that's just fine. But even in a medium-sized room, gesturing big can help lift energy and emphasis during a speech.

When we're completely comfortable with what we're saying, our gestures seem totally natural and match what we say. But when we're not quite sure of the verbal, the visuals can get weird quickly. Just look at politicians running for office. There is often a woodenness to them, sometimes because their gestures seem out of sync with what they're saying. We spend a lot of time watching debates, and sometimes it seems like there's an advisor standing behind the camera yelling, "MOVE YOUR ARMS!" at the candidates, who respond by doing just that. However, the gestures often seem completely disconnected from what they're saying, which can lead to comic results (think John Kerry, Mitt Romney).

Political candidates and corporate executives who've worked hard enough on their speeches will use gestures to enhance their messages. For example, during a poignant or emotional story, they will touch their right palm to their heart to emphasize how meaningful, how close to their very core, the story they're currently telling is for them at that point. Look closely and you can also see how they feel about their opponents; we're thinking here of a presidential candidate who was talking about his opponent and just happened to scratch his forehead with his middle finger as he mentioned what the other candidate was saying about him. Anyone watching with the sound off would have wondered why that candidate just flipped off the audience.

One basic mistake many speakers make is gesturing with their palms facing their audience. This can appear defensive, even if you don't mean it that way. Gesture with your palms up (back of your hands facing the audience) and avoid pointing at the audience unless you're recognizing someone for great work. Pointing can be perceived as overly aggressive. That's why President Bill Clinton made famous use of his thumb and knuckle when emphasizing a point or aiming a critique directly at an individual. It took the edge off the gesture. Of course, if your intent is to scare the pants off your audience and get in their face, point away.

Instead of pointing outward toward a person or group, some speakers point downward with their index figure to help them punctuate a point. Both Barack

Move your arms.

Obama and George W. Bush emphasize key points, beliefs, or assertions by jabbing at the air or tapping their index finger on the podium in front of them. (Yes, presidents get to use podiums; it comes with being the leader of the free world and having a really cool presidential seal. We still don't like podiums, but presidents outrank us—and they control Seal Team Six—so we'll defer just this once.)

Avoid pointing at the audience.

Lots of speakers don't know what to do with their hands when they're standing in front of a room. It's pretty simple: stand facing the audience, with your feet, knees, hips, and shoulders square to the room full of people. Keep your hands at your sides, and then raise them to gesture as you tell a story or make a point. Take that walk from side to side as you present, and you'll find that the gestures seem natural, as does the walking, eventually. (It takes a bit of practice at first to go from a stiff march to a casual stroll.)

The Physics of Smiling

Have you ever watched Richard Feynman talk about physics? It's fascinating. Go to YouTube and watch the "Feynman 'Fun to Imagine'" series. He's smiling the entire time. The 1965 Nobel Prize winner is talking about jiggling atoms and stuff we can't comprehend on a typical day. And then four minutes in, it hits us: we're smiling too.

Feynman loves the subject matter so much, and explains it with such simple, everyday illustrations as a cup of coffee or rubber bands or magnets, that we can't help but like it too. Maybe you should keep this in mind when pitching "enterprise software or IP telephony" or life insurance.

Feynman, "The Great Explainer," was to physics what Ronald Reagan and Bill Clinton were to politics and world affairs: master communicators. Feynman liked to say that if a topic could not be explained in a freshman lecture, it was not yet fully understood. By keeping it simple and using mind-expanding words like "imagine," he made science easy to understand and fun to follow. But it's the smile that sucked you in.

Cesar Millan, nicknamed "The Dog Whisperer," once said that dogs introduce themselves to other dogs through energy rather than names or identities. "It's energy before anything else," he explained to a troubled dog owner.

Smile.
Just smile.

Presenters are a lot like dogs. It's about energy before anything else. If you walk on stage with positive energy, then the audience will be more open to your message. If you look as if that conference or presentation is the last place on earth you want to be, then—guess what—it's also the last place on earth your audience wants to be.

Before the "voice of God" announces your name at the next industry event and before you ever walk on stage, go to your happy place. Do whatever it is you have to do to get into a comfortable, confident zone. One client goes for a run the morning of big presentations. Another executive has his assistant limit him to one cup of coffee before big speeches—we've seen her quite literally pull the second cup from his grasp—because that second jolt of caffeine makes him too crazy.

Here's one last, simple application: smile. Just smile. A longtime client of ours who was the chief technology officer of a content management software company says it's now the first thing he does when he stands in front an audience of any size. He smiles. And he's noticed that a funny thing happens to the faces in the crowd. They return the favor and smile right back.

Sometimes the simplest things, in words and gestures, can have a profound impact.

YOUR HOMEWORK

Watch and analyze Sheryl Sandberg's December 2010 TED Women talk, "Why We Have Too Few Women Leaders" (http://tinyurl.com/WLted). It's one of the best presentations we've seen in recent years, and it's worth watching in its entirety. It's a great example of the first four chapters coming together and coming to life on stage. What you'll see is a very polished presenter who has clearly put in a lot of time rehearsing—and rehearsing the right things.

Sheryl's use of stories. We all remember stories—they stick more than anything else. Sheryl uses her stories strategically to illustrate her key points, to bring in some humor and personality, and to make her key messages memorable. The first comes at 1:45 into the presentation, and it's the most memorable. It reinforces her major message, includes humor, and gives her an immediate likability.

As you watch, note these elements

Sheryl's signposting. Note Sheryl's use of "verbal bullet points" to organize her narrative. At 4:08, after hitting the headline, citing some problematic statistics, and telling a memorable story that brings it to real life and makes it personal, she says "there are three" messages for those women who want to stay in the workforce. Very nice. You'll also notice her hands: when she says "there are three," she nonverbally reinforces it with three fingers up in the air. She then clearly calls out each of the three at the right points, "Number one..."

Sheryl's headline that sets up her entire presentation. At 0:40, Sheryl says, "We have a problem. Women are not making it to the top of any profession anywhere in the world." Strong. (We would have moved it to 0:04 from 0:40, since every part of her presentation falls from this headline.)

Sheryl's use of statistics to reinforce her major point.
Listen for how Sheryl backs up the headline with a few surprising—and credibility enhancing—numbers.

Sheryl's use of the stage. We talk about "movement with purpose," which is what you see in this presentation. She walks purposefully in a small arc to open herself to each side of the audience, and stops and talks there for a while before slowly walking to the other end of the arc.

Sheryl's roll-with-it approach. Audiovisual and other technical problems happen sometimes. They just do. How you respond is what separates good presenters from bad. You'll notice a microphone glitch and a lot of static. So they bring her a handheld microphone and she just rolls with it. She didn't make it a bigger deal than it actually was.

Sheryl's comfort screen. This we don't like. There's way—way!—too much text on the downstage monitors. This is a danger-zone issue. She clearly knows her content, and she doesn't need this much stuff on her downstage screen. In fact, it could cause more trouble later on. You just need a stat or a word or two. You'll notice she regularly looks down to the screens. When you're looking down you're not connecting with your audience. This was a miss.

Sheryl's lip smack. This is a common distraction. She needs to bring a bottle of water to the stage and sip between the major sections of her presentation.

Sheryl's inflection at 7:15. "NO ONE gets to the corner office..." Nice emphasis.

Sheryl's pauses. Throughout the presentation, Sheryl's built in and rehearsed some good pauses for emphasis and effect. However, she's not pausing enough for laughter and applause. She's talking through and over them. Let your audience celebrate you and your presentation. Don't rob them of that euphoria or rob yourself of that stronger audience connection.

Sheryl's ending. Strong. She wrapped up with major statistics, themes, and a personal touch that tied back to her headline.

So that's your homework.

5
you must prepare

Danah Boyd should never have taken the stage at Web 2.0 in 2009.

She simply wasn't ready.

But she did. And she regretted it.

Boyd researches youth culture. She's based near Boston, and as folks in that part of the world sometimes say, she's "wicked smart" (only in New England they'd call her "wicked smaaaart").

But the audience at Web 2.0 Expo doesn't care how smart you are once the presentation begins. They care if you can get to the point, make them think about your subject, and make them care about your point of view.

Boyd had written a paper, "Streams of Content, Limited Attention: The Flow of Information Through Social Media." It received compliments from those who read it. Trouble is, Boyd chose to read it out loud at the podium to hundreds of people, and things went sideways.

Because she was reading, she stumbled over her words. Her brain was moving faster along her script than her mouth was capable of. Because she was reading, her eyes were looking down at her paper rather than at the audience to whom she was speaking. Because she was reading, her language and delivery didn't sound natural. She hadn't translated the written word into the spoken word. Because she hadn't prepared, she hadn't built in pauses to give herself and her audience a breather.

Because Boyd didn't really pay attention to the staging, she didn't realize there was a massive projection screen behind her containing a live Twitter feed of attendees' comments.

Her audience revolted, and the Tweets started to pop up on the screen. Here are three of the nicest Tweets that ran over Boyd's head:

> @billyger: *danah boyd from microsoft is talking way too fast. It's hard to follow and I have no idea what she is talking about. #w2e*
>
> @dandam: *Danah Boyd loves coffee. #w2e*
>
> @andybudd: *Wow, people are bleeding out of danah boyd's somewhat dry and academic lecture*

Which led to this mea culpa several days later on Boyd's blog: "Unfortunately, my presentation at Web 2.0 Expo sucked. I knew something was wrong because folks started laughing in the audience."

We agree that this experience is a commentary on how awful we can be sometimes as humans. No one should have to endure what Boyd did, particularly when she had the courage initially to take the stage and lay herself and her ideas out there for public consumption and criticism. In fact, we strongly recommend that you never—ever—accept a speaking invitation at a conference where a live Twitter feed runs over your head and behind you.

Of course, hindsight is 20/20. No one is perfect, but Boyd has definitely learned from her 2009 speech. The hard way.

That said, the entire debacle was ultimately Boyd's fault. Had she rehearsed out loud—away from the script and on camera—this all could have been avoided. The humiliation. The hit to her confidence. The lasting image. The YouTube video. That doesn't make the audience's behavior right. It's simply a reminder that the success of a presenter lies squarely on his or her own shoulders. It's the presenter's job to rock it. Sometimes that's a hard lesson to learn.

Staging

There is a lot of important but generally unseen work to do between rehearsal and game day.

Do you know what the room looks like? Is the stage five feet off the ground, or is it a floor-level platform? Is the seating like a theater, or are the seats flat on the floor? Are there comfort screens downstage so you can see your notes? Can they give you a lavalier microphone so you can walk and talk? Is there a podium?

These are just a few of the questions that should be in your game preparation for every presentation.

Remember, podiums suck; don't get us started.

The conference coordinator can send you a diagram of the room for a large audience presentation, and the executive assistant can send you a photo of the conference room for your next sales meeting. The point is, you don't want a single surprise when you enter the room the morning of your presentation. Surprises affect your confidence. And a flustered, frazzled speaker will have a tough time getting the audience's attention or gaining the prospect's trust.

For example, we typically insist on having a small round table to our left for a bottle of water and our laptop—because we want to drive any videos or visuals ourselves. We never let a production company run it from the back of the house. Never. We want control of everything, particularly the ability to jump to a video that's relevant to the flow of the session.

Lots of professionals use checklists to make sure things go smoothly—think airline pilots or surgeons—and you should too. Here's a pre-presentation checklist for you to consider. You won't look like a diva if you request some or all of these accommodations, and would you really care if you did? You'll simply look like a seasoned presenter who knows what you need to be comfortable.

A Partial Presentation Checklist

- [ ] How big is the stage and is there a podium?

- [ ] Will you have a lavalier (lapel) microphone so you can walk and talk?

- [ ] Will the placement of the projector allow you freedom to move on stage?

- [ ] Do you want to run your presentation from your laptop on stage or will the AV team run it from the back of the room?

- [ ] Who will run your backup slide deck (if you use one)?

- [ ] You do have a backup of your slides, right?

- [ ] Do you need flip charts or props of any sort on stage?

- [ ] Do you need a printout of your slides for reference?

- [ ] Will you videotape your presentation?

- [ ] What's the dress code for the event?

- [ ] Is there a sound check/AV check set for your presentation?

- [ ] Do you need handout materials of any sort? And if so, how will you distribute them?

- [ ] Do you need handheld microphones for audience members (if you're going to have audience participation)?

- [ ] Make sure you have water on stage.

- [ ] Do you know how long your presentation slot is, and will there be a question and answer period afterward?

- [ ] Be sure your cellphone is completely switched off or away from your computer. No coins in your pockets. No earrings that make noise.

- [ ] If you don't need Web access for your presentation, turn off your computer's WiFi to prevent any unwanted instant messages or e-mail notifications.

- [ ] Are you bringing your own clicker?

- [ ] Will you get evaluated as part of the conference follow-up, or do you need to solicit your own feedback?

- [ ] And, finally, it sounds basic but don't forget the power cord for your computer. These are pretty straightforward questions, but you'd be amazed at how many speakers from brand-name companies neglect to ask them.

You can download the worksheet at ElevatorSpeech.com.

Practice Out Loud

This one's easy. You practice, you'll be better. You don't, and you won't.

Too many presenters don't practice out loud. We can't tell you the number of times company executives have blown off presentation rehearsals because their "slides aren't done yet." Slides should be the last things you focus on, not the first.

That lack of preparation really shows on presentation day—not only in the length and content of the presentation but also in the delivery style. Incoherent content is what draws out those ums and ahs and distracting nonverbal tics. And that's when your audience checks out.

When we asked a group of executives what they wanted to get out of our coaching session, one person got almost confrontational when anticipating our teaching points:

"I had a personality test conducted twenty-five years ago, and it showed that I'm at my best when I'm spontaneous. So I will *never* practice." Practice, he went on to explain, took away his authenticity.

Sigh.

You practice, you'll be better.

We responded by asking whom he thought was the most spontaneous, authentic speaker he'd ever seen. His response? Apple's Steve Jobs.

At this point, we suggested he work on his definition of never. We also shared one of our favorite anecdotes from the January 5, 2006, edition of *The Guardian* in London (http://tinyurl.com/WLjobs).

For every forty-five-minute keynote Steve Jobs used to deliver at Macworld, he'd spend two full days in dress rehearsal on the same stage at the Moscone Center in San Jose. Two full days, out loud, on stage, in dress rehearsal. That's not counting all the weeks of prep time, message development, and effort leading up to those rehearsals.

Word is the doors were locked and there was even a Porta-Potty in the corner of the room. Do you know anyone who commits that amount of time to rehearsal? We don't either.

That's one of the reasons Jobs stood apart as a master presenter. He recognized that presentations were part of his job and required the same degree of focus, discipline, and preparation as any other executive responsibility. And that level of preparation was why—on game day at Macworld—it appeared to our client and the rest of the world as if Jobs hadn't practiced at all.

The key is to build muscle memory. The more you practice something, the better you get at it, and the less you think about what you're doing while you do it. It's the same in sports, music, acting, carpentry, and yes, presenting.

(Years later, still no word from our executive with the personality test. We assume that's because he's busy practicing for his next "spontaneous" Jobs-like presentation.)

There was an interesting documentary some time ago about *The Silence of the Lambs,* the 1991 thriller in which Sir Anthony Hopkins won an Academy Award for his chilling portrayal of the cannibal Hannibal Lecter.

So how does one prepare to inhabit a character like Lecter? Hopkins admits that he has a "little bit of an obsession" when it comes to rehearsing. "What I do is I go over and go over and go over it. I take a section of the script, and I go over it twenty times, thirty times. And as I build up to two hundred fifty times, I know that I know that I know it. As Hamlet says, 'The preparation is all.' You can't wing these things. You must prepare and prepare and prepare."

Can we get an amen from the congregation?!

From that preparation came an Oscar.

Now two hundred fifty times is staggering. But imagine if you read through your "lines" for your next speech twenty-five times, or even 2.5 times. You'd own your material and be able to take the stage with a great deal of performance energy while simultaneously appearing relaxed and confident. These are the marks of a true master communicator.

Want to see us go crazy? Have a CEO (like the executive above) tell us, "Oh, I don't like to practice too much for my speeches. I like to wing it." When this happens, the CEO is mistaking diligent rehearsal and careful calibration of materials for "winging it," because it appears so natural and comfortable that audiences think the speakers must be winging it.

The best presenters who appear effortless on stage or on screen are more often than not the ones who practice more than anyone else.

Practice presenting out loud.

Winston Churchill was said to prepare forty-five minutes for every one minute of speech he delivered, even in the midst of war. Martin Luther King Jr. practiced fifteen hours each week for his Sunday sermons—when the civil rights movement was tearing at the fabric of the country.

There's no substitute for out-loud practice. If they can do it, so can you.

It sounds simple enough, but few presenters practice out loud. Fewer still record rehearsals on video and play it back—the ultimate preparation process. No camera? Do it in front of the bathroom mirror, in the shower, in the car, on your morning walk, or into your voice mail at work. Just do it. That way, you get used to the rhythms of your speech; you understand what to emphasize and what to edit. Be merciless in what you remove. Not sure what works or what doesn't? Deliver the next five to ten minutes of your next presentation to a colleague or a group of friends. You'll rapidly find out what works and what doesn't.

We watched it firsthand with Kevin Hogan, then CEO

of Zurich Global Life Insurance, a massive insurance company based in Switzerland. Each year the company gathers approximately three hundred of its top business leaders in one place to kick off the year's efforts.

Hogan had done a lot of thinking about what he wanted to say. He had written several pages of notes and thoughts. After a few telephone conversations and edits to his script, we met in a conference room at the Newark Airport Hilton over the holiday break in January 2012.

He embraced seven hours of work on his narrative for his two major presentations, much of it on camera. We played back the recorded rehearsals and collectively critiqued his words and delivery to build upon his existing strengths and ideas. By the end of the session, we had crafted a new opening and structure for his two presentations—which were only two weeks away. We also left him with a video camera to take back to Switzerland for additional practice.

It's infrequent that an executive makes that next commitment. Their job usually gets in the way of subsequent rehearsals, and the awkwardness of videotaping yourself is easily avoidable. But Hogan—like Jobs—recognized that presenting is part of his job. CEOs are called on to inspire, rally teams, deliver hard news, and bring clarity to complex business issues. That all takes a lot of work.

To our surprise and delight, Kevin did his homework, literally. He set up the video camera in a back room in his Zurich home and recorded the next iteration of his narrative and delivery. The Sunday evening before his Wednesday-morning kickoff, we received links to several videotaped rehearsals. Each version was progressively better.

On Wednesday, he took the stage with this opening,

"I'm going to do something a little bit different. I'm going to talk about three things today. I'm going to talk about engines. I'm going to talk about hedgehogs. And I'm going to talk about sherpas."

That unexpected opening gave a creative, memorable hook to his primary messages, and stories illustrated each of the three.

Hogan delivered his thirty- and forty-five-minute presentations without notes or a comfort screen, accompanied by only a few photos on his slides. He employed a conversational tone and a smooth walk-and-talk delivery up and down a catwalk stage.

This was no small feat. Weeks earlier in Newark, we had prepared for a theater-in-the-round stage arrangement. Without an early arrival and a lot of at-home practice, this staging surprise could have chipped away at his confidence.

Confidence comes in no small part from figuring out the words first. Kevin Hogan's "talk track" was the basis for the rest of his presentation, it's vocal cadence and its visual staging. Even though it's only 7 percent of Mehrabian's findings, it's a critical 7 percent that essentially triggers the rest of a good presentation.

The problem in most corporations is that people prepare backward—they develop their slides first instead of figuring out the talk track. Or worse still, they cobble together a presentation by cutting and pasting a mishmash of previously used slides from colleagues, creating a "blob" of visuals with no discernible point or narrative.

On Wednesdays at 30 Rockefeller Plaza in New York, writers and actors from *Saturday Night Live* sit around a big conference table. They all hold scripts for the coming Saturday's show, and they perform what's known as a "table read." They're trying to find the talk tracks for the various skits. They know that's the critical thing when you have millions of people watching you on live television.

If SNL prepared like corporations, they'd design sets, put on makeup, wear costumes, consider lighting, and then—and only then—they'd look at all those visuals and think, "Gee, wonder what I'm going to say here?"

That'd be insane. But it's how most corporate speakers get ready for a presentation.

Break that mold. Find your talk track first, then like Kevin Hogan, you'll know that what you say provides the right launch pad for how you say it and what your visuals look like.

 There are two steps to your homework— one right before your presentation and one right after. Each step employs the same tools: video and evaluations.

Video: For the next two months, make your company's presenters rehearse out loud two to three weeks ahead of their next presentations. No PowerPoint. Just talk out the content: the messages and the stories. Videotape it and play it back. Then repeat. It will have a tremendous impact.

There's a reason that coaches in sports as varied as golf, football, and soccer watch game film before and after contests: that film often shows very clearly what went right and what went wrong. It's the same situation for speakers. If you're videotaping and watching rehearsals, you'll see what's working and what isn't. If you watch the "game film" after a speech—a sort of presentation postmortem—you'll know what the audience saw, and you'll be able to see if those messages you worked so hard to develop actually got through.

By some estimates (including ours), each minute of a fabulous speech will require roughly one hour of preparation.

If you think that's a lot, consider the cost of not preparing for that critical presentation to your boss, employees, prospects, partners, customers, shareholders, or reporters. The good news is that once you've endured the preparation once, you can often shorten it considerably for future variations on the same speech.

Evaluations: You've practiced your presentation diligently. You've got clean, simple slides. You feel good when you get in front of the audience, and they applaud mightily at the end of your speech. Heck, you feel great. But how do you know that you're hitting the mark? How do you know your message is embedded in the brains of all the audience members?

Here's how.

An evaluation form is an efficient way to solicit instant feedback from your audience during rehearsals and on game day. It's not always possible to get such feedback, but if you can, you should. Too many speakers are scared to ask for feedback; we think that's a huge mistake.

Here's what we've done at various corporate clients. The Coaching Session Feedback form on page 105 is printed and available in the room. Let's say you speak to forty people in a conference room. The form is in front of each person or is handed out immediately after your speech. You, or someone else on your team, then say something like:

Evaluation Form

Thanks for coming to Dave's speech today. We appreciate you being here, and we want to make sure it was a good use of your time. There's an evaluation form in front of you; please spend sixty seconds filling it out and please DON'T put your name on it. We're only interested in candid comments, not who said them. You can fold the forms in half and put them in the box by the door before you exit. Thank you so much.

You'd be amazed at how useful this simple exercise can be for speakers, during rehearsal or after the official presentation. When we coach senior executives, we videotape them presenting and often use this form so the entire audience can provide input. The execs get an earful from us, and they see themselves on video. They also get peer feedback from colleagues who understand the business like they do—that's insight almost no one else can provide.

The feedback form has three basic buckets: verbal, vocal, and visual. Verbal is of course what you say—the words that come out of your mouth. Vocal is the rhythm, pacing, and cadence—giving feedback on the use of any non-words or whether you are speaking too fast or too softly. Visual is everything else—how you look, how you move, and your eye contact.

Combined, the video footage and the evaluation forms will give you precious insight into what your audience hears, sees, and absorbs from your presentation.

Be brave. This particular homework assignment will be uncomfortable; no one likes being videotaped or critiqued. Do it anyway. It will make you and your team better presenters.

So that's your homework.

Coaching Session Feedback

Rate from poor to excellent:	1	2	3	4	5	COMMENTS
VERBAL						
Clear Point						
Examples						
Stories						
Language						
Jargon						
VOCAL						
Projection						
Variety						
Non-Words						
Speed						
VISUAL						
Posture/Stance						
Movement						
Gestures						
Expression						
Eye Contact						
Dress/Appearance						
OVERALL						
Energy						
Passion						
Q&A						
PowerPoint						

You can download the worksheet at ElevatorSpeech.com.

Summary

Let's go right back to where we started. In summary, our counsel to executives boils down to one simple acronym: **S.T.O.R.Y.**

On page one of this book we introduced you to Jim and his forty-five-minute, sixty-slide presentation with its three hundred "um-ah" stammers. For us that is a relatively common scenario. Executives with years of experience and mountains of industry knowledge still make fundamental mistakes when it comes to speaking well. They don't tell stories, they use too many slides, and they don't practice out loud.

It's not complicated; in fact, it's so far from rocket science it falls into the category of what Dave's dad used to call "the bleeding obvious" (which was our second favorite title for this book). But if you do your homework, if you stop the slide tsunami, if you tell great stories, if you organize your speech so it flows beautifully, if you pay homage to what Mehrabian found about believability, and if, above all, you prepare meticulously, then you will ascend to membership in that exclusive club of truly effective speakers—and a place from which your career can often skyrocket.

"Dr. Elmer provides a valuable and tin_____ially as the face of world missions is changing. No longer is missions from the ...est to the rest,' but from 'everywhere to everywhere.' This delightful trend in missions makes Dr. Elmer's book even more significant. Today, Peruvians face culture shock in China, and Taiwanese are challenged to understand Sudan. Missionaries in multinational teams need to learn to work with their colleagues as well as with host-country nationals. *Cross-Cultural Connections* is filled with sound principles and fascinating stories. I will be sending copies of the book to each of our personnel directors."

Jim Plueddemann, International Director, SIM

"With his candid humor and personal applications, Elmer knows how to instruct adults. This is not just a book but a training manual that incorporates some good andragogical principles of adult education. . . . Elmer doesn't just take us to the field, but treats the oft-neglected topic of reentry. The appendix, while directed to a debriefing of a longer term cross-cultural experience, could well be a separate manual to debrief the many short-termers who need post-trip evaluation."

John H. Orme, Executive Director, IFMA

"Today's world demands the awareness, mindset and skills that Dr. Elmer delivers in *Cross-Cultural Connections*. Multicultural interactions, once reserved for the world traveler and missionary, are now everyone's experience. For success in missions trips, business trips and in a demographically changing U.S., every Christian needs the insights in this book . . . every day."

Wayne Shabaz, Cross-Cultural Business Consultant and Author of *The Corporate Genome: Unleashing the Power of Our Diversity*

"Dr. Duane Elmer makes complicated and technical material easy and practical. He has a gift of connecting both theory and practice in such a way that they become usable. Although written with Western readers in mind, the book reflects Two-Thirds World thinking. It works both ways—for those who wish to cross the cultural limits from the West to the Two-Thirds World or vice versa. For this reason I recommend this book not only to the Western readers but also to Two-Thirds World people."

David Tai-Woong Lee, Director, Global Missionary Training Center, Seoul, Korea

"Starting with the story of a monkey 'rescuing' a fish from 'drowning,' Duane Elmer shows the rest of us primates how to jump into the chilly waters of another culture and learn to swim with the fish. As one who has seen him do this effectively with business personnel, I am delighted that his insights are now available to far more who are making the plunge—especially those doing so for Christ's sake."

J. Dudley Woodberry, Professor of Islamic Studies and Dean Emeritus, School of World Mission, Fuller Theological Seminary

"Some of us work the same way whether we are at home or abroad. *Cross-Cultural Connections* will help and prepare you to see the core values commonly shared by the receiving culture, which determine how they make decisions and interact in everyday life. Although I live and travel constantly between different cultures, I was able to reflect on a couple sticky situations of my own with the wisdom offered by this book."

Janson Chan, president, CMR International Corp, China

"Once again, Dr. Elmer has provided us with an excellent, insightful and interactive guide for preparation for cross-cultural ministry at home or abroad. The applications to interpersonal relationships are many. This is a 'must read' for any Christian anticipating wider involvement in service for our Lord."

Howard Searle, M.D., executive director, Emmanuel Hospital Association (USA)

"Duane Elmer has a very special gift: he helps people become more comfortable with each other and with themselves. . . . His gift for clarity and meaning is revealed for the reader in terms of the practical illustrations and stories of events that seem to leap off the page full of meaning. By putting his own wealth of experience together with the skill of an architect, Duane Elmer shows clearly the difference that culture makes in the feeling of things, the meaning of things and in the perspective that transforms experiences into wisdom."

Ted Ward, Professor Emeritus of Educational Administration and Research, Michigan State University, and Professor Emeritus of Educational Studies, Mission, and Research, Trinity International University

Cross-CULTURAL CONNECTIONS

Stepping Out

and Fitting In

Around the World

DUANE ELMER

IVP Academic

An imprint of InterVarsity Press
Downers Grove, Illinois

InterVarsity Press
P.O. Box 1400, Downers Grove, IL 60515-1426
World Wide Web: www.ivpress.com
E-mail: email@ivpress.com

InterVarsity Press®️ is the book-publishing division of InterVarsity Christian Fellowship/USA®️, a student movement active on campus at hundreds of universities, colleges and schools of nursing in the United States of America, and a member movement of the International Fellowship of Evangelical Students. For information about local and regional activities, write Public Relations Dept., InterVarsity Christian Fellowship/USA, 6400 Schroeder Rd., P.O. Box 7895, Madison, WI 53707-7895, or visit the IVCF website at <www.intervarsity.org>.

Cover photograph: Glen Gyssler
Cover design: Design Concepts

ISBN 978-0-8308-2309-3

Printed in the United States of America ∞

Library of Congress Cataloging-in-Publication Data

Elmer, Duane, 1943-
  Cross-cultural connections: stepping out and fitting in around the
world / Duane H. Elmer.
    p. cm.
Includes bibliographical references.
  ISBN 0-8308-2309-3 (pbk.: alk. paper)
  1. Intercultural communication—Religious aspects—Christianity. 2.
Christianity and culture. 3. Missions—Theory. I. Title.
  BV2082.I57 E46 2002
  261—dc21

                                                                      2002005715

P	23	22	21	20	19	18	17	16	15	14	13	12	11	10	9	8
Y	22	21	20	19	18	17	16	15	14	13	12	11	10	09	08	

Dedicated to my sons . . .

each a master in his own way in the fine art of connecting.

SCOTT,
wonderfully deep and loyal.

MARC,
wonderfully natural and inclusive.

Contents

SECTION 4: *Cultural Differences That Confuse*

SECTION 5: *Returning Home*

Preface

YOUR SOJOURN INTO ANOTHER CULTURE will probably be fun and frustrating, exhilarating and exhausting, stretching and stressful. It may be among the toughest things you have ever done and also the most rewarding. The purpose of this book is to help you become aware of the realities in making a cultural transition—in business, in short- or long-term missions, as a bivocational person or in whatever capacity you may find yourself. Awareness of the issues you will face gives you an advantage because it causes you to have more realistic expectations, which diminish the jarring effects of a new environment and give you the presence of mind to employ coping skills that will move you forward in cultural understanding and adjustment, and in strong relationships among the people of the other culture.

While the title of this book contains the word *cross-cultural,* many have found this material helpful as they try to connect across ethnicities. Thus, the same skills necessary for making cultural transitions apply to domestic situations as well.

The contents of this book have been used at home and abroad by thousands of business people, short-term mission workers, missionaries, relief and development workers, bivocational people and educators. Many sectors of the secular community, such as multinational corporation personnel, medical workers, refugee resettlement workers and private sector groups, have also found the information useful. In my opinion, if the ideas of this book were applied more broadly in the mar-

ketplace, Western organizations would be more successful in their cross-cultural ventures and in the spreading of international goodwill at the same time.

Thus, the concepts, principles and skills in this book have been taught and applied in a large variety of Christian and non-Christian situations and cultural contexts. The focus is on helping you make a successful transition into another culture. Behind the skills are concepts and principles that will help you live your life more effectively no matter where you may be.

* * *

BOOKS ARE RARELY WRITTEN BY INDIVIDUALS, more often by a dedicated team of participants. Among the many, I wish to acknowledge a few who played major roles in whatever quality this book may possess. Heather Webb, my teacher's assistant at Trinity Evangelical Divinity School, worked with graphics, proofing and editing. Cindy Shabaz contributed significantly with timely insights and fitting illustrations. Muriel Elmer, my beloved wife, gave unceasing encouragement and provided invaluable help in shaping the content and development of the book. Thank you wonderful people.

GETTING A PERSPECTIVE

Monkeys, Mission and Us

To be surprised, to wonder, is to begin to understand

JOSÉ ORTEGA Y GASSET

IS IT WORTH YOUR TIME TO READ THIS BOOK? Such a question is legitimate to ask of this and any other book you are about to read. Here are my thoughts on why this book is worth reading—it may make the remainder of the book more meaningful for you.

In my thirty years of teaching at the college/university level, the majority of my students have been in my cross-cultural communication classes. Most seem eager to learn, but sometimes a bold person will ask, "Why should I be here? Why can't I just go to a country and do my ministry?" To some, all the time, courses and money seemed like a gigantic waste. "People are dying every day while we are just sitting here doing nothing. Can you tell me why I should be here?"

Similar questions arose during my fifteen years of training in the corporate world. Some in business felt that understanding people from other cultures was a waste of time. Those in my workshops had their technical skills and just wanted to get on with the job. Such a view, however, is quite shortsighted and potentially dangerous. The reason? These people see the job as a task to be done with little or no concern for genuine relationships with local people. A strong task orientation without first establishing friendships can lead to disappointing if not disastrous outcomes.

Early in my career these "why bother" statements would cut like a knife. Since I am a cross-cultural trainer, my profession and my whole life seemed under attack. Defensiveness would surface and I would mut-

ter something about requirements by sending organizations and statements like "It will do you good" and "Someday you will understand." I doubt I convinced any skeptics. As you read this book, you might wonder the same. Why bother? Why not just get on with it? Is all this preparation necessary? I have a better answer to that question now, and it begins with a story.

THE MONKEY AND THE FISH

A typhoon had temporarily stranded a monkey on an island. In a secure, protected place, while waiting for the raging waters to recede, he spotted a fish swimming against the current. It seemed obvious to the monkey that the fish was struggling and in need of assistance. Being of kind heart, the monkey resolved to help the fish.

A tree precariously dangled over the very spot where the fish seemed to be struggling. At considerable risk to himself, the monkey moved far out on a limb, reached down and snatched the fish from the threatening waters. Immediately scurrying back to the safety of his shelter, he carefully laid the fish on dry ground. For a few moments the fish showed excitement, but soon settled into a peaceful rest. Joy and satisfaction swelled inside the monkey. He had successfully helped another creature.[1]

About monkeys. Like others who have heard this story, you may wonder about the intelligence of this monkey—a valid first impression. But let's look deeper by asking questions and discovering some important insights. Take a moment to answer the following questions.

1. What was the monkey's motivation?

2. What words would you use to describe the monkey as he went out over the raging water on a precarious limb to "help" the fish?

3. Why did the monkey help the fish by taking it out of the water?

4. What did the monkey assume about fish culture?

5. How do you think the fish felt about the help it received?

6. What advice would you give the monkey for future situations where he would like to help?

Lessons. In what ways might you be like the monkey? Write down three to four parallels between the monkey and yourself as you consider entering another culture to help the people. This will help clarify your thinking and help you remember the important lessons from the monkey.

1.

2.

3.

Here are my thoughts on the story. First, the monkey was courageous, had good intentions and noble motives. He also had zeal. However, his

motives were misdirected because of his ignorance—he could not see beyond his own frame of reference. He believed what was dangerous for him was dangerous for the fish. Therefore, what would be good for him would also be good for the fish—a crucial assumption. As a result, he acted out of his ignorance or limited frame of reference, and ended up doing damage rather than the good he intended. Unfortunately, the monkey may not even have known the damage he did, because he may have walked away leaving the fish "resting."

IMPORTANCE OF CROSS-CULTURAL TRAINING

Training in cross-cultural ministry is important so that we don't act like the monkey. We demand competence, skill and expertise from people who serve us. Suppose a person went through a year of medical school and then concluded, "All this learning is a waste of time. People are dying every day. I need to get out there and help them now." Would you consider going to such a physician? We would find such people foolish and dangerous, and would avoid them. What about nurses, lawyers, electricians, builders, pilots and food manufacturers? Don't we require the highest standards from them? Of course we do. We want the best because lives are at stake.

WHY BOTHER?

We bother because we do not want to be "monkeys." Because the eternity of people is at stake, we want to be the best possible representatives of Christ. If people refuse to become followers of Jesus, we hope it will not be because we were obnoxious, reckless, sloppy, irresponsible, ill-prepared—or because we were well-meaning but badly informed "monkeys." We can do better.

WHO ARE THE "MONKEYS"?

While this book is written primarily for North Americans, monkeys can come from anywhere—the monkey problem is universal. Since this

appears to be true (at least my observations suggest it is), this book should have broad application. I was a missionary for seventeen years. I have been on numerous short-term trips, trained businesspeople and missionaries, conducted cross-cultural training seminars in dozens of countries and had considerable exposure to inner-city work in the United States. I've seen more monkey behavior in myself than I ever want to admit. But I have tried to identify it and extract from it principles, which seem to work across ethnic groups in North America, cultural boundaries around the world and generational differences. In a curious way, they even help marriage partners understand each other. Now I pass these insights on with the prayer that you will be able to learn from my experiences and those of others. In doing so I also pray that God will reward your effort and make you effective for his glory.

D I S C U S S I O N Q U E S T I O N S

1. What doubts do you have about your need for cross-cultural training? Why?

2. Have you seen anyone act like the monkey? Have you ever acted like the monkey? What was the result?

3. List the things that you think the people will need in the culture you will enter. How can you discover whether what you listed will really meet their needs?

2
Your Part of God's Story

God so loved the world . . .

JOHN 3:16

And you will be my witnesses . . . to the ends of the earth.

ACTS 1:8

FOR MANY CENTURIES GOD HAS BEEN PUTTING TOGETHER a mosaic of people who have followed him to the ends of the earth. He continues to do it today. Perhaps you are reading this because you are thinking of entering another culture as a missionary, short-term worker or businessperson. This book is intended to help you be more effective in understanding the challenges of making the cultural transition. In anything you do, preparation is important. We expect it in all professionals. Preparation is even more important for the person representing Jesus Christ.

WHY ARE YOU IMPORTANT?

It is quite simple. Over six billion people inhabit the earth. Missiologists tell us that about one-half do not have a follower of Jesus in their community. Most have never heard that Jesus Christ offers them life eternal. Are you a Christian? Then you have some part to play in making Jesus known. It may be in another part of the world or it may not. You need to find out how and where God is leading you. Across the street or across an ocean, it doesn't matter as long as you are using your gifts and abilities to serve the Lord where he has placed you. If you are going somewhere where the people are not like you, this book will help you adjust and, hopefully, you will have a positive experience while fulfilling your goals.

In Another Culture

Entering most cultures of the world puts you in the minority—at least if you are white-skinned and living in North America or Europe, which, by the way, includes me. It was hard for me to think of myself as a minority person, because most of my life I looked around and nearly everyone looked like me. That made me a majority person. I felt good being in the majority. But I had a small perspective.

Let's get a sense of the world we are in. While that may seem a bit overwhelming, it is good to see things in proportion. Sometimes it helps us realize that God does not limit his attention to our part of the world. It is good for us to see beyond ourselves. But it is also good to see that we are part of God's activity in this world.

Here are some numbers that give us a glimpse of the global picture. Imagine a village of 1,000 people that represented the world's population.

- 206 would be Chinese
- 167 would be Indian
- 79 would be from Central and South America
- 50 would be from the former Soviet Union (Eastern European)
- 51 would be North American
- 45 would be Western European
- 33 would be Indonesian
- 21 would be from Japan
- 22 would be from Bangladesh
- 21 would be from Nigeria
- 24 would be from Pakistan
- 118 would be from other sub-Saharan African and other Asian countries[1]

The median age of those in the more economically developed countries would be about thirty years, while in the developing countries it

would be under sixteen years. In this global village, on a typical day there would be about twenty births: twelve Asian babies, three African, two Latin American and one each from North America, Eastern Europe and Western Europe.

Note the following statistics: The 114 North Americans, Europeans and Japanese (just over 11 percent of the population) own nearly 90 percent of the wealth in the world and consume more than half of its products. The fifteen richest countries have a per capita income of $11,500 (in 1987 U.S. dollars) while the fifteen poorest countries have a per capita income of $190.

Religiously, the global village of 1,000 people would look like this:

- Christian: 330, leaving 670 non-Christians
- Muslim: 198
- Nonreligious: 126
- Hindu: 135
- Buddhist: 60
- Ethnoreligionist: 38
- Atheist: 25
- New-religionist: 17
- Sikh: 4
- Jewish: 2
- Other: 65[2]

The intent of this chapter is to provide a perspective on the world outside our own context. Sometimes we fail to see beyond our experience and fail to realize the vast array of differences. Those differences can be a bridge to discovery and fascination or cause us frustration and endless headache. As the next two chapters suggest, we can handle the differences like the proverbial monkey or we can take a better approach.

D I S C U S S I O N   Q U E S T I O N S

1. How do you think being American affects your view of the rest of the world?

2. More specifically, write down three to five words that come to mind when you think of the country that you may be entering.

3. List three to five words that you think people of other cultures might use to describe Americans.

4. From a biblical perspective, what is the Christian's responsibility to the other parts of the world? What part would you like to play?

5. What do the statistics quoted in this chapter tell you? Have you changed your view of the world? Why or why not?

6. What, in your opinion, are some of the big needs in the world today? Where is help most desperately needed? How might you make a difference?

7. In what ways might people of other cultures help you?

3

Right, Wrong and Different

I had to believe that others were wrong in order to believe that we were right . . . in order to give validity to our existence.

GLADIS DEPREE

FOR MANY YEARS, SIDNEY HARRIS WROTE a widely syndicated editorial column for the *Chicago Tribune*. Among his penetrating insights, I remember one in particular. He stated that "every book that is ever published, every article ever written and every speech delivered should have the subtitle 'How to Be More Like Me.' " His point: We all believe that our way is the right way, our beliefs are correct and our culture is superior. So whenever I write or speak, the subtle message that transcends my words is: "You would be wise to change your ways to be more like me."

Wasn't that the monkey's message to the fish in chapter one? Is that the message you want your neighbors to hear? What about people in the new culture you plan to enter? I assume your answer is a quick and resounding no! Yet, it is not so easy as the monkey and fish story indicated. Transforming the way we think takes careful reflection and humility.

This chapter is intended to reveal and help reverse that subtle superiority that so many of us unconsciously carry. I will offer a series of insights on attitudes and behaviors that, if practiced, may help you enter and adjust to a new culture more effectively. These insights will also help you find fruitful, lasting relationships and represent well the Lord who goes with you and before you.

RIGHT, WRONG AND DIFFERENT

Let me share something from my life that will help us think about how our history influences our behaviors. We are all products of a heritage that cannot be set aside. It is good to acknowledge the positive contributions, affirm them and even build upon them. At the same time, it is good to become aware of the negative pieces of our history so we will not be victimized by them.

I grew up in a Swiss-German home in Southern Wisconsin. The Swiss are famous for magnificent alpine mountains, accurate and dependable watches, and trains that always run on time. Precision and punctuality are important Swiss values that support a larger value that "there is a right and wrong way to do everything," a phrase I often heard from my father and grandfather.

While right and wrong were familiar categories as a child, later I began to think more about the category of "differences." I define differences as "all those things, which the Scripture does not directly or in principle identify as sinful, wrong or destructive." (See Paul's handling of differences in Romans 14 and 1 Corinthians 8.)

In a way, the line below represents the values I grew up with in my home. Things were categorized as right and wrong and, if one searched long and hard, one or two things that might fall into the category of differences

RIGHT	DIFFERENCES	WRONG

Could just about everything in life be explained in terms of right and wrong as I had been taught?

School, to a great extent, supported this right-wrong mindset. On math tests, answers were either right or wrong. No negotiation. When I got my first English essay back, it looked like it had bled to death! The rules of grammar were not negotiable. To this day I hate red ink and refuse to use it in evaluating papers.

Sunday school and church had me traveling the same road. It seemed everything fell into one of two categories: right or wrong. Over time, it dawned on me that the things I put into the category of "right" were the things that were like me and the things I pegged as "wrong" were the things and people that were unlike me. Sidney Harris was right. However, this kind of thinking will likely cause serious problems since we live in a world bursting with differences, which should not be categorized as right or wrong. God reveals his multifaceted nature through the variety and diversity he has placed in his world. Difference was born in eternity—God as Father, as Son and as Holy Spirit, each different yet each fully God. Much of what we see and experience in this life does not belong in the right or wrong categories, and to force them into one or the other would be counterproductive, if not destructive. Some of us need to cultivate and enlarge this difference category to be more effective in human relationships.

I don't want you to get the impression that my home was unhappy. My parents were good, godly and loving. Like most parents they did the best they could; but they were products of their own cultural heritage. Similarly, over the years, our two sons have helped my wife and me by pointing out where we drew rigid right-wrong lines unnecessarily.

However, the Bible does speak of right and wrong. The modern tendency to categorize everything as a difference—"your thing" or "whatever"—leads us to very dangerous ground. A mindset where everything is "just different"—and nothing is judged by Scripture to be wrong or sinful—must be rejected. Contemporary culture has shifted from the rigid right-wrong categories of my childhood to the opposite extreme where virtually everything is different and nothing is declared wrong. Throwing out all absolutes doesn't solve anything. Both extremes need to be avoided. In this chapter you might get the impression that I am a cultural relativist—right and wrong are relative to the culture. That is not true. If we treat everything as right and wrong, we do a great disservice to the human diversity God has placed in his creation. If we treat everything as

a cultural difference, we do a great disservice to the God who authored an uncompromising word of truth. I attempt to respect both God's world and the Scripture.

THROUGH THE GENERATIONS

Where to draw the lines has always been murky business. Each generation often rejects many of the previous generations' lines and draws its own, believing them to be superior. However, when their children come along and take the liberty of drawing their own lines, the battle starts over again. Young people are happy to draw their lines differently than their parents. Yet, when they have their own teenagers, they will also find it difficult to allow their children to freely draw their lines wherever they choose. At some point, obviously, we stretch the range of differences too far, at which time we have violated a biblical absolute and entered the area of wrong or sin. Trying to determine when that happens is not my intent here. The issue in crossing cultures is the tendency to judge cultural differences as wrong and to do so with little thought or understanding. So bear with me as I try to develop this idea. Consider the three generations in my family.

My Father's Lines:

RIGHT	DIFFERENCES	WRONG

My Lines:

RIGHT	DIFFERENCES	WRONG

My Sons' Lines:

RIGHT	DIFFERENCES	WRONG

Observe that the range of differences grew greater with each generation. Each Christian generation felt they drew the lines more in keeping with Scripture. I will give my opinion on the matter shortly.

Western Culture's Lines:

RIGHT	D I F F E R E N C E S	WRONG

Most Christians would reject the lines that Western culture draws where nearly everything seems to be in the category of difference and little is labeled as right or wrong. But it is not so easy to draw the lines when all three generations (as shown above) represent Christians who love the Lord, are active in the church and try to follow our Savior in obedience. So who is right? Do you know what is right? That may be the wrong question. It assumes lines can be drawn once and for all. I believe it may rather be a life-long struggle to know where the lines are. Consider this: maybe everyone is partially right given a particular moment in history. And maybe everyone needs to adjust, given ongoing conversation around the Scriptures, which respectfully include the perspectives of generations, ethnicities, cultures and genders. I am not sure any one person or group knows the mind of God well enough to be able to draw right-wrong-difference lines in an absolute way for all time. But if we come together and learn from each other, I think we can get closer to the mind of God in how we ought to order our lives.

For example, think about how the dress of men and women has changed over the years. What about jewelry? At certain periods neither women nor men were allowed to wear jewelry. Now it seems accept-able—it is not considered a sin by most in the Western church. Women wear makeup and jewelry. Men wear necklaces, bracelets and maybe ear-rings. Currently, tattoos seem to be in the category of different and, there-fore, acceptable in many circles. In most Western cultures, women can wear a short-sleeved dress or jeans without thought of immodesty. Yet in certain parts of the world this is considered immodest and wrong. The lines are not easily drawn, and so we keep bringing our life choices hum-bly before the Lord and asking for guidance.

MAKING SENSE OF ALL THIS

How does all of this apply to us? There are two levels of meaning and appli-

cation: one applies to you exactly where you are; the other applies to you as you prepare to enter another culture. Let's take a brief look at both.

Where you are. Look again at the four lines that represent the three generations and Western culture. Place the letter M next to one of the four lines that most closely represents you. Then place the letter P next to the one that represents your parents or guardians. Place initials next to the one that most represents your spouse, closest friend(s), supervisor or other significant relationships. Finally, place the letter C next to the one that most closely represents your church.

Now take a look at the letters you have placed. What does this picture tell you? Is there anything that you see that surprises, concerns or troubles you? Is there anything that you think should be changed? Is there anything you should talk about with someone important in your life?

Below are the lines that I tend to draw compared to those of my sons. Their category of differences is wider than mine—some things they put in the difference category, I categorize as wrong. These are potential points of conflict in my relationship with my sons. On the other hand, there were things I counted as right and worth fighting for, but which were mere differences for my sons. Their attitude about things in that zone was, "We can take it or leave it. It doesn't matter to us." This was difficult for me because the things I put in a right or wrong category were convictions that I wanted my sons to share. When they treated my convictions as matters of difference, I often became aggressive in trying to convince them they should change and be like me. My attempts to "help" them usually made matters worse.

My Lines:

RIGHT	DIFFERENCES	WRONG

My Sons' Lines:

RIGHT	DIFFERENCES	WRONG

Over time I have come to realize that many of my convictions about

what was right, wrong or different were culturally based. In my Christian history, card playing, dancing, movies, drinking (even modest) and bowling (where alcoholic drinks were served) were considered sinful. Christians were marked more by what they refrained from than what they engaged in. Later generations did not see things the way I did. For example, in current Christian culture, many think drinking is okay, but not drunkenness. Movies are okay with discretion. Dancing is okay but don't let it lead to sin. These may still be strong convictions held by some, but I have observed people who place these in the difference column and are committed to Christ, actively involved in building his kingdom, devoted in worship to him and demonstrating the fruit of the Spirit.

Your turn. Think of an important relationship you currently have where there is significant disagreement on what belongs in the right, wrong or differences categories. Look at the lines that follow. Place your name in the designated space. Place the other person's name in the other space. If you want to change the distance between categories to more accurately represent the situation you are thinking of, feel free to do so. Next, identify those things over which you disagree and write them in the category—right, wrong or difference—that they best fit for you. In what category do you think the other person would place those same items? Finally, think about what you might do with this information. Can you share it with the other person for purposes of clarification and understanding? Can you make some personal adjustments so the disagreements do not become or continue to be divisive? What other options might you have with the information shown below?

_____ **Lines:**
(Your name)

┌───┐
│   │
└───┘

_____ **Lines:**
(Other person's name)

┌───┐
│   │
└───┘

Entering another culture. We have taken considerable space discussing right, wrong and differences. Why? Because entering another culture is about encountering differences, every day, all day. How you handle them determines your level of comfort, ability to function, level of satisfaction and degree to which God can use you.

If I have a narrow category of differences, I will try to force nearly everything I see in the new culture into the categories of right and wrong. Furthermore, I usually make the decision of what belongs in which category by what looks like me or my culture—that would go in the category of right. What does not look like me would go in the category of wrong. I have established my culture and myself as the norm, the standard by which I judge others and their culture. People with a narrower category of differences have a greater tendency to do this, and this is a problem we all must guard against.

It Gets Worse

As we examine this situation more closely, things actually get worse. When we encounter cultural differences, we usually make an immediate judgment. When we judge quickly, we usually place that cultural difference in the category of wrong, not in the category of differences. As soon as we label it as wrong a new series of responses begins. First, I want to correct it. If it is wrong, it should be made right. But what is right? Obviously, what is like me is right. Most of this goes on at the semiconscious or unconscious level, and we will realize what we are doing only if we take the time to stop and analyze our reactions. Second, once I have placed something in the wrong category, I no longer need to try to understand the cultural context. It is wrong; therefore I can reject it. But now I have lost the opportunity to learn about the new culture. Third, I am disturbed by the wrong and spread the word to others who may sympathize with me. Together we can change things. Fourth, if the people of the new culture resist my wisdom and arguments for change, I may withdraw or try to inflict some kind of sanction. If they can't be reason-

able, I may try to use force—for their own good, of course. Now it is not just a cultural practice that I have named as wrong, but I begin to place people in the category of wrong too. It is easy to see how people become adversaries, even enemies.

After thirty years of international travel, I must confess I still fight this tendency to categorize anything different from me as wrong. At the same time, my experience has shown me that the overwhelming majority of things I experience in other cultures are actually different and not wrong. Furthermore, a number of things I experienced in other cultures are superior to practices in my home culture. And yes, a few are wrong by clear biblical standards. So what should I do when I encounter things that I judge to be wrong by biblical standards?

If you have been in the new culture only a short time you may not have earned the right to enter this potentially sensitive area. But I have found it best once I've reached this point to ask how the local church leaders feel about this matter. Is it an item of discussion among the pastors and Bible teachers? What Scriptures speak to the matter? What is the current thinking? In other words, I want to discover what local Christians think about it and the current state of any discussion. If anyone is going to place a wrong cultural practice under the authority of Scripture, it is best done by the Holy Spirit guiding the local church rather than someone from the outside imposing a "correct" theology. If the Holy Spirit is guiding them, the authority of Scripture will emerge as an internal conviction that will promote deep and lasting cultural change. If the decision is made by an external person or group, change may be only superficial and temporary.

HANDLING CULTURAL DIFFERENCES

If we can label most of our encounters with the new culture as differences, it liberates us in a variety of ways.

• Seeing most of the cultural expressions as different relieves us from the stress of dealing with so much that is wrong.

• We can see differences as neutral, freeing us from being prone to negative judgments.

• Interactions with people will be more open since correcting others will not be first on our mind.

• Practicing acceptance and trust will be easier while keeping fear and suspicion under control.

• Differences allow us to inquire, learn and understand the tapestry of the culture in a way that reveals God to us in wonderful new ways.

• While comparing the new culture with your home culture is inevitable, we can now relax and say, "Oh, that's different."

THE WISE PERSON

One expression of wisdom is knowing more and more how to interpret and respond to life's experiences. In looking back on my own life, I wish I had been able to categorize more things as merely different instead of thinking of them as wrong. Often I fought for the wrong things. Whenever that happened, everyone experienced pain and bondage.

I went to see one of my missionary colleagues from South Africa who was in a hospital in the United States. A brain tumor was stealing his life, and I wanted to spend some time with him again. With forced cheeriness I entered his room with a "Hi Uncle Irl, how are you doing?" He did not return the greeting. Abruptly, he took me straight to the preoccupation of his mind. "Duane," he said, "I've learned that the most important thing in life is not the length of a person's hair." My mind raced to capture the meaning of this statement from a man whose words, as well as days, were now numbered. Why would he use his limited breath to say this?

Years earlier, in the late 1960s and early 1970s, the long hair craze had hit South Africa. One of Irl's sons let his hair grow to shoulder length. The son argued it was simply a difference, but Irl insisted it was wrong. His son's resistance brought strong efforts from Irl to change him. Both became more stubborn and entrenched. The relationship broke.

Now as Irl lay on his deathbed, he agonized over a distant son who was the casualty of a battle that need never have been fought. Forcing a difference into the category of wrong and then fighting for his own rightness and his son's wrongness brought a heavy price—one that would not have been necessary.

Uncle Irl taught me much in our sojourn together in South Africa. His most important lesson for me came on his deathbed. He helped keep me from making some of the same mistakes for which one lives long in regret and grieves a price too heavy.

I close this chapter with a definition of maturity of unknown origin that puts difference and maturity in perspective: "Maturity is knowing more and more what is worth fighting for and what is not worth fighting for."

DISCUSSION QUESTIONS

1. Give examples of how you see right and wrong differently than your parents, spouse, colleagues or friends.

2. In what ways does your culture try to influence you on matters of right and wrong? Who is the most influential in helping you form your beliefs?

3. How do you typically react to new situations or new people? Are you more open and flexible to differences or more cautious and deliberate?

4. How do you think your attitude toward differences will help or hinder you in a cross-cultural setting?

Dealing with the New and Different

4

Culture Is Everywhere, and It Sneaks Up on You

*One of the greatest stumbling blocks to understanding
other peoples within or without a particular culture is the
tendency to judge others' behavior by our own standards.*

JAMES DOWNS

"HOW MANY OF YOU ARE HERE FOR A CLASS on cross-cultural communications?" Usually all hands went up. Then I would say, "Fine. But this will probably be the best class you will ever take in preparation for marriage." This usually brought a number of awkward snickers since most of my college students were not married. The few who were married gave a knowing look as if to say, "I think I know what you are saying. I thought I knew my spouse well, but marriage has been a real eye opener about our differences."

This is how I open every class I teach for people who are interested in cross-cultural ministry. Married people in my classes usually confirm that the material has been helpful in understanding their spouse as well as preparing for ministry in another culture. The single students have been given new categories to use in thinking about the people they are dating or engaged to.

CULTURAL KNOWLEDGE HELPS RELATIONSHIPS
The material in this book will help you if you are going to do some kind of work/ministry outside your own cultural context, whether in another

region of the United States or Canada or in another country. You may think, *I am only going to be painting or digging ditches or building.* Or you might be thinking, *I am just going to do my work; and since I know my job, what else is there?* Those are fair questions. A few brief answers will give you a perspective:

• All ministry, whether it is digging ditches or closing a business deal, is for and with people, so ultimately work/ministry is relational.

• How you do your job affects how people see Christ and respond to your message of Christ's love. How you communicate Christ and his love depends upon how people in the other culture perceive you.

• If you are insensitive to their traditions or remain distant from the people, they will assume that you think you are superior to them and they will be unlikely to respond to your message.

• You communicate all the time, but most of it is without words— nonverbal communication. People read you all the time. Are you warm and friendly or do you cluster with your own kind, building only minimal relationships with local people?

• If you have the right attitude and can use the right skills to creatively interact with cultural differences, you will have a satisfying experience and will leave a positive, lasting impact for the kingdom of God.

• You represent Christ in your cross-cultural ministry. You will want to do it right. That is what this book is all about.

THE PERFECT GIFT

Now let's try to tie some of these ideas together in an illustration from my own marriage. I want to show you how sneaky cultural differences are and how quickly they cause problems if we don't handle them wisely. Also, I will try to show how these principles will work with your schoolmates, your parents, your work relationships, your siblings and with people who are culturally different from you.

My wife and I had been married for nearly a year, and I knew I would have to find a special gift for our first anniversary. I put consider-

able thought into it, because I wanted it to be right. I decided the gift had to meet two objectives: It should be expensive to communicate my love and appreciation for her. And because we would be moving several times over the next few years, the gift should be practical, something she could use, not something decorative that would sit on a shelf and gather dust and maybe get broken in our moving around. This line of reasoning made sense to me. It even seemed like the smart thing to do.

On a chilly mid-December evening I took my bride of one year outside to present her with the "perfect" first anniversary gift. I had prepared her for the event by telling her how much thought and planning had gone into it. With pride I extended the open palm of my hand toward the brand new pair of snow tires on the car. Top of the line. Already mounted on the rims. Shiny black with whitewalls. Metal studs for extra traction. Expensive and practical. The perfect gift.

I noticed a small tear form in the corner of my wife's eye. Thinking she was overcome with joy at my generosity I began congratulating myself on this smashing success. It was my first crack at an anniversary gift and I hit a home run. I began bracing myself for the big hug that would come momentarily. Instead, she turned away and went back inside. *She's too cold to hug right now,* I reasoned. But as I followed her inside she began to cry profusely—tears not of joy but of bitter disappointment.

My gift reflected the cultural context in which I grew up. Not only was it a rural farming environment but quite a male-dominated one. Life was practical and functional, and my gift reflected this heritage.

My wife, on the other hand, grew up in Zimbabwe (then Southern Rhodesia), Africa. After living with the Shona people for seven years, she went to boarding school where she was transformed into a polite, sophisticated young lady after the British tradition. She grew up attending tea parties with fine china, having men of all ages stand as she entered the room and enjoying the refined life. Born of missionary parents, she was not rich, but was surrounded by a culture that treated

women differently than some of us did growing up in the Midwest farming culture of the United States. In both cultures women were valued, but valued very differently according to the dictates of the environment.

So I was doing something that naturally grew out of my cultural history, but her expectations were set in an entirely different direction. Our cultures collided.

Because I did not understand her cultural history, I did not understand why she reacted so negatively. How she could have ever married such an insensitive creature as myself was beyond her. Both of us experienced some culture shocks, because we assumed that the other person saw the world pretty much as each of us did.

By now you have probably concluded that I was really clueless to give my wife snow tires. Even though I have tried to explain my perspective, I doubt that you are persuaded about anything, except that people do not get much dumber than that.

Culture is like that. It sneaks up on us, and we tend to make decisions based on our cultural background rather than trying to understand the cultural background of the other person first. When something goes wrong we tend to judge negatively and quickly. To withhold or suspend judgment means that we refuse to think negatively about the other person or culture until we have made deliberate attempts to understand. Now, let's finish the story.

THE REST OF THE STORY

We were poor, sometimes having to wait a few days for a check to come so we could buy milk or bread. My wife was putting me through school by working as a public health nurse. Her job took her into the really poor and often dangerous areas of the city. With the winter days growing dark before she would leave these areas and with snow piling up, I feared for her safety. I sensed she was anxious too. The snow tires might bring her an added sense of safety and a little more peace of mind for both of us. I cared for my wife deeply and wanted to show it in the best

way I could. But was this the best way? Probably not. Yet, you see my frame of reference. So did my wife. Enlarging our frame of reference may not make things right, but it helps us understand and be less harsh in our judgments.

FRAME OF REFERENCE

We usually communicate from our own frame of reference. Snow tires communicated from my frame of reference and my cultural heritage. But the gift completely missed my wife's frame of reference and her cultural heritage. It caused her pain when I wanted so desperately to bring her joy. It put a strain on our relationship when I wanted to make it stronger. It communicated insensitivity when I wanted to communicate love and devotion. Fortunately, my wife is a forgiving person and usually sees my heart when my actions miscommunicate.

What should I have done? Knowing what I know now, I should have given her some roses or perfume or a necklace or something that would have been appreciated from her perspective and said later, "Oh, by the way, I put some new snow tires on the car because I love you very much and want you to come home safely every night."

Principles. From this experience we learn the following principles that can help us effectively enter another culture and live peacefully with those in our own cultural context.

1. All of us are products of our cultural heritage, which dictates how we see the world and how we interact with the world, including gift-giving. Everything we say and do reflects our heritage.

2. We tend to think that everyone else sees and interacts with the world the way we do. So we become confused when they do not appreciate our gifts or acts of kindness.

3. Judgment comes quickly—my wife thought I was totally insensitive, and I thought she was an ungrateful snob. We both concluded negative things about the other.

4. When we learn about the other person's cultural heritage, the person's perspective and intentions, we are better able to understand and accept more quickly.

5. Withholding judgment can be the best gift we give to another person, whether spouse, parent or person from another culture (or within our own culture). This allows us to stay open-minded toward them in order to accomplish the next step.

6. Asking why the other person behaved in a certain way or said something in particular, accomplishes four things:

   • It prompts us to suspend judgment until all the facts are in.

   • We learn about the other person's cultural heritage as the other person explains the reasons for feeling/acting in a certain way.

   • We understand how a particular behavior fits into the other's cultural context and becomes a natural way of life for the person.

   • It allows us to change in ways that communicate our true feelings.

However, getting answers can be a bit tricky. Often local people do not know why they do something. Often Westerners do not know why they do certain things such as elbows off the table or church at 11 o'clock on Sunday morning. Some things become habit and we have lost the reason for its existence. If you ask a local person why something is done in a certain way, the person may feel defensive, thinking that you are asking a judgmental question. Or the person may feel some shame if the answer is not known. So ask your questions of local people with whom you have built trust, unless you are asking questions they can answer. L. Robert Kohls[1] offers fifty questions that you can ask in most social situations. Another way of asking why is to find "cultural informants"—people in the local culture who understand Westerners. Ask them since they will be familiar with dealing with people outside their culture. You may also ask questions of another Westerner who has successfully adjusted and has excellent relationships with local people.

How you pose the question is very important. If you ask the question in a condescending way or in a tone that suggests frustration or displeasure, then you may find the response defensive or evasive. If you ask in a winsome voice that communicates positive intrigue, caring and a teachable spirit, then you should find people enthusiastically helping you understand.

Another way of discerning what you should do in situations that are new to you is to ask a friend what your behavior should be. For example, a visitor in this country may be confused about what to do when the nation's flag is presented. Is it okay just to imitate those around you or is a different behavior expected of you? "Why" questions seek understanding, whereas "what should I do?" questions seek the appropriate behavior. Determine which you need.

Look back on the six principles. If you practice these insights, will they help you with your friends, colleagues, parents or siblings? In many ways, like my wife, they represent another culture even if you are of the same family.

Over the years people have heard the snow tires story and have shared their own with me. A man had just bought and moved onto a farm about the time of his wife's birthday. Obviously he was thinking about things that would be required to make the farm successful. So for her birthday gift, he bought her a brand new manure spreader. For city folk who may not be tuned into rural life, just know it was a necessity on every farm.

We act out of our cultural heritage and it seems natural. Our culture can be male or female, old or young, parent or child and different ethnicities or races. It is most important to remember that each of us acts consistently with our culture—different people will do things differently. Caution must be taken not to judge quickly just because people are different. My wife has never agreed that snow tires make a good anniversary gift, but we both learned more about each other's frame of reference, making the last thirty-seven years of marriage more pleasant for both of us.

D I S C U S S I O N   Q U E S T I O N S

1. Have you ever made a snap judgment about someone or something only to realize you were wrong? Give an example.

2. Explain in practical terms how you can suspend judgment and look at situations more objectively every day.

3. Has anyone made a snap judgment about you? How did you feel?

4. In what ways has your heritage affected you? What aspects of it might interfere with your view of others and their views of you? What aspects of your history might be an advantage for you as you enter a new culture?

5

Culture Shocks

The more we retreat from the culture and the people
the less we learn about them;
the less we know about them,
the more uncomfortable we feel among them;
the more uncomfortable we feel among them,
the more inclined we are to withdraw.

CRAIG STORTI

NEARLY EVERYONE WHO CONSIDERS TRAVELING to another country hears the dreaded words "culture shock." What is it? How do I recognize it in myself and others? What causes it? And how do I deal with it?

Most people have experienced mild forms of culture shock simply because so many of us have had a wide range of experiences. Growing up in rural southern Wisconsin among rolling hills, forests and streams, I could meander for miles in any direction and always find my way home. Then, at age seventeen, I was plopped down in the middle of Chicago where traffic, skyscrapers, slums, busy streets, incessant traffic lights, crowded subways, panhandlers, crime and strange smells bombarded my senses. It was too much. For weeks, all I wanted to do was go home. I couldn't survive in Chicago. How could anyone survive? So I stayed in my room a lot, clung to the one good friend I had made, pondered how I ever got in this mess and how I would escape. I quickly realized there was no escape. I was committed to Bible school for three years. So how would I survive? I was in culture shock, big time! All the skills I had learned for navigating rural Wisconsin were useless in nearby

Chicago. Even though the distance I had traveled was only a couple hours, the culture shock was intense.

Perhaps you grew up in the city or suburbia. You navigate confidently. Everything comes easily and you accomplish your goal with little effort. But, if you wandered the forests and hills of Wisconsin for a couple hours, I doubt you would know how to return home. In fact, the odds are strong that you would get completely lost. Lost! That is the feeling of culture shock. You do not have the tools to navigate this new situation, and it is embarrassing, frustrating, frightening and humbling. You feel helpless and want to get out of this situation, which makes you feel so uncomfortable.

CULTURE SHOCK DEFINED

"Culture shock is when you experience frustration from not knowing the rules or having the skills for adjusting to a new culture." That is my definition. Here are some others, which may give other dimensions so you can recognize culture shock when it happens to you or someone else.

"Culture shock is the disorientation we experience when all the cultural maps and guidelines we learned as children no longer work."[1]

Two researchers speak of culture shock as one's reaction to the lack of fit between one's former experiences and what one is experiencing now.

Kalervo Oberg, who has studied culture shock extensively, says that culture shock is the "anxiety that results from losing all the familiar signs and symbols that help us understand a situation."[2] If we stop and think about it, we are always interpreting situations so we know how to act. If we cannot interpret a situation we do not know how to act, making us vulnerable to embarrassment, mistakes and even danger.

WHY CULTURE SHOCKS

Upon entering a new culture, the differences are massive even if an American goes to a Western European country. Surface differences like clothes, smells and language bombard you, but eventually you experi-

ence the deeper differences, like values, thinking patterns, space and nonverbals. When the differences are great, we are not sure how to respond. What we did back home does not work here. It is all very confusing. Our physical and emotional energy is taxed just to make it through each day.

When you feel the confusion and frustration, remember this: culture shock is normal. It happens to virtually everyone in varying degrees of intensity. People from other cultures experience culture shock when they come into American culture. Everyone feels it.

Actually, experiencing culture shock has some good news. It can be a means of knowing God better. Sometimes Westerners tend to unconsciously believe that God reveals himself only to the Western church and Western culture. Underneath, many Westerners carry this assumption. In fact, God reveals himself through all the cultures of the world and all the peoples within those cultures. When we see the differences of others, we may well be seeing more of God. He cannot be contained in or explained from only one cultural perspective. Thus, culture shock may be a means whereby we see God more clearly in all his glorious diversity.

SATAN IS AT WORK

Christians can easily draw some wrong conclusions about their experiences with culture shock and the results can be dangerous. Satan would like to use it to distort your wonderful adventure, whereas God wants to use it to show you more of himself. Here is how Satan can distort your thinking.

I am experiencing culture shock because
- I am abnormal.
- I am unspiritual.
- I missed God's call.
- God is punishing me.
- I am not skilled for ministry.

These five statements may represent lies that Satan will use to try to

- discourage us from getting involved in ministry
- rob us of the excitement of being in the new culture
- disrupt our learning of the new culture and growing from it
- get us to blame others: the person who got us involved, the local people or even God
- get us to focus on ourselves and not the people we want to serve

Culture shock is probably not a spiritual problem; it happens like catching a cold or getting motion sickness.

GOD'S PERSPECTIVE

Jesus, as the sinless God-Man, had to deal with cultural differences all the time. But the greatest cultural gap he had to bridge was between God and humankind, heaven and earth. Read Hebrews 4:14-16 and consider the following questions:

1. What were some of the major challenges Jesus faced in his transition from the culture of heaven to the culture of earth?

2. Jesus successfully bridged the heaven-to-earth cultures. What can we learn from the way Jesus adjusted to earth culture?

3. What resources are available to us from the text in Hebrews and other Scripture references?

4. What other Old and New Testament characters were successful in making cultural transitions and living cross-culturally?

FROM JOSEPH TO JESUS

From my perspective, Joseph shows us how to bridge cultures like no human being other than Jesus. His story in Genesis 37—47 is astounding. This seventeen-year-old was rejected by his brothers and sold into slavery in Egypt. He learned a new language and culture, was wrongly accused by Potiphar's wife and thrown into prison. He was the victim of broken promises and on it goes. Yet there is no record that Joseph ever complained or doubted that God would keep his promise. The God who took Joseph to

Egypt is the same one who takes you to a place of service. As he was faithful to Joseph, he will be faithful to you.

SYMPTOMS OF CULTURE SHOCK

Symptoms are important for maintaining health. Like an early warning system they can tell us when something may be wrong. The physician diagnoses and treats the problem based on an accurate description of the symptoms. If I ignore the symptoms, things may get worse, causing more serious problems.

Experts on culture shock suggest the following can be symptoms to alert you:

- wanting to withdraw from the local people
- excessive sleeping
- hanging out only with your friends
- obsessing over missing favorite foods
- craving for news from home
- doubts about being in the new culture
- wishing you were somewhere else
- feeling physically ill (from the emotional stress)
- blaming others for your negative feelings
- reluctance to leave the house to socialize
- excessive daydreaming about home
- criticizing local people and their culture
- general sense of anxiety and discomfort
- sense of dread, fear, paranoia
- lethargy, depression, lack of vitality or energy
- spending enormous time on the phone or Internet with friends back home

Virtually everyone experiences culture shock to some degree regardless of what country they come from. It is quite normal to have some of the above symptoms. However, people process culture shock symptoms differently. Some externalize and express their thoughts and emotions.

Diagnosis is easy in this case. Others internalize—they hide their real thoughts and feelings and try to tough it out hoping it will get better. Outwardly they seem to be functioning well, but they are hurting inside. Thus, in the early stages of exposure to the new culture, it is good for people to talk about what they are observing, thinking and feeling. Regular debriefing times are necessary to reveal the emotional state of people. Private conversations may be required for those who tend not to talk. When people talk about their reactions, issues get clarified, and everyone discovers they are in this together and will get through it together by God's grace.

CAUSES OF CULTURE SHOCK

Usually no one cultural factor causes culture shock. We can handle one or two differences, but it is when the differences collectively descend upon us that we have difficulty coping. I've provided a brief description of some of the more common cultural realities that cause people discomfort and, sometimes, culture shock. Knowing them will help you adjust your expectations and be a bit more prepared to cope.

Language. North Americans rely heavily on verbal means—talking—to communicate. Much of our life centers on being able to converse with one another. We can accomplish things, reduce confusion and establish meaning by talking. But if you are not fluent in the language of the culture you plan to enter, it can be very frightening: you cannot converse, you cannot reduce the confusion you feel and you cannot make sense out of the situation. You feel like a helpless child. You may have to rely on someone else to talk for you—an interpreter—which compounds the embarrassment and humiliation. Perhaps you try to use the language. You ask the merchant for a soft drink and you get a fish head. You are so humiliated you walk out with the fish head.

So what do you do?

• Relax, people expect you will not know everything.

• Relax, people will admire you for trying to learn and use their language.

• Relax, learn two or three words a day. Use them and it will surprise you how much you have learned in a week, month or year.

• Relax, because others like to see that Westerners are not as high and mighty as they are perceived to be.

• Relax, lighten up and laugh at yourself. Most situations are not life and death ones, so don't treat them as such.

When your language inability embarrasses you, remember this story. While living in another country, an American took his car to the local mechanic. Even though the mechanic spoke basic English, the American wanted to impress him with his language ability, so he used the local dialect to say, "My engine is not working well; please change the spark plugs." The mechanic, on hearing this in his own language, doubled over in laughter, as did some others who overheard. The American was quite embarrassed but resisted the temptation to take his car and leave. Instead, he said, "What did I say that you found so funny?" The mechanic, still trying to control himself, managed to say, "You told me that your car will not give birth and I must change its bananas," and he began to laugh again as did the others.

Each time the American saw the mechanic, the mechanic broke into laughter. Later, someone asked the American, "Don't you feel embarrassed that this person always laughs at you when you meet?" The American had a wise answer, "I do, a little, but I prefer to look at it this way. Every time we meet I bring a little cheer into his life and I think that is a good thing."[3] So relax.

Relationships. Friends and relatives give meaning and stability to life. Leaving them can be traumatic. Any extended stay in another culture causes you to wonder if you will see these people again. You feel empty and lonely as the old meaningful relationships are stripped away, and everything and everyone is new, different and unknown. The social and geographic confidence you knew back home has been replaced by a total

lack of knowing how to function. It's like being an actor in a play and coming out on stage one night to find that you are in a completely different play. You haven't rehearsed, you do not know the lines, where to stand or what will happen next.[4]

So what do you do?

• Thank God for bringing you to this place and being with you.

• Keep a cool head; others have done this successfully and so can you.

• Put up some family pictures and familiar objects that remind you of home.

• Remind yourself that God has special and beautiful people everywhere, and they will not be hard to find with a little time.

• With a friendly smile and warm enthusiasm, introduce yourself to the people who will be part of your new life: neighbors, gas station attendants, the person delivering your mail, the pharmacist, the check-out clerk and others who seem like they may be a part of your life in this new country. Show yourself friendly and the rest will take care of itself.

• Realize that building new relationships, while not always being able to replace the old ones, can be one of the most rich and rewarding experiences you can have; so go for it.

• Watch how the locals do things; usually it is okay to imitate.

• Remember the word *yet*. "I can't do it . . . *yet*. It will come. I will get it."[5]

A story is told about a woman in severe culture shock. Instead of going to the meat market herself to make her purchases and develop a comfortable relationship with the merchant, she isolated herself and had her maid go. Thereby she avoided her cure for her culture shock and missed out on the specials the butcher sometimes offered the expatriate customers. Another woman ventured out into the marketplace, but with two large Doberman pinschers, one leash in each hand. Neither woman had the solution to culture shock.[6] We are tempted to employ our own tactics to put a distance between us and the things that confuse or frus-

trate us in the new culture. Such behaviors send loud negative signals which most of us want to avoid. Say it often in the early days of your cultural transition: "I can't do it . . . yet." You will be rewarded.

Routine. Nothing is the same overseas. Change is the name of the game. You will notice changes in shopping patterns—why do we have to argue about the price? Just put it on a label. There are changes in transportation, banking, recreation, cooking, the amount of time to do anything. There are even changes in taste (I would give anything for a good pizza), medical care, sports, music, TV programming, driving habits and patterns of communication. Even holidays are different. Changes show up in the workplace as well: the equipment, technology, lines of accountability, styles of leadership, accounting, conflict resolution, expectations (the unwritten, but important rules) and means of fitting into the church or business practices of the organization.

So what do you do?

• Every move requires adjustments to the new and different; this move just requires extra effort because it is not a new state, but a new country. Be patient; what seems confusing and irrational to you now will eventually make more sense as you learn the patterns of life.

• Remind yourself that difference is not wrong; therefore you can learn new ways and fit in. Repeat silently to yourself: *It's not wrong; it's just different.*

• Give yourself some time. The feeling of awkwardness eventually goes away and you stop thinking about it.

• Give yourself some extra space and treat yourself a bit more charitably; the adjustment process is emotionally taxing, so give yourself more opportunity to rest, to take a relaxing break and to treat yourself to something special.

Physical health. Can I drink water out of the tap? What foods can I eat and not eat? What medical care exists? Can I trust the food on the street? In the restaurants? Cooked in the home by local people?

So what do you do?

- Look around; do most people appear upright and mobile? Like them, you can survive.
- Contact other international people like yourself and ask them what they have learned about maintaining physical health.
- Don't be foolish and eat everything; the little bugs can get you, but there is usually medicine to kill them after they have made you miserable for a day or two.
- You are not invincible. If you do not take the proper precautions, the malaria mosquito will find you, the parasite, bacteria and virus will find a way to make you run fast to the toilet numerous times a day. These little critters have learned all the tricks and you are new. Remember that.

I always carry some towelettes with me in case I need to wash my hands and soap and water are not available. As a reminder, do not leave home without all the vaccinations necessary for protecting yourself in the new country. The local public health department or the Centers for Disease Control and Prevention in Atlanta can help you. If you get sick, seek immediate medical attention. Usually it will be something common, quickly diagnosed and easily treatable. Above all, stay hydrated, especially if you have vomiting or diarrhea. It would be wise to take some packets of oral rehydration mix with you—available at your pharmacy, they are well worth the small investment.

Both our sons were born in South Africa. When we returned to the United States, they experienced frequent sickness, colds, sore throat, congestion and other small problems. We assumed that the States was a healthier place to live than most other places of the world; not so for our sons. They had built up natural immunities to a variety of small illnesses in South Africa but did not have the immunities to the illnesses in the United States. It takes time for the body to adjust because sickness is everywhere.

Making a cultural transition can be one of the great adventures of life. It will have some bumps, but being realistic about what awaits you is an important beginning. Culture shock is real, but it hits people in different

degrees. People respond to it differently—some get hit intensely, while others not so much. Be compassionate and encouraging to those who struggle. Don't compare yourself with others. Keep working at relationships, understanding the culture and avoiding the tendency to criticize and blame others. God guides you to new places and promises to be with you there. He will never abandon you.

DISCUSSION QUESTIONS

1. What scares you most about traveling to and living in another culture? What steps can you take to deal with these fears and prepare yourself?

2. Have you ever experienced culture shock in America or your home country? What were the symptoms and how did you deal with it?

3. In very practical ways, how can you depend upon God when experiencing culture shock?

4. What resources can you use to help you navigate a new culture?

6

Identifying Expectations

The great common door through which most
forms of negativity enter is pre-mature expectations.

HUGH PRATHER

But, as with anything else . . . there are unforeseen
complications lying like crocodiles among the green river grass.

ST. KILDA

EVERYONE HAS EXPECTATIONS ABOUT life in another culture. These gremlins hide in our pockets and sit unseen on our shoulders. We are usually not aware of our expectations, but they do their devious work at the worst, most unexpected times. Think of it this way: every disappointment or frustration you experience is a result of some expectation that has been violated or unfulfilled. You expect one thing and something else occurs. Usually that something else is not as good as what you expected, leading to disappointment and frustration. This chapter will help us identify our hidden expectations, achieve more realistic ones and provide some thoughts on how to cope with the unexpected.

EXPECTATIONS CAN BITE

A man and woman are dating—one expects the relationship will conclude in marriage; the other is thinking about how to break up. An employee believes that a promotion is imminent. Instead, a termination slip arrives. A secret is shared with a best friend, who reveals the secret to several others, causing much embarrassment. The best-friend relationship ends. The common theme here? Shattered expectations. Unmet

expectations can be devastating. Realistic expectations protect us from major disappointments and problems. There will still be surprises, but hopefully they will not be so destructive.

We live with expectations everyday. When expectations are not fulfilled we can have a mature or immature response. Immature responses include outbursts of anger, resentment, criticism, blame, negativity, fear, possessive controlling and pent-up irritation. I have seen all these reactions; in fact, I have experienced many of them. I am as guilty as anyone of not handling violated expectations maturely.

Important guidelines can help cope with these pressures. These guidelines will lead to mature godly responses when we face unmet expectations. But first we must get a better grasp of how the problem functions. With this knowledge we can deal with the root of the problem not just the symptoms.

EXPLORING YOUR EXPECTATIONS

It's a good idea to explore our subconscious expectations. By raising them to a conscious level we can name them, own them and then control them in such a way that they will be less likely to cause negative attribution, miscommunication and stressful relationships. As you anticipate a venture into a culture different from your own, think about the categories in table 6.1. Try to identify several expectations that you have for that category. For example, in the Reality column, write what you believe will be the most likely situation. Get the answers for this category, not from wishful thinking or Hollywood stereotypes, but from asking people who have been there and done well, from good books, *National Geographic* magazines, documentary films, historical novels, web sites and classes at the local community college or university. Newspapers may or may not be helpful. They often focus on the sensational bad news, and we then believe that what happened in one location is true of the entire country. This can produce a strong fear reaction toward that country. Don't be naive. But don't be controlled by fear either.

Table 6.1. Expectations and Reality

Category	My Expectations	Reality (As best I can know)
The local people's feelings about Americans		
My living situation		
The food		
My/our task		
Personal hygiene and sanitation		
Noises/sounds/quiet		
Relationships with local people		
Travel/vehicles		
Language		
People's concept of time (yours and theirs)		
Worship:		
• starting time		
• dress		
• style		
• length		
• music		
• prayer		
• sermon		
Sports/recreation		
Relaxation		
Climate:		
• temperature		
• rainfall		

Fill in the "My Expectations" column now. Then do your research and fill in the Reality column as you get information. After you enter the new culture, review what you have written and make adjustments in the Reality section.

As you can see, we carry many expectations. As a result, being realistic about another culture is not always easy. The wider the gap between your expectations and reality, the more difficult and disappointing your experience will be. If you can close the gap by this exercise and other information in this book, you will have a more positive experience, leave a positive impression and have a greater impact for the kingdom of God. In the final analysis, your single, most important goal is to represent Christ to the people in the other culture. That is more likely to happen when you are not struggling with all kinds of unrealistic expectations.

Keep in mind that God has placed beautiful Christians in every country of the world and they have the same goal as we do: to represent Christ to us and to their community. It is a great privilege when we can join hands with them in some common endeavor.

VIOLATED EXPECTATIONS

So what do we do when our expectations are violated? It will surely happen. So it is best to be prepared.

The problem. Not long after our arrival in South Africa I was confronted with a situation that confused and frustrated me. Six teenage missionary children lived with us in addition to one of our own in diapers. So we hired Eunice to help us with the housework and cooking.[1] She was a good worker and we were fortunate to have her. One day while we were sitting around the dining room table, we heard a dish drop and break in the kitchen. I called out, "Eunice, did you break the dish?" There was no harshness or judgment in my voice, but for some reason it seemed important to verify what I heard. Eunice replied, "No, the dish fell from my hand and it is dead." Her response struck me as odd and certainly not what I was expecting.

I wanted the world to be like me, and Eunice did not respond the way I wanted. I was troubled by this and remember thinking, *This behavior is not normal; she is not normal. What is her problem? Obviously she has difficulty accepting responsibility for her actions.*

Analysis of the problem. Before we continue the story, let's analyze what has happened so far. First, when we are confused or frustrated, we make negative attributions. That is, rather than trying to understand, I assign a negative attribute to the other person: Eunice doesn't accept responsibility. Note how many I made. Second, these negative attributions locate the problem in someone else. Third, if the other person is the problem, then we are freed from making any adjustments or seeking understanding. This means the other person must change or we must help bring about the change. Finally, this kind of thinking takes different forms, but is usually known as colonialism, imperialism, paternalism or neocolonialism.

I decided to give Eunice another chance to simply admit she made a mistake so that this would all be cleared up. So I said again in an even lighter tone of voice, "Eunice, did you mean to say that you broke the dish?"

Eunice responded in a firmer voice, "No. The dish fell from my hand and it is dead." She did not admit what she did and I wondered what "fell from my hand" and "dead" was all about. The proof was there——Eunice refused to accept responsibility; she would not be accountable. That she was not responsible was now a fact in my mind. We needed to watch her more closely since she seemed not to be trustworthy. My confusion and frustration led to negative attributions and they quickly became fact without any attempt to understand.

Notice the progression: something happens that I do not expect and do not understand. I assume it must be bad, and I make negative attributions. I believe everything I have done is based on "fact." I choose a course of action based on the "facts," which begins a downward spiral of suspicion and mistrust. A new pattern of behavior emerges—watch her more closely.

My problem was making hasty judgments without getting the facts from the *other person's* perspective. Somebody does something I don't understand, and I get confused, suspicious, frustrated or angry. If it is not like me, then it must be inferior or even wrong. I dislike ambiguity and confusion; I want clarity and I want it now. So I fill in the blanks quickly by jumping to a conclusion. When I do, it is almost always with a negative thought about the person who caused me the confusion. By making the other person the problem, I am no longer responsible. This is a natural tendency whenever I find that people are not like me! Do you ever do this? Don't panic; just be aware of it. Awareness represents a good beginning to the solution.

Are you normal? Ponder this question for a moment. Do you think you are normal? Many people are not sure how to respond, so they try to avoid a direct answer. Deep down, most of us believe that we are normal, and in most cases this is quite acceptable—it is fine to believe you are normal. However, there are some who are dangerously abnormal who believe they are normal. But since they represent a small minority, we won't consider them in this discussion. Most of us consider ourselves normal and we probably are. Believing we are normal does not get us into trouble; something else does.

There is a fine line that we unconsciously cross that causes the majority of the problems. When we think we are normal, we make a rather fatal slip into believing that we also are the *norm* by which everything and everyone else can be judged. We do this without thinking. But every time we make a negative attribution we risk saying rather loudly to those around us, "That's not like me, therefore it is inferior, wrong and unacceptable." Most of us do not wish to communicate this message, yet it happens with disturbing frequency. Identifying our expectations and comparing them with reality as best we can before actually entering the new culture gives us an advantage. We will be less likely to assume that we are the norm, and it will help us realize that there are many legitimate norms. So if I assume that certain behaviors are normal for you, even

though they are not part of my patterns, I can more easily adjust my expectations to the reality I am in. Instead of saying, "That is not like me, it must be inferior or wrong," I can now say, "That is not like me and I do not understand it . . . yet. But that is *you*, and I can accept you and your ways."

From a biblical perspective there are things that are definitely wrong. Some behaviors cannot be rationalized into something good simply by saying it is the culture and therefore acceptable. If God says it is wrong, it is wrong. The overwhelming majority of experiences you will encounter in another culture will not fit in the category of right/wrong, but in the category of cultural differences. I have a high respect for God who has placed wondrous diversity in his world and a high respect for people who bear the image of their Creator. At the same time I recognize that sin from God's perspective cannot be explained away by cultural norms, mine or anyone else's.

DEALING WITH VIOLATED EXPECTATIONS

Let's get back to Eunice and see how things worked out. It all started when I expected Eunice to be normal—like me. At the point I think people must be like me, I have crossed the line from believing that I am normal to also believing I am the *norm*. If I believe I am the norm and you are different from me, then I am free to judge you. When Eunice was not like me in that she did not fulfill my expectations, I judged her to be abnormal. This opened the door to a variety of negative attributions. What I failed to realize at the time is that all this happened in seconds and at the unconscious level. I was not aware of what I was doing, what was happening, what was really being communicated and what the impact would be if things did not get sorted out. I was on dangerous ground and did not even know it! How can this kind of mistake be avoided? Three very simple steps can save us embarrassment and hurt feelings.

Stop. When you are confused, frustrated, angry or disappointed, do only one thing—stop! That is the first step and a difficult one for many

Westerners who prefer to act quickly. Think about what just happened; think about your feelings and what those feelings are telling your brain. Monitoring the negative thoughts that go through your mind is a great beginning. If you are not sure what to say or do, say and do nothing. Let someone else take the lead or just let the situation pass.

Suspend judgment. The ability to suspend judgment is a critical second step in these early encounters with another culture.[2] However, before you can suspend judgment, you must realize that you are making a judgment, especially a negative one. This requires that you monitor your thoughts. Catch the negative thoughts and stop them before they slip through and cause damage. This takes discipline and work early on, but the more you do it, the more you will find your experience enjoyable, even fascinating. Moreover, suspending judgment is a life skill that builds and preserves relationships. More important, you will better reveal the presence of Christ in your life.

Suspending judgment takes us further toward a positive experience with the culture. It helps us become proactive in discovering why something happened or why someone said/behaved in a certain way. With Eunice, I moved very quickly from hearing her response to making a judgment. I did not hesitate; I was even comfortable with my interpretation and conclusion. I assumed there was no other way to see it.

Suspending judgment does not mean never making a judgment. It does mean that when confused, you keep from making a judgment because you know it is likely to be premature and wrong. Suspending judgment allows us to keep an open mind, seek further information and pursue understanding. When a judgment gets fixed in our heads, we close our minds to new information and do not pursue understanding. The negative attributions now become "facts." To make matters worse, we act on those facts.

Americans may see suspending judgment as a sign of weakness—being too hesitant or indecisive. Culture has trained them to size up a situation quickly, make a decision and then make it work. Though being

quick and decisive may be an American value, it can work against you when entering and living in another culture.

Ask why. It never occurred to me to ask why Eunice responded the way she did. Frankly it was much easier and more time efficient to jump to a conclusion—a negative one, of course. The third step of asking why leads us to a better understanding of the culture where we are guests.

Over time I began to discover the whys—they were wonderful, enlightening and fascinating discoveries. And then I began to understand Eunice. In Eunice's native tongue, the Zulu language, people tend to use the passive and stative voices with about as much frequency as we use the active voice. The way she spoke in her native tongue was the way she would use English:

"Eunice, did you break the dish [active voice]?"

"The dish fell from my hand [passive voice] and it is dead [stative voice]."

Further inquiry led me to discover that many language groups of the world used the active voice infrequently because it implies intentionality. Thus, for Eunice to respond, "Yes, I broke the dish," would in her mind be saying, "I intentionally broke the dish," or "I wanted to break it," which obviously was not true. By using the passive and stative voices, she was communicating that it was an accident, not intentional.

I must confess, I was relieved! Living in a world of quick judgments, negative attributions and suspicions is a bondage that robs one of the joy of beautiful relationships based on understanding and trust. I had misjudged her because of my own failure to act properly. Stopping to monitor my thoughts and suspending judgment would have kept me from making negative attributions and helped me to pursue understanding by asking why.

By the way, were you getting a little frustrated that it took me so long to explain Eunice's response? Life is like that. Understanding comes to those who patiently seek answers to their confusion. Recently, I told the

story of Eunice to a group of missionaries in Namibia—a country in the southwestern corner of Africa. A missionary told me that when her husband was dying she could not tell any Namibians that he was dying, because using the active voice would communicate, "I want him to die." So what could she say? Mostly, someone in that situation would say nothing or something like, "We are praying."

Entering another culture can be both wonderful and fearful. Identifying our expectations and managing them when they are unfulfilled can make the difference between a happy, productive experience and one in which you grit your teeth and merely endure.

DISCUSSION QUESTIONS

1. Can you think of a time when your expectations were not met? How did you react? How do you feel about it today?

2. What did you learn from the expectations exercise (table 6.1 on p. 56)? What surprised you the most?

3. Do you think you are normal? In what ways do you expect others to be like you? In what ways is it okay for people to be different? What guidelines can be found in the Bible?

4. As you think about entering another culture, what aspects of that culture might you find most difficult to adjust to? What steps can you take to learn about that now?

7

Square Heads and Round Heads

We have been created in the image of God,
and it is God-likeness we share. . . .
Thinking that people are all like me
can only lead to disillusionment.
Am I the center of the universe?

GLADIS DEPREE

BEFORE THE HUMAN RACE, diversity existed in the Trinity. God was diverse: three persons. Then when God decided to create, the array of diversity was staggering. The human race began with diversity: male and female. God apparently loves difference; he created so much of it. Most of us, however, prefer sameness. Difference makes us feel uncomfortable because we are not sure how to respond. Entering another culture is to encounter daily difference. Comfort in another culture occurs only when you understand difference. Prospering in another culture is learning how to celebrate difference. This chapter takes us a step closer to being able to do just that.

A NEW GAME

Imagine you are a good athlete. You are good at your sport and enjoy the game, say baseball. Someone across town invites you to play a game that looks similar to your sport, and you agree. But the game, called cricket, has different rules and requires different skills. Balls and bats are used, but in a different way. You try to play, but mostly the game is frustrating. Trying harder does not work. Sometimes you want to give

up rather than adjust to this new game. It would be easier to go back and play the game you know so well. But you decide to hang in there. Soon you learn the new rules, develop the skills and enjoy playing cricket. You have grown into something new and different and feel better for the experience.

Entering a new culture is much the same. The rules and skills that were natural for you in your home culture do not work very well in the new culture. People of the new culture do things differently. Language, transportation, dress, food, shopping and a variety of other things are different. People have different values and attitudes that seem strange to you. You can't play this game very well, at least not yet. But with patience you can learn the new rules and begin to enjoy being in the new culture. The balance of this book is designed to help you learn the rules and build the skills for a positive experience in another culture.

PICTURE IT THIS WAY

As we enter another culture it is important to get the right perspective. We grow up looking, for the most part, like the people around us (figure 7.1).[1] We share a common language, core values, patterns of behavior and the basic rules for conducting our lives. If we grew up in square culture, we would look square. If we grew up in round culture, we would look round.

When you leave the comfort of your own culture and enter another, you don't leave your squareness (cultural baggage) behind; you take it with you (see figure 7.2). You become the proverbial square peg in a round hole. At this point you have a choice, as seen in figure 7.3: you can maintain your squareness, or you can choose to adjust, knock off some "corners" to fit in and identify more and more with your host culture. By adapting to the local ways, you will find greater fulfillment for yourself and greater effectiveness in the activity God has placed before you.

People grow up looking very much like the cultural background in which they were raised. If your cultural background is "square," you turn out to be square. If it is "round," you are round.

Figure 7.1. Square and Round Cultures

When you leave the safety of your own culture and enter another, you do not leave your cultural baggage behind. You take it with you. And you may feel like the poverbial square peg in a round hole.

Figure 7.2. Fitting into Another Culture

But you can adjust; you can fit in. You can adapt yourself to this new culture. You can make the transition effectively and gradually identify more and more with your host country colleagues. The result is greater fulfillment and productivity for you and your employer.

Figure 7.3. Adjusting and Refusing to Adjust

At the bottom of figure 7.3, notice that some from square culture maintain their squareness. They choose not to adjust to the local culture but to remain the same as if they were in their home culture. Ponder this: By refusing to change or lose any squareness, what messages does the square-headed person send to the round-headed people? Write your responses below.

Here are some of my responses. The square person communicates, "I don't care if I adjust to your situation, learn your language or do things the way you do. I am better educated. My culture is more technologically advanced. My way is better than yours, so why should I change?" Round people could read this as insensitive and arrogant.

What messages do the round-headed people receive when the square person does not adapt to round culture? Write your responses below.

Here are my responses to this situation. Round people feel that the square person does not care enough to make any changes. Round people may think that in order to establish a relationship, they must lose their roundness and become like square people. How unfortunate that people of other cultures receive any of these messages from us even though, if we send them, we do so unintentionally! Even so, the people of the host culture will still receive the message. We are always communicating, verbally and nonverbally. Therefore, we must be vigilant, aware of how and what we are communicating.

Notice the better option in figure 7.3 where another square person is entering round culture. Slowly over time the square person takes on some roundness as a result of experiencing the culture. This symbolizes the adjustment process of fitting into the culture. Amazingly, you dis-

cover that any squareness you lose was never important.

What are some of the ways in which we can lose our squareness during the time we are in another culture? Make a list of at least six things you can do to help yourself take on roundness or, conversely, lose some squareness—even if you plan to be in another culture for just a short time.

1.

2.

3.

4.

5.

6.

My list of adjustments would be to

- learn greetings and key words in the new culture
- buy and wear some pieces of local clothing
- smile frequently
- resist making negative statements about the people or culture
- ask questions and listen attentively
- spend as much time with local people as possible and minimize the time spent with people of my culture
- eat the local food as long as it is safe

As the square person becomes more round, what is the message that is being communicated to the round people? Write down your responses.

The messages the round people are likely to receive are that square people enjoy round people, even respect them. Our (round) ways must be good since square people are adopting some of our behaviors and values (becoming a little like us and not trying to change us to look like them). Square people are humble, willing to adjust. Square people are

willing to learn from us. They think we are important, they want to communicate with us, they want to be our friends, and they think of us as human beings equal to them.

As you can see, very powerful messages are sent simply through our willingness to make some adjustments to the new culture. The things we set aside from our home culture in order to adjust to the local culture are usually not core values, but less important things. Yet the impact of those adjustments makes an enormous difference in how effective you will be in the ministry God has for you.

Obviously, when it comes time to return to square culture, the person who has lost some squareness will have won the respect of the local people and will have left behind the sweet aroma of Christ. You will also discover that you return richer because God has added new beauty to your life. What you give up is nothing compared to what you gain. Multitudes who have gone before you attest that the benefits of adjusting and fitting in far outweigh any sacrifices.

BUSINESSPEOPLE AND SQUARENESS

There is another side, however. Businesspeople want to return to their home organization and incorporate some of the things they learned while on their international assignment. One automotive executive, after three years in Spain, was eager to share some of his thoughts with his U.S. colleagues. His enthusiasm died when his colleagues greeted him with statements like "Bet you're glad to be back in civilization."[2]

Everyone struggles with squareness. Anyone going from one culture to another must deal with squareness and roundness. Businesspeople struggle, as do missionaries, tent-makers, short-termers and anyone who tries to establish a meaningful relationship with local people. Businesspeople often face an extra challenge because they may have limited time to adjust, arrive with a heavy task assignment, have little or no preparation on how to be effective in the new culture and gravitate to other expatri-

ates. It takes determination to break out of squareness, but it can be done.

The latest story I heard was about a businessperson who was given three days by his U.S. company to get a signed contract on a big competitive deal in South America. Instead, a European company got the contract. The reason, I am told, is that negotiators from the European firm spent ten days in the South American city with the local company. The first seven days were spent in getting to know each other—in social and recreational time together. During the last three days, they hammered out the details of the contract. When asked by the U.S. firm, the local officials said the difference was that the European negotiators took the time to get to know them as people, to build the relationships. One local person said something like, "You Americans had a better product, but you never took the time to know us."[3]

In the United States (square culture), people judge the merits of the product and pricing and make their decision based on those facts. In much of the world (round culture), it is not so much the merits of the product and price, but the merits of the person and the relationship. When square people cannot or will not become round in their thinking and behaving, their message and goals are likely to be ineffective. Becoming round—taking time to build a good relationship before plunging into the task—is not a matter of right or wrong but of difference. We are free to adjust to cultural differences, and the wise person will do so.

This situation works both ways. Often, people from round cultures will come to the square culture—the United States or another Western country—to do business or for some kind of project. The round people will take excessive time (by square culture standards) in small talk, social time and relationship building. The square person may interpret this as wasteful and unprofessional and may seriously question whether the round person can meet deadlines and be efficient. We can easily misinterpret each other without intending it. Later, several chapters are given to value differences in round and square cultures.

D ISCUSSION Q UESTIONS

1. What cultural baggage are you willing to shed in order to better fit into another culture?

2. In what practical ways can you show acceptance of people in another culture?

3. Have you ever felt like a square peg in a round hole? When? How did you respond?

4. While there are differences, what similarities do you see between people of differing cultures?

5. How can you use these similarities to connect with people cross-culturally?

6. Do you identify more with the businessperson from the square culture or with the businessperson from the round culture? Why?

8

Cultural Adjustment Map

If the relationship is strong, then the truth will be accepted.

BURMESE PROVERB

WHENEVER YOU ARE TRAVELING TO A NEW PLACE, a map is a good idea. The same is true when entering a new culture. The cultural adjustment map[1] in figure 8.1 was created by a group of people experienced in cross-cultural travel and adjustment.

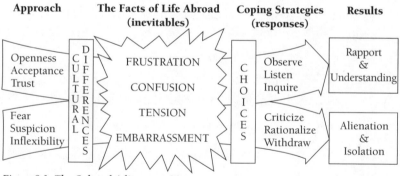

Figure 8.1. The Cultural Adjustment Map

For purposes of simplicity, let's look at the cultural adjustment map as having two tracks—the upper track, which begins with an approach of openness, acceptance and trust, and the lower track, beginning with an approach of fear, suspicion and inflexibility. Everyone tends to approach a new culture more on one track than the other, but no one travels one or the other exclusively. In fact, we will probably flip-flop

between the upper and lower tracks many times during our cross-cultural experience.

THE INEVITABLES

Note the section on the map called "The Facts of Life Abroad." It suggests that everyone will experience some negative emotions like confusion and frustration as cultural differences are encountered. Many people tend to overlook these inevitables since they believe that God has called them and given them such a love for the local people that they will not experience any negative emotions. Usually they are in for a rude awakening.

Everyone who spends any time in direct contact with a new culture will experience these negative emotions in varying degrees of intensity and duration. It signals that you are very much alive and very human. Therefore

• having negative emotions does not signal Christian immaturity or lack of spirituality.

• falling victim to the negatives does not mean you are out of God's will. Paul is clear that those who try to follow our Lord will have challenges and difficulties (2 Timothy 3:12; 1 Peter 3:8-17).

• it does not mean that you don't have a long-term future in this culture.

• it does not mean that you never should have come.

• it does not mean you will be ineffective or should give up.

• it does mean you are normal; so get on with learning the culture and practice the insights in this chapter.

THE UPPER TRACK

The person approaching a culture with more openness, acceptance and trust will still encounter cultural differences, feel the inevitables and need to make a critical choice. But the critical choice will more likely be to remain on the upper track and choose a positive coping strategy.

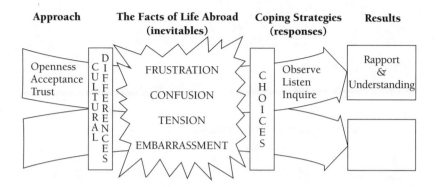

Figure 8.2. The Upper Track

Observe. Keeping your wits about you in spite of the negative emotions you may be feeling allows you to do something important: observe—look around and assess what is happening. In some cultures I get quite uncomfortable because the local people stand very close to me during conversation. I get the sense that they are pushy, overbearing and aggressive (note the negative attributions). I feel uneasy and a little anxious. I back up a step, they move closer again. I take another small step back, trying to get a little space between the other person's face and mine, but also hoping I will not offend them. *What is it with these people?* keeps racing through my mind while I try to stay positive and figure this out. Eventually, the conversation concludes, much to my relief. But now I need to understand. Over the next few days I observe how close people stand to each other when talking. It does not take long to realize that people stand close to each other in three kinds of circumstances: during moments of anger, during moments of debate or bargaining and during moments of friendship building. My experience fell into the latter category. Now I interpret the situation in the positive light that the other person actually intended—in fact, a Middle-Eastern proverb speaks of friendship as the "sharing of one another's breath."

Listen. Listening is another important skill for coping with cultural differences. Focused listening should prompt more questions, which

should bring more listening, which provokes more questions and so on. Most people err in not listening well, even if they do ask some good questions. Often people listen only as a courtesy until they can speak. Think of listening as an act of loving. Perhaps nothing shows respect for others more clearly than listening to them and then probing their thoughts more deeply.

Inquire. Inquiry is simply the art of asking questions. A good dose of curiosity helps. All my life I have been curious as to why things work, why they happen and why people act the way they do. So I have made it a habit to ask lots of questions; a habit, as it turns out, that has served me well in other cultures. Keep in mind that there is a wrong way to ask questions. The wrong way to pose a question is to imply inferiority, judgment or deficiency. For example, "Why do you drive on the wrong side of the road?" suggesting driving on the right side is correct. Rather, one might say, "I would enjoy hearing about the history of why you drive on the left side of the road. It is different from my past, and I am wondering how we inherited these two ways." In many countries you will learn that driving on the left side was inherited from their colonizers. The more you have built trust, the richer the dividends of your inquiry.

Failure to inquire can cause major problems. A United States government agency was building latrines (outdoor toilets) to improve the hygiene in a poor, largely Muslim community in Asia. When the project was completed, the foreigners were proud of the contribution they had made to the health of the local people. However, it was soon discovered that none of the local people were using the latrines. In fact, they were using them as storage sheds. Why? A couple questions revealed that all the latrines were facing Mecca, and no respectful Muslim would use the facility while facing their holy city. A brief inquiry before the project began could have saved the foreign agency this embarrassment.

The person who follows the upper track on the cultural adjustment map will delight in the results: understanding and rapport. Understanding means you are grasping how the cultural pieces fit together and make

sense. As you understand the local culture you will gain appreciation and respect for it. Rapport means that you sense a bond with the people and value the relationship. Of course, this does not happen all at once. The insights accrue over time, and there are plenty of bumps along the way.

Yet one of the great pleasures of life is to plunge into another culture, figure out how it works and find yourself enjoying it as the local people do. It does not mean rejection of your culture nor does it mean that you accept everything in the new culture. It does mean that you are learning to dance to the rhythm of the new culture and, having done so, find yourself much more effective in accomplishing your goals.

One needs to travel that upper track many times before sensing the rhythm of the culture. But each time one treks that upper track successfully, it builds stronger openness, acceptance and trust. A chapter has been dedicated to each of these three crucial concepts later. Next, we need to look at the lower track, a place I've visited more times than I like to admit.

THE LOWER TRACK

If you approach the new culture with large doses of fear, suspicion and inflexibility, then the cultural differences will not only produce increased frustration and confusion, but you are now likely to make negative attributions about this new culture. Much of this happens at the unconscious level, but the effect remains the same: you will still be faced with a choice about what to do when those feelings occur. But this time, instead of suspending judgment, you will jump to a negative conclusion about the new culture.

Fear. Think about the fears you might have as you approach cross-cultural ministry and list them below. It is very important to label them so that they do not unconsciously sabotage you later.

The fears that I can think of are

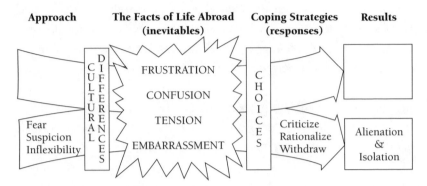

Approach	The Facts of Life Abroad (inevitables)	Coping Strategies (responses)	Results

Figure 8.3. The Lower Track

Rank your fears from the greatest to the least. Being honest and realistic are necessary for successful adjustment.

Where did your greatest fear come from? Can you think of a number of sources for that fear? Maybe something happened in your past or maybe recent news from the country you are entering caused the fear. Maybe you even picked up the fear from someone else and made it your own.

Let's take one fear and work it through. Teaching at the university level most of my life, I have had lots of international students in my classes and I have enjoyed knowing many as friends. One thing many of them will admit after they get to know you is that they were scared when they came to the United States. "Scared?" I would exclaim, "Of what?" They would then sheepishly answer, "Scared of being murdered." I would often laugh because the thought was so absurd—not that it could not happen but that it was so unlikely. Yet it was the greatest fear of many. This fear emerged during the era when a city in the United States had the highest murder rate among the economically developed nations and had the reputation of being the murder capital of the world. Television carried the image around the world.

The same thing happened when my wife, our two sons and I lived in South Africa. There were places where violence, crime and murder were

very high. My family in the United States expressed fear for us and prayed daily for our protection. I assured them that we were quite safe. I cannot remember one time that I felt fear for my physical safety. In my extensive travels my wife and I have taken together and separately, we have rarely felt fear. Usually we are impressed by the courtesy and kindness of the local people. I think this will be your experience as well.

At the same time, I do not want you to think that you can just wander anywhere at any time and you will be fine. There are evil and malicious people everywhere in the world and one must always use good sense. There are places both in the United States and abroad that I would not visit at night. Seek and listen to the advice of the local people whom you trust. Err on the side of caution, especially if you are new in the culture.

Suspicion. This is the opposite of trust. It thinks the worst of others, or at least doubts the best. Sometimes you will have evidence to support suspicion, but take it in stride. For example, merchants discovering you are not a local person may raise their prices. You may feel they are taking advantage of you. In a sense, perhaps they are. Locals tend to think all Westerners are wealthy, and usually we are by comparison. While you may think that they are trying to take advantage of you, they think that Americans hoard their wealth. For example, if bargaining is a practice in the culture you enter, feel free to bargain, but usually you will not get the price the local people get. Yet, if you concentrate more on building the relationship and less on getting the best price, you will win in two ways: you will win friends and your friends will not try to take advantage of you. Furthermore, the resulting relationships can lead to meaningful sharing.

Inflexibility. This refers to the tendency to reject anything that does not look like you. It is the opposite of acceptance. Inflexibility, a form of rejection, is the square-headed person's refusal to change and adjust to local ways. Such a person has a strong sense of being right in most everything. This person has a narrow range of differences, believing what is right is what looks like me and what is wrong is what does not look like

me. Local people will probably sense superiority in such a person.

Superiority may surprise you. Most of us do not think of ourselves as superior. In fact, equality remains a high value in North America. Yet, many North Americans are still accused of an attitude of superiority. In part, I feel this is true especially for citizens of the United States who are accustomed to being told that we are a superpower, economically, militarily, technologically and in other ways. Some of this seeps into our thinking and we believe, not consciously or overtly, that we as a people and as a country are superior. Of course, there are many ways in which other countries are superior to the United States, but we rarely hear of it. If we do, we may not think it significant.

One U.S. corporation has humility as a corporate value. When their clients outside the United States were asked how these Americans demonstrated humility, their answer was, "They don't." Obviously many Americans are humble and demonstrate it, but maybe only other Americans recognize it because we define humility according to our cultural norms. Other cultures may define it differently and, therefore, demonstrate it differently.

Another reason for others perceiving superiority in many from the United States concerns natural cultural differences and how they are misinterpreted. Many Americans are outspoken, task oriented, goal driven, decisive and assertive. Many believe these qualities made America great, and promote and reward them. However, in most Two-Thirds World[2] countries, those qualities are not valued so highly. So when an American comes along and suggests what might be done, the local people who do not want to shame the guest by not taking the suggestion, move ahead on it even though they know it may not be the best way to go. The American receives gracious appreciation for the work done and continues the assertive, get-the-job-done attitude. Eventually this wears thin for the local people because they are constantly giving in to the unsuspecting American, who should have caught on to the ways of the local culture by now.

Generally, Americans think that if they are doing something wrong, someone in the local culture will tell them. Yet correcting a guest is considered very rude because it would cause the Americans to lose face and feel shame—something to be avoided at all costs. We will deal with this later. While exposure to Americans and their ways have brought some changes, allowing some local people to be more direct and confrontational, this would usually not be true of poorer people, rural people or anyone who has minimal contact with Westerners. Rather than blurt out your suggestions and ideas, encourage the local people to teach you to do it their way. They may insist that you know better because you are educated and from a highly technical culture, but don't give in quickly to this expression of cultural courtesy. There is a cultural dance going on. Get in step.

If you carry high levels of fear, suspicion and superiority and face a host of cultural differences, you will experience higher degrees of frustration, confusion, tension and embarrassment. But even worse, you will more likely make a bad decision when you come to the point of choosing a coping strategy. Negative attribution will kick in and you will jump to a negative conclusion about these people and their culture. If you are not careful at this point, you will easily slide into a variety of unproductive mindsets:

• Comparison: it takes twice as long to get things done; we can do it back home in half the time.

• Blame: these people are at fault for my frustration.

• Criticism: these people are really backward.

• Rationalization: it's impossible to understand these people and their culture.

• Withdrawal: I will do my job but I will not get emotionally involved with these people.

Notice the repetition of "these people."

"THESE PEOPLE"?

Monitor the two words "these people." When they frequently appear in

your speech and thoughts, it is a sure sign that you have not formed the kinds of bonds that make you think in terms of "we" instead of "they" or "these." Also, when you hear yourself think or say "these people," it may be a convenient way of not taking responsibility for your own feelings. If you blame your frustration on someone else, then you do not have to assume responsibility or consider making any changes. Slipping into that frame of mind will dull your ability to observe, inquire and listen. When that happens, learning and understanding stop.

USING THE CULTURAL ADJUSTMENT MAP

Suppose you have had a rough day and feel bad because of the negative emotions you felt ("The Facts of Life Abroad—Inevitables"). You also realize that you made some bad choices. Take a look at figure 8.1, the cultural adjustment map (p. 72), and answer the following questions.

1. What cultural difference prompted the negative emotion?

2. Which negative emotion(s) did you feel?

3. What thoughts ran through your mind during the negative emotion(s)?

4. Did your negative feelings prompt any action(s) you now regret? If so, describe.

Your answers will help you to name and describe a situation that took you on the lower track. The next step is to ask yourself, *How can I handle it better in the future?*

5. If you could do it over again, what would you do differently? Look at the upper track. Be specific about what you might have done differently.

6. Look at your response to the fourth question. Is there some way you might have broken trust with someone? What can you do to restore that trust?

7. Looking at the upper track and assuming that negative emotions will arise at some future point, what options did you have? Or what options would you prefer to exercise in future situations?

These simple steps force us to reflect, evaluate and plan. By doing this regularly, you will find yourself making wiser decisions, staying on the upper track and building stronger relationships. Eventually you will look back on your cross-cultural excursion as a high point in your life.

EXPECTATIONS REVISITED

In an earlier chapter we talked about expectations. You might want to review your expectations to assess how many of them were positive and how many were negative. The more your expectations are positive (while also being realistic), the more likely you will approach the culture with openness, acceptance and trust. If your expectations tend to be negative, you may be prone to fear, suspicion and inflexibility. In this case, you would be more vulnerable to making negative attributions about the people and culture whenever anything confuses or frustrates you. So if you are already biased toward fear, suspicion and inflexibility, you are more likely to experience more and more intense negative emotions during contact with the new culture. You might also act out some of those negatives so that the local people will realize you are not happy and at peace in their homeland.

The purpose of this chapter was to provide you with a cultural road map to help you navigate your way through the new culture. Should you get stuck somewhere or make a wrong turn, the map may help you identify where you went wrong and what you might do to correct things. The map also gives you a realistic picture of what is ahead of you both in challenges and in the joy of new friendships, hopefully, lifelong ones.

DISCUSSION   QUESTIONS

---

1. Describe your feelings when you realize that frustration, confusion, tension and embarrassment will be inevitable in another culture. Why do you feel this way?

2. Before entering the new culture, what can you do to increase openness, acceptance and trust? What can you do to reduce fear, suspicion and inflexibility?

3. How do you typically cope with difficult situations? By reflecting on those, what do you learn about yourself? What might you do to change how you handle difficult situations as you think about a cross-cultural experience?

4. When you offend someone, is it easy or difficult for you to apologize and make amends? When you think you have offended someone in another culture, what do you think the appropriate response(s) should be? Is it the same or different from your home culture?

5. How do you think the cultural adjustment map helps you understand the relationship between God and yourself?

Attitudes and Skills for Cultural Adjustment

Openness:
How to Be Approachable

Until the day you can greet a man as a man
and not be conscious of his face,
except for its individual beauty,
you are still acting as judge.

GLADIS DEPREE

HAVE YOU HAD SOME PEOPLE IN YOUR LIFE whom you really enjoy seeing? What is it about them that makes you feel good when you are around them? My experience suggests that those people express openness, acceptance and trust in relationships. These topics will occupy the next three chapters. Practicing openness, acceptance and trust will give you a big advantage in building wonderful relationships in your new cultural venture and will enrich your life wherever you are.

Remember the cultural adjustment map in the previous chapter? Openness, acceptance and trust are three skill sets we need to take as we approach another culture. They get us started in the right direction and help us stay on the upper track toward building positive connections with people who are different.

OPENNESS

Openness is the ability to welcome people into your presence and help them feel safe. A similar word is approachable. What is it that signals to people that they are welcome to approach us? Openness and approach-

ability sound simple enough, but many people are not naturally good at it. I know I am not. I must work at it.

An attitude, like openness, is an intangible that expresses itself in ways we can see. We can look for acts or behaviors, which reveal an attitude of openness. Once we are aware of what an open person does, we can observe and practice those behaviors until people sense that we are open too.

Someone in my life who best illustrates this quality is my wife's adopted mother, Helen. My wife, Muriel, a missionary kid, lost her father when she was just over two years old. Her mother continued living in rural Zimbabwe as a missionary. At seven years of age, my wife was sent away to boarding school in the city and later to a missionary children's home. One set of "parents" at the missionary children's home adopted Muriel, a relationship that has lasted for fifty years. When Muriel and I were dating, these parents, who had returned from Zimbabwe for furlough, adopted me too. I didn't realize it, but before I knew it, I was family. In fact, we are so much family that we, along with other adoptees, are part of their will. These amazing people best illustrate openness. I have tried to analyze how they do it.

I have had similar expressions of openness expressed toward me in nearly all the seventy-five countries I have traveled in. In this chapter, I am attempting to put my observations in concrete form through the life of one person who lived so successfully in a second culture. Please remember that openness, acceptance and trust, which are important qualities in every culture, may be expressed differently in different parts of the world. For example, eye contact, which communicates openness and equality in most Western cultures, communicates arrogance and even insolence in other cultures, especially if a younger person looks an older person in the eye. It is considered polite and proper for the younger person to look down toward the floor or lower than the eye level of the other person. In some cultures eye contact between a man and a woman has sexual overtones. Women in these cultures usually look down when a man approaches. Thus, you need to discover the cultural nuances in the

place you will be and make appropriate adjustments.

Smile genuinely. A genuine broad smile always greets us when we enter Helen's home. She lives near us, and nearly every Sunday, her small, unassuming house is the gathering place for ten to twenty people for dinner and the afternoon. Less than half the crowd is made up of blood relatives. New people are always being introduced. If they live in the vicinity, they soon become "family." Spontaneous laughter frequently erupts throughout the house as people connect. One might think this is a happy-go-lucky family with few cares in the world. Actually, not so. The family has seen its share of sorrow and hardship. Yet, Helen's smile to so many continuously warms the home, making it a safe place to relax and be ourselves.

Reach out. Helen proactively reaches out to people. She moves toward you either by seeing you coming and holding the door open or by physically drawing near as you enter. An eager hug awaits if you are so inclined. A touch on the arm and an enthusiastic "I'm so glad you could come," gives you the distinct impression that your presence has made her day. Immediately, you are also glad you came. During your visit she connects to find out how you are doing. She keeps moving toward you, yet remaining sensitive not to intrude.

Ask questions. I feel valued when people ask about my life, work and activities. Helen remembers everything about our lives just as though we were her own children. Her questions reveal honest interest. She listens well and follows up with more questions. The exchange unfolds naturally and in various directions. Her own thoughts and concerns flow gently into the stream of shared conversation. Unconsciously, the event becomes another bonding experience between parent and children.

Engage people. If Helen cannot engage you in conversation, she will invite you into a game or some creative project she has recently started, or ask your opinion on some matter. Yet, it is okay to quietly read a book or paper, doze off in a chair or watch TV. Her home is your home, and people are encouraged to do as they please. But she will do her best to make sure you feel welcome, comfortable, relaxed and, most important, safe.

Suspend judgment. When I first met Helen, I noticed she was slow to judge and tried to give everyone the benefit of a doubt. Before judgment she would try to find the facts and keep an open mind about the other person. It seemed she found it difficult to believe something negative about another person. When she did, it would be shared in the most gracious spirit. Then she would continue to make it a matter of prayer. This attribute contributed significantly to the safe atmosphere she built in her home.

Expressive. One might be inclined to think that Helen has few opinions and, perhaps, a wimpy spirit. Actually, she has quite strong opinions, sticks to her values, is in touch with her emotions and reveals all quite freely. I have often wondered how Helen can be open and accepting while also being quite confrontational on sensitive matters. After watching her for a couple years, I have noticed two qualities: First, her confrontation comes in the form of inquiring questions (as opposed to judgmental questions). She seeks to understand the other person's perspective before forming and expressing her own position. Second, she shows genuine interest in you as a person and in a commitment to sustaining the relationship. Thus, the positive atmosphere she has created becomes the loving context in which she may confront. Confrontation in this atmosphere usually produces positive results.

One healthy outcome of her open expressiveness is that you are rarely in the dark about her feelings. You know where you stand with her—no game playing or charades.

Generous. Helen quickly offers food, drink, candy or little gifts revealing that she is thinking about you and values you. She discovers your birthday and the entire extended family showers you with gifts on your special day as well as Christmas and whenever she may feel like it. Mostly you realize that she gives of herself for the benefit of others. The tangible expressions let you know what is in her heart.

Slow to bid farewell. I must confess to relief when certain people leave my house. One never gets that impression when you leave Helen's house. Her face and words reveal genuine regret that you must leave so

soon, in spite of the fact you have been there for four hours or longer. "Are you sure you can't stay a little longer?" are frequent words as my wife and I signal it is time for us to leave.

Invitations to return. Often Helen calls to find out if we can come to Sunday dinner and stay for the afternoon. Part of it is to plan for the food, but more of it is to let us know that she wants us to come. It is a good feeling to be wanted. We always feel welcome and safe. People from other cultures have felt her openness in the same delightful ways.

These are some of the qualities that I have noticed not only in Helen, but also in people everywhere who communicate openness. It is a great gift to receive and a great gift to give.

D I S C U S S I O N   Q U E S T I O N S

1. Are there any other ways that people you know express openness?

2. Of the expressions of openness mentioned in this chapter, which ones do you need to work on to be a more open person?

3. Rate yourself on the behaviors of openness. On a scale of 1-10, how do you rate yourself? (1 = very poor; 10 = very good).
   - Genuine smile of greeting   _____
   - Reaching out to others   _____
   - Asking nonjudgmental questions   _____
   - Active listening   _____
   - Engaging others in conversation   _____
   - Suspending judgment   _____
   - Expressing yourself   _____
   - Generous   _____
   - Slow to end the meeting   _____
   - Looking forward to the next meeting   _____

Do your scores show that you are an open person?

4. Can you identify any areas where you could improve? How? Thinking about the culture you plan to enter, might any of these be culturally unacceptable? Which and why? How can you find out?

5. Sometimes it is a good idea to see if others see us the way we see ourselves. Give this list to three to five other people and ask them to score you according to their perception of how well you express each of the characteristics on the list. If the scoring was done anonymously, you might a get more honest set of scores from the others. Then compare their scores with your own.

Acceptance: How to Be Positive

We stand in awe of the ocean,
The thunderstorm,
The sunset,
The mountains;
But we pass by
A human being
Without notice
Even though
The person
Is God's most
Magnificent
Creation.
AUGUSTINE

I HAD NEVER THOUGHT OF ACCEPTANCE as an important biblical concept until several years ago when I heard a respected Bible teacher say, "What John 3:16 is to the non-Christian, Romans 15:7 is to the Christian." Most of us know what John 3:16 says, but after three years of Bible school and a seminary degree, I did not have a clue about what Romans 15:7 said. Yet, I did not want to show my ignorance so I mumbled something about "interesting insight." Then I raced home and read the text, which says, "Accept one another, then, just as Christ accepted you, in order to bring praise to God." Are you surprised that the Bible professor placed this verse in such importance for Christians? I was, until I began to examine the word *accept.* Then I understood the wisdom of his statement.

ACCEPTANCE DEFINED

Acceptance is the ability to communicate value, regard, worth and respect to others. It is the ability to make people feel significant, honored and esteemed. Though acceptance appears to be a passive concept like tolerance—meaning to indulge the person, put up with or endure the person—acceptance is not passive, but proactive. It means to intentionally extend regard, honor and esteem to others.

There are several reasons why acceptance deserves its own chapter in this book and why we must practice it in all our relationships. First, Paul uses acceptance as the key instructional point to guide the Roman Christians in dealing with the cultural differences that were dividing them. Second, Paul uses Christ as the example of acceptance that we are to follow. Third, we must show acceptance toward all people, because deeply rooted in the soul of every person is dignity. God himself bestowed dignity upon every human being when he shared his image with us (Genesis 1:27).

ACCEPTANCE: PAUL AND THE ROMAN CHRISTIANS

The church at Rome faced a crisis that threatened to divide the congregation. Two groups disagreed over some matters of conscience, which grew out of their respective cultural traditions. Paul calls the two groups "the weak" and "the strong" (Romans 14:1-4; 15:1), terms which probably do not refer to the spiritual character of the groups but which more likely refer to the sensitivity of conscience toward certain customs, such as eating food offered to idols (Romans 15:1). The weak probably referred to a group of mostly Jewish Christians who were concerned whether the food they ate was prepared according to Jewish custom and whether they could celebrate special days on the Roman calendar. Their conscience was sensitive, and they did not want to violate it.

The strong referred to Christians from a Gentile cultural history. Their conscience regarding food and special days was not so sensitive, and they saw no reason to be so concerned.

Paul mentions that these differences were about "disputable matters" (Romans 14:1), suggesting that the issues separating the two groups were not core doctrinal differences nor were they critical moral issues. They were just differences—the issues were not worth breaking fellowship and splintering the body of Christ. So how does Paul propose to solve these deep cultural differences that threatened the church and its testimony in Rome, the nerve center of the world, at that time?

ACCEPTANCE IS LOVE

To accept others, is to love them. From Romans 12:1 through chapter 15, Paul emphasizes the centrality of love in relationships (Romans 12:9-10, 17-21; 13:8). Paul appeals to both Jewish and Gentile Christians to put that love into practice by accepting one another and not passing judgment on each another (14:1, 10, 13). Neither side should judge the other side as inferior, for God has accepted them both (14:3).

Paul concludes, "Let us therefore make every effort to do what leads to peace and to mutual edification. Do not destroy the work of God for the sake of food" (14:19-20). That last sentence could be read as as "Do not destroy the work of God for the sake of our cultural traditions."

LESSONS

We can learn a few principles from the Christians at Rome.

1. People see things differently, and those differences often come from cultural traditions.
2. Differences can alienate members of the body of Christ, which disrupts the work of God. We must make every effort to keep this from happening (Ephesians 4:3).
3. Acceptance is a powerful expression of love. To accept people is to love them as God does and as he commands us to do.
4. If something irritates you about another culture and its people, "keep [it] between yourself and God" (Romans 14:22).

5. If differences are culturally based and not a violation of Scripture, we can accept people, honor and respect them, and learn from them since God also accepts them.

6. Christ accepted us while we were yet sinners, suggesting we must find ways to communicate acceptance to those who have not yet bowed to the lordship of Christ and who live in violation of his law (Romans 15:7).

CHRIST: THE EXAMPLE OF ACCEPTANCE

The power of acceptance may be seen more clearly by looking at the opposite: rejection. Rejection ranks among the most painful words in the human vocabulary. Physical wounds certainly are painful, but emotional wounds seem worse for they hurt the deepest part of our being. Many emotional wounds are a result of some form of rejection—from a best friend, parent, spouse, relative or some trusted person. Rejection is harsh. It takes a long time for the wound to heal and the pain to fade.

Now consider the fact that Christ had every right to reject us. Think about what that would have meant. Rejection by others is painful. But rejection by Christ would be eternally worse, because the consequences are forever. We would be outside his love, condemned and without hope. Looking at rejection makes Christ's acceptance of us among the truly beautiful statements of Scripture—"Accept one another, then, just as Christ accepted you, in order to bring praise to God" (Romans 15:7).

Christ accepted me and held me in esteem, not because I was good or somehow worthy, but because the Creator placed his own image in me and all of humanity, bestowing upon us dignity. Because of this divine dignity, Christ accepted us.

How did he accept us? In love, without conditions, just as we are. He did it proactively, not waiting for something from me. He did it irrevocably and unconditionally as an act of love. What Christ did for me, I

must be willing to do toward others: "Accept one another . . . just as Christ accepted you."

F O R   R E F L E C T I O N

As you think about your environment—the office, school, home, neighborhood—who do you have the most difficulty accepting?

- Think about why that may be so.
- Think about how that makes God feel.
- Think about how God sees that person (those people).
- Think about what it does to the image of God in those people.
- Think about how it affects your own relationship to God.
- Think about how you might begin to change your attitude.

Practicing acceptance of "one another as Christ accepted you" in your immediate context will give you the right mindset, the right attitude and the right skills to practice it with people in another culture.

D I S C U S S I O N   Q U E S T I O N S
---

1. In what ways do you show acceptance toward others? How have others shown acceptance toward you?

2. In the culture you are entering, in what ways do you think they might show acceptance toward you? Do you think you can show acceptance to them the same way you would toward someone from your own culture? Explain your answer.

3. What kinds of people are hardest for you to accept? Why?

4. What does it mean to you personally that Christ accepted you?

11

Trust: How to Build Strong Relationships

*Was it the nature of faith to create barriers, or, was true faith
intended to eradicate barriers?*

GLADIS DEPREE

THIS CHAPTER IS ABOUT TRUST, which may be the most important idea you
will get from this book. Think about the following statement: "Nothing
significant happens between people unless there is a strong bond of
trust." Do you agree? Would you say that the major characteristic of best
friends is that they trust each other, even with their deepest secrets? If a
doctor says, "Take this medicine," and you do, is it not because you trust
her or his competence? The criteria for trust may be competence (cre-
dentials) or credibility (being trustworthy) or both. Regardless, trust is
the glue of all good relationships.

If we don't trust people we probably will not spend much time with
them, listen carefully to what they say, follow their advice or put much
energy into the relationship. Trust makes all the difference in the quality
of a relationship. This is especially true if you are sharing something of
great importance, like the possibility of following Jesus. People will take
you seriously only if they trust you. If you have built trust, people are
more likely to listen to you and consider your message. If you have not
taken the time or put in the effort to build trust, it is less likely that they
will listen. Most people do not change a lifetime of patterns because
someone new comes into their culture and announces that they ought to
change their ways.

PRIOR QUESTION OF TRUST

A prior question of trust in its simplest form asks what would build trust with a particular person or group.[1] Remember the snow tires that I gave my wife for our first wedding anniversary? I asked myself *What would build trust?* but forgot to add *with my wife?* If we ask only the first part of the question—"What will build trust?"—we can easily answer it from our own frame of reference and then end up looking like the monkey.

Just as I needed to ask what would build trust with my wife when buying a gift for her, we must intentionally ask ourselves what would build trust with others with whom we desire to build relationships, especially in another culture. I say "intentional" because it is so easy to forget. Eventually it will become natural. Remember to ask the entire question: "What will build trust with this person in his/her cultural frame of reference?" Do this several times a day at critical points. If you fail to do this, you will slip back into your own cultural patterns and you will be offering snow tires instead of perfume, flowers or something appropriate to the person. But it is not quite so simple when you are in an unfamiliar culture. The monkey discovered this when he tried to help the fish!

TRUST IS CULTURALLY DEFINED

In many cultures, my way of building trust does not work. In fact, it communicates the opposite. Let me explain by using a generic story gleaned from a variety of situations. Mary and Joe Smith, working in another culture, decided they would like to build a relationship with a local couple. Joe worked with Koko at his job and believed a friendship would be possible.

Joe talked with Koko, and he and his wife agreed to come to Joe and Mary's home for an evening meal. Everyone had a delightful evening. Now the Smiths waited to see if the local couple would do something to show they wanted a friendship—perhaps an invitation for the Smiths to come to their house. Several weeks went by and nothing. The Smiths

decided they would try it again and essentially went through the same routine. The other couple came again, the evening was wonderful and everyone departed happy. Weeks went by and nothing came from the couple that would signal interest in pursuing the relationship.

Miscommunication. At this point, it is important to know that both couples wanted a friendship, but both had concluded that the other couple did not want it. Why do you suppose the local couple would conclude that the Smiths did not want a friendship? It seemed pretty obvious, at least to us. Would you have done anything different if you had been in the Smiths' place?

In much of African, Hispanic and Asian culture, setting a time, place and agenda for an evening together signals that you want a more formal, prescribed relationship, not a friendship. One signals a desire for friendship by stopping by the person's house, *unannounced*. Often it's called "popping in." Popping in at mealtime is all the better; now you can eat together and spend the evening chatting. This causes many North Americans discomfort. First of all, you don't just stop by—that is rude according to our etiquette experts. Second, we do not like people stopping by unexpectedly because we put a premium on having a clean house for guests and making sure we cook a special meal. What do we do about enough food if people just pop in? Third, the evening meal in many Western homes is considered family time because of the way our lives are structured. So we assume it is family time for everyone else as well. We do not want to be interrupted during family time, and we would not think of doing it to others.

But in many cultures of the world, people will generally cook more than they need because people are always popping in. Or, if they do not have enough, the children will eat later or be sent to a relative's house where they may have some extra food. The condition of the house is not nearly so important as the fact that someone has chosen to stop by and spend time with them. Neither are they so preoccupied with whether things are tidy but more with celebrating the arrival of guests and enjoying time together.

Be culturally sensitive. Be alert to discovering how people build trust in the culture where you will be. You can do several things: observe what people do; ask veteran Westerners who have built many solid relationships in that culture; listen to conversations among friends and ask a local person what you can do to build a friendship with a person in that culture. I would use the word *friendship* instead of *trust* because there is less ambiguity with friendship. (Did you notice the "observe, ask/inquire and listen" in this paragraph? They are the important coping skills from the cultural adjustment map in figure 8.1, p. 72.)

TRUST IS PERSONALLY DEFINED

Not only is trust culturally defined, it is also personally defined. The snow tires story is a good example, but here is another. Another husband, newly married and quite the outdoor sportsman, purchased a new shotgun for his wife's birthday. He presented it to her in a nice case so it would be protected from scratches. With the gift came this message: "I think this shotgun will help us develop more intimacy in our marriage. Now we can walk out to the woods together, shoot some animals together, process the meat together and eat it together while rehearsing the hunting memories." She was not impressed.

He was completely sincere but certainly did not understand the indoor preferences of his wife. My friend bought an expensive gift, had good intentions and ended up a failure. His wife did not enjoy hunting or any sports for that matter. Like the monkey (remember the monkey and fish story) my friend had acted out of his own frame of reference. He wanted to express love and build trust but was unsuccessful because he neglected to add, "with my wife." As we practice answering this question in our own culture, it will be easier to ask and answer in the new culture.

Trust, or the lack thereof, defines all relationships. Let's not be naive. We cannot just barge into someone's life and have instant credibility. If we try, we will be giving snow tires instead of a clear message of love. Or,

as the apostle Paul said, our witness will sound more like a "clanging symbol" than genuine love (1 Corinthians 13:1).

Circles of trust. Trust is necessary every day with everyone—we can practice trust daily with everyone around us, even those with whom trust has been broken. However, it is best to focus on specific people when thinking about trust.

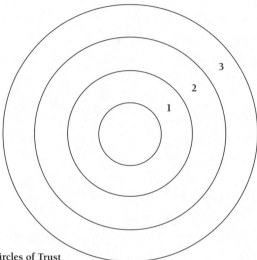

Figure 11.1. Circles of Trust

Figure 11.1 has concentric circles. Put your initials, representing you, in the smallest circle. Then, place the initials of people who are closest to you, the people you trust the most, in circle 1. In the second circle, place the initials of those you trust to a lesser degree. Next, inside the third circle, put the initials of people you trust only a little or those you do not trust at all or with whom trust has been severely broken. Do this now and please do not read further until you have given three to five minutes to put initials where you think they belong.

Now think about the following questions:

1. Where did you place your parents? Siblings? Uncles and aunts?

Grandparents? Spouse? Colleagues? Add new initials of people if you wish.

2. Where did you place Christians? Non-Christians?
3. Are there any people farther away than you would like? Should they be closer to you? How can you make this happen?
4. Are there some who are close to you but who have an unhealthy influence on you and maybe should not occupy such an influential place? How should you respond?
5. Do you have any other insights from this activity?

The circles applied. I had just finished teaching a session on trust. As I absorbed the warm sun on a mountaintop outside Puebla, Mexico, a young man of college age joined me. "I heard what you said about trust this morning," he started. "What was important for you?" I answered, believing he wanted to say more. "My dad and I haven't talked for three years, and it doesn't seem right," he blurted. "It's not that we don't ever talk. We just exchange greetings and maybe something about the weather, not much more," he continued. "You would like to change that?" I countered. "Yeah, I will be leaving college and moving away soon, and I want to have a more meaningful relationship with my dad."

Becoming more direct, I said, "What do you think you can do to begin that process?" Because the young man could not find an answer to that question, I had to ask it in several different ways. I finally said, "When your dad is enjoying himself, what is he doing?" "Working with wood," he answered quickly. "He loves making things, and he does a beautiful job." "Have you seen any wood around this place that has caught your eye?" I asked. My grandfather loved wood, and I love refinishing old furniture, so I was on familiar ground. At this the young man brightened. "Interesting you should ask. I notice wood all the time, and there is some unusual wood around here." Now we were get-

ting somewhere. "So how would your father interpret it if you sent him a nice slab of wood from Mexico?" (Note: I was asking him to put himself into his father's frame of reference—what would build trust with his father.) Now he sat upright and became animated. "He would really like that! I can do it!"

The young man realized his father had been in one of the outer circles and wanted to change that. He just needed a conversation to nudge him in the right direction. The process of a better father-son relationship had begun. Building trust is not hard, but it does take a little thought.

TRUST TAKES TIME

Two brief thoughts remain. First, it takes time to build trust. If trust has been violated it may take more time to build it, but usually you will find people ready to respond. Be patient. Keep checking to make sure that your attempts to build trust are not based on your own frame of reference but on that of the other person. The people in the new culture have probably had previous experiences with people from your culture. This history may have influenced them toward openness and trust toward you or, perhaps, to be more cautious.

Second, trust is built in slow progressive steps. We may want to build or rebuild trust with one giant act. Usually it does not work that way, particularly if trust has been broken in the past. Even in new relationships, trust starts with small acts and builds into a solid and healthy relationship. Patience pays off.

FOR REFLECTION

1. How has God built trust with you over the years? What does he do? Make a list of items.

2. What insights does this list give us in our attempts to build trust with those around us and our friends in other cultural settings?

D I S C U S S I O N   Q U E S T I O N S

1. Thinking about the culture you are going to, are there ways in which you can learn how the people build trust?

2. What kinds of behaviors from you would tend to undermine or break trust with the people you will be with?

3. Among the people you know, with whom have you had difficulty building trust? Why it has been difficult? Can you think of what else you might do that will build trust from their perspective?

4. Can you think of a time when trust was broken with you? How did you feel? What did it take (or would it take) to rebuild the broken trust?

5. Why does it feel good when someone builds trust with you?

12

Skills for Cross-Cultural Effectiveness

To be surprised, to wonder, is to begin to understand.

JOSÉ ORTEGA Y GASSETT

YOU ARE THINKING ABOUT SOME KIND OF ACTIVITY in another culture. You are motivated to do a good job and make a difference. But the monkey and fish story in the first chapter showed us that good motives and good intentions are not enough to be effective. You really need a set of insights and skills to give feet to your good intentions and motives. This book is exactly about that: giving you skills to do the job well, so well that the people will want you to come back and stay longer.

This chapter attempts to do two things: first, to reinforce in a different way some of the skills we have talked about; second, to introduce some new and useful skills and ideas that will help you. When something happens that you are not sure how to handle, hopefully, one of these insights will provide you with a way to understand that situation and deal with it. I have found that acronyms help lodge ideas in people's memory.

IT TAKES TIME (ITT)

Cultural adjustment does not come quickly and, for some, not easily. Therefore, don't be so hard on yourself. Go into the new culture realizing that there will be bumps. But keep in mind too, that tens of thousands of others who have gone before you also had bumps and still made a

positive impact for the cause of Christ. They did it, and you can too.

So don't give up. That is exactly what Satan would like for you to do. But God has an important purpose for you being right where you are. He has something important for you and for the host country people. By persevering you will see the wondrous things God has in store. Virtually anything important will have some struggle attached to it. Those struggles will make you stronger and wiser if you don't give up.

A friend of mine who worked for one of the big three auto companies in the United States was sent to a Spanish-speaking country on a two-year assignment. He had little cultural orientation yet plunged into his work. He found the cultural issues overwhelming and, in a few weeks, found himself unable to function effectively. Before the end of his first month he returned to his U.S. office. He felt terrible, a complete failure. He was also confused. What went wrong? Why couldn't he adjust? Others had. What was wrong with him? My own analysis, apart from his having no cultural orientation, was that he tried to do too much too fast without attempting to get acquainted with his new office and living environment. It takes time to adjust, and if we ignore the adjustment process, we may pay dearly.

MONITOR, MONITOR, MONITOR (MMM)

What should we monitor? Our emotions! Why? Because they usually cause quick, unthinking reactions that can damage relationships. There are several steps involved in monitoring our emotions.

Step one. Think about what you are feeling. If the feelings are negative then put yourself on alert so you don't do anything that you will regret. So monitor your emotions, especially when they are negative.

Step two. Name the negative emotion: anger, frustration, confusion, embarrassment, fear, tension, anxiety, jealousy, envy, superiority or maybe a vague, but real discomfort. Try to give it a name. You cannot proactively deal with something that is not identified. If you cannot identify it, you tend to react; reactions usually cause other reactions and

things quickly go out of control. Now everyone becomes a victim. That inability to identify and properly manage a negative emotion quickly sabotages our well-meaning efforts.

Step three. Ask yourself what is causing the negative emotion. While step two was naming your emotion, step three is naming the situation that triggered this emotion in you. Describing the situation in your mind may accomplish several things. It disarms the emotional content by letting your mind take charge. It gives you a second or two to judge whether your emotions are justified or not. It also gives you a moment in which to replace reaction with a planned action, one that will give you more positive results.

Obviously, if you feel immediate physical threat, the thing to do is get out of harm's way. That reaction is wise and natural. But most of the time the situations you face will be of the more common cultural variety that can be dealt with in a more thoughtful way.

Step four. What options do you have? Options fall under several categories:

• Thoughts—be guided by the positive, the good and the constructive, resisting the tendency to blame and fault others.

• Speech—be guided by words of grace and sensitivity, resisting the harsh and judgmental.

• Actions—be guided by acts of love, gentleness and kindness, resisting the sharp and abrasive.

Step five. Choose the best thoughts, words and acts to express yourself even though you are frustrated enough to punch somebody's lights out. It is okay to feel that way sometimes, just don't act on it.

The bottom line is to figure out what is happening and turn it into a positive learning experience. Keep that goal in mind and work hard to get there.

PRIOR QUESTION OF TRUST (PQT)

Even though the last chapter focused on trust, I am mentioning trust

again here because it as an extremely important concept. Also, in the last chapter I spoke of it as an attitude, and in this chapter I am presenting trust more as a skill.

Most of us tend to react when we feel stress or frustration. Our reactions may be understood in our home culture but often are misunderstood in another culture and result in hurting innocent people. My experience suggests that when we hurt others, they usually do not tell us about it, at least not directly. It would cause us shame and loss of face. They would never dishonor us in this way.

Building trust, as I said earlier, is culturally defined. Let me illustrate. An automotive supplier in the United States had employees from an overseas customer visit his site for training on some new technology. Over a period of fifteen months, the American found the guests to be very inconsiderate because they asked personal questions and seemed to be more interested in small talk about family, hobbies and such. The guests thought the Americans were very inconsiderate because all they thought about was business and never seemed interested in the guests as people who were away from their families, strangers in the United States and isolated. Each group judged the other as inconsiderate because of the different cultural rules each had for building trust. Needless to say, the project was less successful than the respective companies had envisioned.

That which builds trust in your culture may not build trust in another culture. In fact, it may break trust. It would take several books to talk about how each culture builds trust. In most cases, we do it so intuitively in our culture that we do not even know it. If someone asks us how we build trust, we shrug our shoulders and say something like, "I don't know; it is something you just do." The same is true of other cultures.

So how do you learn to build trust? Some things are universal: smiling when meeting someone and frequently as the friendship develops; speaking positively about people of the host culture, their culture, their family, their country (everyone is proud of their homeland); expressing happiness in having the relationship; reciprocating in kind deeds and

gifts; and being willing to spend time with the people. In some cultures, trust is built by doing what you say you will do in the time you said it would be done. In other cultures, the time given to building the relationship builds the trust more than keeping a schedule.

Still, one must learn the local ways as well. How does this happen? Primarily through observation. Watch what good friends do with and to each other. How close do they stand to each other? Many cultures stand closer than the American who likes more space. What role does touch play? Some cultures are far more high touch than others. In fact, in some countries, two males or females who are good friends may walk down the street arm-in-arm or holding hands. Such physical expression has no sexual connotation—it is a way to show trust and friendship. If you are building a good friendship, do not be surprised if, without even thinking, the other person grabs your hand as you walk along and keeps on holding it. Your reaction may be to pull your hand away. But review the steps in the previous section on monitoring your emotions.

A friend of mine was walking down the sidewalk with a friend from the local culture. Suddenly she realized she was walking in the gutter. Her friend was walking so close and speaking right into her face that she unknowingly had kept moving away until she found herself off the sidewalk and in the gutter. She quickly monitored the situation, realized what was happening and, returning to the sidewalk, enjoyed the ongoing conversation knowing not to pull away.

STRATEGIC WITHDRAWAL STRATEGY (SWS)

Sometimes your system will get overloaded with all the new things around you. You need a break to settle yourself, get your bearings again and come back to the situation refreshed. This is strategic withdrawal, and it is important to utilize it rather than explode, go into culture shock or get bitter and cynical.

Strategic withdrawal is like counting to ten to cool off and is a good idea when the pressure gets too intense. Hence the word *strategic*—when

it is just too much to stay involved in your activity and you feel like you are going to explode, cry or have some kind of outburst, take the time to withdraw. Physically remove yourself from the situation that causes the unbearable pressure or strain. The withdrawal should be relatively short depending on how long the pressure has been building up. For example, if you are at a party and you are feeling stressed out, take a five-minute strategic withdrawal to the bathroom, take a short walk or hang around people who relax you; then, when the pressure is back under control, reenter the situation.

Perhaps this is one reason why God gave us a day of rest—not only a day of worship but a strategic withdrawal from the burden and pace of the work world. God himself rested after the creation of the world. Taking a day or two off each week or taking an extended vacation each year are ways of keeping ourselves healthy physically, mentally and emotionally. When we are overseas my wife and I may go out for an evening to a nice Western restaurant or spend a weekend in a Western style hotel. The wonderful atmosphere not only refreshes but restores energy and perspective.

Keep in mind that strategic withdrawals taken too often or for too long may be a sign not of wise management of a situation but of culture shock. Physical and emotional isolation from the local people to listen to music, read American magazines or books, sleep, or hang out with your Western friends for extended periods signal culture shock, and this needs to be handled quickly. If you find yourself disengaging for large blocks of time, reread the chapter on culture shocks. Employ the aid of friends and senior people who have worked through these issues. They will help you laugh, understand and achieve objectivity as you work through the adjustment process.

LAUGH AT YOURSELF, LAUGH AT LIFE (LAY-LAL)

Having a good sense of humor gets us through many of life's tough spots. Humor relieves tension. It puts situations in perspective. It keeps us

from exploding or imploding. It gives everyone a chance to step back from a potentially damaging situation and try to turn it into a productive one.

But beware of the dangers of humor. While it is usually acceptable to laugh at oneself, it is risky to laugh at someone else until you are quite versed in the culture and the trust is strong. If you are in a group joking and having fun in a public place, local people may be glad to see that you are happy. However, they may also wonder whether you are laughing at them, especially if your humor is loud and accompanied by pointing at something or someone.

Humor rarely translates well across cultures. Usually one must be an insider to appreciate humor. If you are in a group of people of your own culture and people from the local culture are with you, they may not understand your jokes and remarks. It would be good to explain why a given story or remark causes you laughter. This accomplishes two things: the local people realize that their culture is not the object of the humor and they begin to understand the humor of your culture.

IT'S DIFFERENT (ID)

"It's different" may be the most useful little statement you can daily rehearse along with the Prior Question of Trust. The next section is on cultural differences that confuse us. Usually, when we get confused we look for someone or something to blame. Remember Eunice? She spoke in the passive and stative voices, which confused me. I blamed her for my confusion. Something was wrong with her and I needed to try to straighten her out. I saw her behavior as wrong, not as different. When I put something in the category of odd, confusing, weird, wrong or whatever, I am no longer able to learn from it. I have put the person or behavior in a category where I am right and the other is wrong. I am now superior and should try to correct the person. This damaging attitude is simple pride and puts up enormous barriers in relationships.

A simple skill I strongly encourage you to develop is found in a little

phrase: "It is not right or wrong; it is just different." Let me hasten to say that some things will fall into right and wrong, but my guess is that most of your experiences will best fit in the category of differences. If you put a confusing person or situation into the category of difference, you are more likely to suspend judgment, remain open and seek understanding. In doing so, your relationships will be maintained, you will get a quicker and better grasp of the culture in all its fascination, and you will have a far more enjoyable sojourn.

D I S C U S S I O N   Q U E S T I O N S

---

1. Rate yourself on the following skills by circling the appropriate number.

   a) It Takes Time (ITT):

   I am a patient person
   Very much   1   2   3   4   5   6   Very poor

   I am a persevering person
   Very much   1   2   3   4   5   6   Very poor

   b) Monitoring (MMM):

   I can monitor my thoughts
   Very much   1   2   3   4   5   6   Very little

   I can identify my emotions
   Very much   1   2   3   4   5   6   Very little

   c) Prior Question of Trust (PQT):

   I build trust easily
   Very true   1   2   3   4   5   6   Not very true

   I think about how my actions will affect others
   Very true   1   2   3   4   5   6   Not very true

d) Strategic Withdrawal Strategy (SWS):

I usually can handle new situations in a positive way
Very true   1   2   3   4   5   6   Not very true

I tend to get angry when things do not go my way
Very true   1   2   3   4   5   6   Not very true

e) Laugh at Self/Life (LAY-LAL):

I can laugh at my mistakes
Very true   1   2   3   4   5   6   Not very true

I take life too seriously
Very true   1   2   3   4   5   6   Not very true

f) It's Different (ID):

Differences intrigue me
Very true   1   2   3   4   5   6   Not very true

I tend to put things in "right" and "wrong" categories
Very true   1   2   3   4   5   6   Not very true

2. What do you see as you look at the numbers you circled? What areas did you mark yourself as skillful? What areas might you need to work on?

3. Note any areas where you marked yourself low. How might that affect your entering and ministering in another culture? What might you do to improve that skill?

CULTURAL DIFFERENCES THAT CONFUSE

13
Time and Event

What do you Americans do with all the time you save?

COMMENT FREQUENTLY HEARD IN VARIOUS
PARTS OF THE WORLD

IN THIS SECTION, I WILL ATTEMPT TO DESCRIBE several values that express themselves very differently in different cultures. I have selected only a few of the more prominent values that Westerners may benefit from knowing about in advance. I hope that this knowledge will ease the cultural adjustment process and hasten your enjoyment of the people and culture.

IMPORTANT PERSPECTIVE

In this chapter I will describe cultures that view time quite differently. Sherwood Lingenfelter and Marvin Mayer call this contrast "time versus event,"[1] terms I am going to use. Others talk about synchronic cultures and polychronic[2] cultures. Keep in mind the following statements as you read the chapters in this section.

1. Neither value—time or event—is better than the other; neither value is more godly.

2. Different cultures may prefer one value over the other but move back and forth on the continuum.

3. Most of us, when our time-orientation needs are satisfied, can easily adjust and even enjoy someone who is event oriented and vice versa. Frustration comes when our time orientation needs are not met first or, for the event-oriented person, when their event-oriented needs are overlooked or ignored.

4. If I fail to start where the other person is, for example, event-oriented, I may be perceived as insensitive or uncaring, which strains the relationship.

5. The person with the servant heart will try to discern where the other person is on these cultural differences and enter into that frame of reference as a basis for building relationships.

6. For the most part, these values are matters of difference, not right or wrong. As such, we are free to communicate openness, acceptance and trust to people who may express these values differently than we do.

7. It is my observation that much of the Two-Thirds World is becoming more like the West and much of the West is becoming more like the Two-Thirds World. For example, younger-generation Americans are less time-oriented and more event-oriented. Two-Thirds World people, with exposure to the West, are becoming more time-oriented. This trend seems to be true of many of the values discussed in this section. Thus, we are seeing a meshing of cultures where there may be more similarity than difference in some of the values mentioned in this section.

Everyone has the same twenty-four hours each day. Beyond that, however, people think about and use time differently. This chapter will help you become more realistic about how differently people in other cultures view time. It will also help you adjust your expectations.[3]

INDUSTRIAL ECONOMIES

In the West and other highly industrialized countries of the world, time is an important cultural value. As the industrial revolution came to dominate the United States, Henry Ford envisioned most of the country being an assembly line producing everything from cars to clocks. The factory assembly line changed everything. It required everyone to show up on time and punch a time clock. Now we could determine who was

on time and who was late. The clock told everyone when to take a break and when the workday was over. Time was attached to wages, productivity and profitability. Thus, time became money. If someone did not show up on time or did not show up at all, the entire assembly line ground to a halt until someone filled the vacant slot. In public schools, Sunday schools and on the job, people were rewarded for being on time and punished if late or absent. On the job workers would get their pay docked. In school, some of us remember students receiving a gold star for perfect or punctual attendance.

Out of this environment came the commitment to time: being on time (punctuality), little or no down (sick) time, wasting time, making time, buying time, finding time, saving time and, of course, not losing time. Concern focused on the amount of production for the work time. Scheduling, efficiency, planning, goal setting and predictability emerged as important values for an industrial culture. The amount of time became the measuring device for life and work. Life was quantified into time frames where seconds, minutes and hours took on significance. Not being late was a virtue. The wristwatch became the most common gift received by grade school and high school graduates who were entering the unforgiving world ruled by the watch. Success was tied to time.

Many of us remember the hectic frenzy around the house trying to get ready on time for church or some event. We arrived on time but at the cost of shouting and tense feelings. Maybe it is still true in your house. Nevertheless, our time orientation served us well for things like gross national product, national emergencies and progress in science. It has, however, often taken its toll on relationships. Thus, a time orientation is good news and bad news. Minimize the bad and everyone benefits.

Industrial economies had to be future oriented. One planned for eventualities that may interfere with the production schedule and quotas. Thus, assuring the continuous flow of commodities and personnel

to keep the factories going became a growing science. Long-range planning became part of every company's administrative structure. Progress required less attention to the past and more to the future. The focus on time and the drive for profitability tempted executives and investors to see people as machinery more than human beings.

As the industrial revolution evolved into the information economy, the complexity of life increased, forcing people to plan more precisely. Nanoseconds, baud, megaherz (mhz) and megabytes per second (mb/s) replaced the vocabulary of seconds, minutes and hours. Time remained the primary currency for defining progress in many sectors of society.

As I noted, many in the emerging generation who are under thirty appear to be in transition away from a time orientation. I am surprised by the number of younger people in malls and parking lots who notice I have a wrist watch and ask me the time. We have given our youngest son three watches, none of which he has ever worn! From my historic time orientation, I often wonder how he survives. Actually, he seems freer of stress, though there have been moments when he wished he had been more time-oriented.

AGRICULTURAL ECONOMIES

Agricultural economies are not so concerned about seconds and minutes or even hours. More important is "seasonal" time when crops are planted and harvested and the timeliness of rain and sun. The days are not divided into small increments but are seen as opportunities to do the timely thing which could be planting, fixing a machine, helping a neighbor, playing with your child, relaxing, welcoming a visitor or rebuilding a strained relationship. Such activities do not fit into time frames. Each event is as long or short as it needs to be. One cannot determine the required time in advance. Time is elastic, dictated only by the natural unfolding of the event. The quality of the event is the primary issue, not the quantity of minutes or hours. One cannot schedule relationships in

fifteen- or thirty-minute segments, not if they are to grow strong. A relationship should take the time it needs to mature and endure.

Since many economies of the Two-Thirds World are agricultural, they often find strict time frames difficult, if not dysfunctional. One cannot predict when friends will stop by. The unexpected friend popping in will get priority over some scheduled appointment. The appointment will be kept, but usually late, after the relationship is properly respected. Local people understand, but those of us from a quantity-time culture must adjust our expectations. It is not an issue of favoritism or respect. If they were talking to you, they would miss an appointment with someone else to sustain the quality time with you.

In many Two-Thirds World countries, buses do not run on a predictable schedule for a variety of reasons. The bus driver may need an extra half hour to load the produce someone is taking to market. The driver may overload the bus causing it to break down. Sometimes, a child runs ahead of the parent to tell the bus driver to wait for an adult who will be along "soon." The driver will wait knowing the next bus is a day or two later. It is the way things happen. Get used to it. The sooner you adjust, the better you will feel and the more fun you will have.

TIME IN THE BIBLE

Doesn't the Bible speak about redeeming the time and discerning the time? Of course, but we read the Bible from our Western frame of reference—our time orientation. In the New Testament the two most common words for time are *kairos* and *chronos*. *Chronos* refers generally to time segments, sequences and what we might think of as a specific time or time period. In today's culture, we might think of it as clock time or calendar time. You might check Matthew 2:7, Acts 7:17, Hebrews 4:7 and 1 Peter 4:3 where *chronos* is used. In Western culture the notion of time is usually *chronos*.

Kairos, used nearly twice as often in the New Testament, approximates the way many people in the Two-Thirds World perceive time.

Time is understood not in terms of specific segments but more in terms of opportunity, the right time, the appropriate time or the meaningful time. Thus, *kairos* people value the moment, the event or the opportunity and try to make it significant and memorable. They do have concern for time frames and schedules but often not as a priority. The more modern versions of the Bible have picked up the distinction. For example, "See then that ye walk circumspectly, not as fools, but as wise, redeeming the time *[kairos]*, because the days are evil" (Ephesians 5:15-16 KJV). Compare this with, "Be very careful, then, how you live—not as unwise but as wise, making the most of every opportunity *[kairos]*, because the days are evil" (Ephesians 5:15-16 NIV).

DEVELOPING BETTER ATTITUDES

Since patience and waiting are not my strengths, I have had to develop a better attitude when living and traveling in cultures that structure their lives around events and opportunity moments rather than linear time frames. As in many potentially frustrating situations one can turn it into an advantage. Here is what I have done.

Read. I usually carry reading material with me, including a small Bible. I always feel better waiting if I can fill the time doing something.

Pray. Spending time in prayer is another good way to use the waiting time.

Observe. I think it was Yogi Berra who said, "It is amazing how much you can see just by looking around." Make a game out of it and mentally note what you are observing. What differences and similarities do you see compared to what you might see in your home culture? As you observe, try to determine the meaning of what you are seeing.

Listen. What are people talking about around you? What does it tell you about their lives? Their culture? Their values?

Relate. Strike up a conversation with someone. Ask questions. Listen. Seek information. What can you learn? People are eager to talk and are a wealth of information.

For Reflection

We have looked at two ways in which cultures may view time. In this chapter and several following, I will present several continuums on which you can rate yourself. The time/event continuum has a scale of 1-10 ranging from a strong preference for time to a strong preference for event. While 1 or 2 shows a strong preference for time, 9 and 10 show a strong preference for event. Keep in mind several things: rural/agricultural North Americans will probably place themselves more toward an event orientation (say 5, 6 or 7) more than urban or suburban North Americans. Factory workers who punch a time clock may place themselves at 1, 2 or 3. African Americans may lean toward event time as well, even though they may work in a time-oriented job—they may slide back and forth on the continuum depending upon circumstances and environment. Much of African and Latin American economies are agricultural, suggesting they will prefer the event side of the continuum. There may be some people, however, because of exposure to the West or because they have lived in a time culture who will lean to the time side of the continuum.

The cultural differences chapters that end with a continuum like the one below are not intended to put everyone in an inflexible category. It is intended to point out tendencies that will help us acquire more realistic expectations and adjust our behaviors to fit in more quickly. In other words, this information will help us to enter another culture—to become less square and more round.

Note the time/event continuum below and then respond to each point.

Time	1	2	3	4	5	6	7	8	9	10	**Event**

1. Place an X indicating where you fall on the time/event continuum.
   Put a P indicating where you think your parents are.
   Put a C indicating where you think your church falls on the continuum.

Use any further symbols that are meaningful to you: S for spouse; F for friends, B for boss.

2. Use NC (new culture) to indicate where you think the people of the new culture will be on the continuum. How much distance is there between X (you) and NC?

You have marked where you perceive yourself and others to be on a scale of 1-10, from time to event orientation. However, I want to emphasize that everyone is, at some point, time oriented and at other points event oriented. All of us actually move back and forth on the 1-10 scale. So keep the following in mind not only for this chapter on time and event but also through chapter eighteen.

DISCUSSION QUESTIONS

---

1. Will your view of time conflict or agree with that of the new culture? How difficult will it be for you to adjust?

2. Do you view your use of time with a right/wrong mentality? What difficulties could this cause you in your new culture?

3. What practical steps can you take to adjust to a different use of time?

4. How have your views about time been shaped by your family and upbringing?

Task and Relationship

As far as I was concerned, she and the cucumbers and the
spring onions were all part of the scenery.

GLADIS DEPREE

BOB, A BUILDER IN DETROIT, AND I HAD DRIVEN twelve hours to Jackson, Mississippi to help Pastor Ron put siding on his house. Pastor Ron was an associate pastor in a predominantly African American church in this city. Ministering among low-income people, Pastor Ron and his wife lived meagerly in a small run-down house. Bob and I offered to help Pastor Ron put on new siding and some other touches that would make the house more livable, especially since Ron had recently married.

Bob and I were on the ladders giving the measurements for the next piece of siding while Ron was on the ground sawing them to size. Each time someone walked by Ron's house, he went out to the street to chat, while Bob and I were left on the ladders with nothing to do. Sometimes Ron's little chats would last five to ten minutes. Bob's earlier optimism and good humor were now turning into a loud silence pierced by an occasional snide remark.

Bob is task-oriented. He sets his sights on a goal and goes after it. This quality made him a successful builder. But now he was "wasting" time because Ron was always drifting off to talk. (Does this remind you of the last chapter on time versus event?) Bob hadn't driven twelve hours and freely offered his skills to be left standing on a ladder. "Are we here to work or talk?" he asked once, trying to get everyone back to the task.

Frankly, I was feeling some frustration as well until I realized what

was happening. I don't always remember to follow my own advice, but this time I did. I asked myself what was really going on in this situation and what values were in conflict to cause my frustration. Pastor Ron had been one of my students during his college years, and I remembered him always socializing with others—even sometimes when he was supposed to be listening in class! He was a highly relational and engaging person. Everyone liked him. He was just being himself as his neighbors passed by.

Furthermore, Pastor Ron wanted his neighbors to become followers of Christ. Being fairly new in the community, he wanted to make every connection he could and get to know the people. Building relationships was an important value to Ron, and it served him well in his pastoral role. Watching Ron talking with yet another passerby, I felt a sense of release, even joy as I realized he was doing exactly what I had been teaching for so many years, "People are more important than projects; relationships are a higher value than the task. Christ died for people not buildings."

Bob and I, on the other hand, had come down to accomplish as much as possible to help Pastor Ron improve his house. Our expectations focused on the task. Because the task was continually being interrupted with Pastor Ron's excursions to the street, our expectations were violated thus causing the frustration.

I mentioned to Bob what I thought was happening. Bob, a wonderfully relational person himself, also began to understand. He relaxed too, and the two of us had some delightful conversations between ourselves whenever Pastor Ron wandered away from his job to do more important things with his neighbors. What started out as a disappointing effort to help someone turned out to be a memorable learning experience.

THE GOOD GETS IN THE WAY OF THE BEST

Traveling through a village, Jesus and his disciples received an invitation from a woman named Martha.

Martha opened her home to him. She had a sister called Mary, who sat at the Lord's feet listening to what he said. But Martha was distracted by all the preparations that had to be made. She came to him and asked, "Lord, don't you care that my sister has left me to do the work by myself? Tell her to help me!"

"Martha, Martha," the Lord answered, "you are worried and upset about many things, but only one thing is needed. Mary has chosen what is better, and it will not be taken away from her." (Luke 10:38-42)

I sympathize with Martha. I like to have the place looking nice, the food prepared and everything organized. It shows respect for the guests. And if it is the Lord himself coming, don't we want everything to be just right? I have often wondered what was going on in Mary's head that she could ignore all the work required to entertain this many guests. How could she be so insensitive as to do nothing to help out? That, to me, seems disrespectful. But as we know, Martha was rebuked for her choice, and Mary was congratulated for her choice. How are we to understand this?

Martha made the same kind of decision that Bob and I made. We valued the task more than the relationship. Ron did not make that mistake. People came first. In the Mary and Martha story, Jesus tells us the same thing. Everyday we make choices. Martha's choice was not a bad one; it simply was not the best choice in that situation. By choosing the good rather than the best, she missed the mark.

Our choices reveal what we value. The astute person realizes this and attempts to assess situations according to the competing values and then chooses the most important value. Many of us, including me, often do what is easiest or most convenient. Given my natural inclination, I am more like Martha. Thus, when I am in other cultures, I try to be sensitive to the values of the host culture—what they consider most important. My experiences suggest that most of the world values the relationship more than getting a job done. Knowing that, I can adjust.

Two attorneys had worked together for thirteen years. Until they

became aware of the different ways they viewed time and event, considerable frustration characterized their relationship. When they became aware of their differences, they were able to capitalize on them rather than become victims of them. So when the time came for the annual company picnic, which they were responsible for, each assumed responsibilities fitting to their particular view of time. One got the task of scheduling, ordering and arranging, while the other connected with people, made sure everyone was happy and comfortable, and generally was the goodwill person. The picnic was a success, whereas the previous ones had been marked by the tension of misunderstanding and negative thoughts and words. The morale of the entire firm was bolstered when two people became aware of their different orientations to time and made the appropriate adjustments.[1]

THE GOAL-DRIVEN PERSON

Some people spend much of their lives achieving goals and getting the job done. They feel good when the job is over. Their identity as people tends to be built around their ability to perform. Their best friends are those who share the same pursuit of goals. These people may even sacrifice their physical and, at times, even mental health for the sake of goal achievement. Many successful individuals also sacrifice relationships with people closest to them. Thus, marriages break up and alienation between parent and child are not uncommon—often because the task took on greater importance than relationships.

The missionaries who went out after World War II were committed to bringing the gospel of Jesus Christ to every tribe, tongue and people. Mission was defined in terms of tasks to be accomplished: language study, translation, evangelism, church planting, discipleship, medical work, education and other ministries. While most of these require some relationship with people, the emphasis was on getting the job done. There was a temptation to value relationships only if they contributed to reaching the goals, or so it seemed to people of later generations.

Hard work defines this type of person. They will get the job done even at considerable cost to themselves or to their families. They are trustworthy, dedicated and sacrificial. My own father-in-law was among the early martyrs for the cause of Christ in Southern Rhodesia (now Zimbabwe). Because the gospel was for all people, he decided it must be proclaimed to villages in the most disease-ridden parts of the country. In less than three years he died of malaria and typhoid fever complications. But the seed had been sown in the hearts of these remote villagers where no one else would go.

When the task-driven person does sit back, relax and relate, one hears the tales of their accomplishments or, more accurately, of God's work. Even in rest, their mind is on the work. Of course, there is always a down side. In my own life, my grandfather, a good man, could not attend the graduation of his oldest grandchild (me) and the first to graduate from college in our extended family. The factory asked him to work that Saturday, and the job came first. In terms of missionary history, many a host-country person has commented, "The missionaries really got a lot done, but we wish they would have spent more time with us."

THE RELATIONAL PERSON

My experience suggests that the majority of the world puts a higher premium on nurturing relationships—talking, relating, interacting, discussing and just being together. Goals and schedules are attended to after a good conversation. Socializing lays the foundation for achieving goals together. The goal is not forgotten, it just does not dictate priorities.

Throughout Latin America, Africa, much of Asia and parts of Western and Eastern Europe, life seems to slow down for involvement with a friend or new acquaintance. The pace stops so two people can connect over coffee or a meal or just standing somewhere to chat. Time seems to stand still for the satisfaction of nurturing the relationship a bit more.

This value finds prominence in business. Latin American business-

people will spend several hours or days in some instances in socializing before moving to the business at hand. During the socializing, Latin Americans will sense whether there is a connectedness that will produce a good business bond. If not, there will be no contract. Similarly, Japanese businesspeople will, during negotiations, close their eyes for a moment (one might think they have dozed off). But they are "reading their stomach"—reading the nature of the relationship to determine whether they should go ahead with the business deal. For the majority of the world, it is relationships that determine whether or not there will be a business deal.

There is a downside to being relational just as for being task-oriented. Relational cultures seem to make much fewer scientific and technological advances. Being so relational seems to limit progress in many areas, yet I notice a peace in their lives and an admirable ability to cope with stress.

EAST MEETS WEST

An intriguing exchange between two world leaders illustrates these two values. When Ronald Reagan went to China, he was asked what he hoped to accomplish with the trip. He responded, "I'll go as a salesman, doing everything I can up to the point of putting a 'Buy America' sticker on my bag."[2] When Deng Xiaoping, premier of China, was asked the same question, he responded, "The presentation of views in a calm way helps increase understanding. I hope to see an enhancement of the friendship."[3] Reagan had his eyes on the task, while Deng planned to build the relationship.

Unless each was able to adjust a little, one can see where there could be some serious miscommunication. In reality, most task-oriented people can be relational, and the more highly relational person can get the job done. Realize, however, that in a relational culture, the job rarely moves along smoothly until a trusting relationship is established. Without trust little effort is made to achieve deadlines, stay within budget or

even cooperate. The same holds true for sharing Christ. Without some sincere effort at establishing a relationship first, your words are likely to come across as a "clanging cymbal" (1 Corinthians 13:1).

WHAT DID JESUS DO?

Reading the four Gospel accounts, we see that the amount of time Jesus spent with people is quite impressive: with individuals, with his disciples, with the masses, in people's homes, on the hillside, on the road, at wells and in the towns. Everywhere he went, he invested heavily in people's lives. At times he needed to be alone. At other times he seemed preoccupied with the task. At age twelve, when Mary and Joseph were in Jerusalem to celebrate the Passover, Jesus stayed behind in the temple. His parents traveled a whole day toward home before they realized Jesus was not with any of the relatives. Returning to Jerusalem, they found him in the temple sitting with the teachers, listening and asking questions. When his parents found him they expressed their anxiety, to which Jesus expressed his task focus, "I must be about my Father's business" (Luke 2:49 KJV). As Jesus neared the time of his death, his task focus grew stronger: "As the time approached for him to be taken up to heaven, Jesus resolutely set out for Jerusalem" (Luke 9:51). Yet Jesus knew that completing the task was for the higher purpose of the Father being able to have a personal relationship with people. Jesus related to people and took time for that, yet he kept his task in focus.

I find it fascinating that task-oriented people tend to focus only on the Great Commission found in Matthew 28:19-20:

> Therefore go and make disciples of all nations, baptizing them in the name of the Father and of the Son and of the Holy Spirit, and teaching them to obey everything I have commanded you. And surely I am with you always, to the very end of the age.

Perhaps this focus should be supplemented with an equal emphasis on the Great Commandment found numerous times, beginning with Matthew

22:36-40. An expert in the law asks Jesus a straightforward question.

"Teacher, which is the greatest commandment in the Law?"

Jesus replied: " 'Love the Lord your God with all your heart and with all your soul and with all your mind.' This is the first and greatest commandment. And the second is like it: 'Love your neighbor as yourself.' All the Law and the Prophets hang on these two commandments."

This commandment appears in some form in Leviticus 19:18 (cf. Deuteronomy 6:5); Mark 12:28-31; Luke 10:27; John 13:34; 15:12; Romans 13:9; Galatians 5:14; James 2:8; and 1 John 3:23. I list the texts for several reasons: (1) Their frequent occurrence startled me. (2) The powerful witness of loving God and our neighbor is that everyone will know that we are Christ's disciples (John 13:35). (3) Mission is at least as much driven by love as by task. (4) I wonder if the current generation of young people is more motivated by the Great Commandment than by the Great Commission.

FOR   REFLECTION

Respond to each point on the following task/relationship continuum.

Task	1	2	3	4	5	6	7	8	9	10	Relationship

Put an X indicating where you fall on the task versus relationship continuum.

Put a P indicating where you think your parents are.

Put a C for whether your church is more task or relationship in its time orientation.

Use any further symbols that are meaningful to you: S for spouse; F for friends, B for boss.

Use NC (new culture) to indicate where you think the people of the new culture will be on the continuum. How much distance is there between X (you) and NC?

IMPORTANT PERSPECTIVE

Again, I want to emphasize how important it is to start where people are. Let us assume you are entering a culture that values the relationship over the task. This does not mean that the people of this culture do not value the task or are incapable of getting the job done. That would be untrue even though some people have built such stereotypes. If you start with a strong task orientation and little concern for relationships, there is a good chance that neither will happen. If, on the other hand, you begin where they are, take time to build trusting relationships, the task will get done. When the relationship values are satisfied, people willingly move to task values and things get done.

Remember the story of Bob, Ron and me at the beginning of the chapter? We got the siding done as well as a number of interior projects. Relational values were satisfied and the task got done. More important, everyone remained friends. All three of us continue to have positive memories of that time together. The more we were able to understand the values that were operating, the more we were able to control negative emotions, suspend judgment and avoid a disaster. It was a wonderful learning experience

A friend of mine says that the international businessperson must carry two briefcases. One briefcase has a time/task orientation and the other briefcase an event/relationship orientation. The question is, which briefcase are you going to open first? The answer will depend upon the kind of culture you are entering. Open the wrong one first, and there is a good chance of failure in spite of a superior product. Open the culturally correct one first and, in due course, the way will be opened for the second briefcase to be opened. As my friend said, "Building the relationship before getting the job done is the first step to getting the job done."[4]

At this point, some may think that I am being a bit harsh on the time- and task-oriented people and too generous on those who give preference to event and relationship. In reality, I am attempting to highlight the per-

spectives and benefits of those who see things differently. If we can understand how cultures outside the West think and function, we are more likely to enter with positive expectations, fit in more easily and open the culturally appropriate briefcase first. Western and Two-Thirds World cultures have so much to offer that we must think in terms of blending, learning from each other and synergizing our strengths. I believe God created every culture to contribute to the orchestra and chorus, which is intended to reveal his majesty. The grand variety of voices and instruments is far superior to any that a single culture may produce.

DISCUSSION QUESTIONS

1. How much do you think you will need to adjust on the task/relationship scale as you enter another culture? As you think of your present relationships, do you have difficulties with people who are different from you on this matter? How difficult will it be for you to adjust?

2. Do you think of the task/relationship in terms of right/wrong? What difficulties could this cause you in your new culture?

3. What practical steps can you take to adjust to differences in task and relationship?

4. How have your views been shaped by your family and upbringing?

15

Individualism and Collectivism

If you want to travel fast . . . go alone.
If you want to travel far . . . go together.

AFRICAN PROVERB

"INDIVIDUALISM LIES AT THE VERY CORE OF AMERICAN CULTURE," wrote Robert Bellah and his colleagues in their bestselling book *Habits of the Heart*.[1] Supporting his point further, Bellah cites the great political and educational philosopher John Locke: "The individual is prior to society"[2]—meaning the individual is to be valued above society. For many outside the Western world this would be confusing if not unthinkable.

Indeed, the individual reigns supreme. We see it in our proverbs: "Pull yourself up by your bootstraps," meaning you can do it on your own, by individual effort. Consider the army motto, "Be all you can be." Or the popular Sinatra songs "I've Gotta Be Me" and "My Way." Or the popular phrase "Do your own thing." These statements imply that North Americans value doing it on their own. Even though they value family and friends, they have a strong value for making their own decisions independent of what others may think or choose. Of course, people do not fulfill these values in absolute ways, but these are powerful guiding principles. Individualism may be giving way to an emerging value of community building due to the postmodern influence on North Americans under thirty years of age. Individualism is still present among them, just not so strong.

I AM WE

In much of the world, one does not think in individualist terms but more as a member of a group, as part of the collective whole. Scholars call this collectivism. Collectivistic people do not make important decisions on their own; they consult family members often starting with a parent, uncle or aunt. One cannot act independently—that would show great disrespect and be dangerous to the harmony of the group. Because each person belongs to the community, the community values and traditions must be lived out in each member. One acts in accordance with the expectations of the group. One's own desires are subordinated to those of the group. One draws one's identity from the community and fulfills its expectations.

A Japanese proverb illustrates this value of fitting in with the group: "The nail that sticks up will get pounded down." Similarly, an Ecuadorian proverb says, "The longest blade of grass is the first to be cut." No one is to act independently of the group or there will be pressure to return to one's place, to conform. Conformity to community norms is expected and enforced. Whereas independence is an important value to Americans and Westerners in general, interdependence is the way of most societies of the world.

For example, in U.S. companies one often sees recognition for "Employee of the Month," honoring the individual. It boosts morale and creates a stimulus for others to strive for the same honor. This is unlikely to happen in a collectivistic society, because to honor one over the others would deflate morale. After all, everyone had to contribute for any one person to be successful. Thus, you cannot honor one person when there were so many who were part of the support team and without whose help the individual could not have succeeded. Thus, in collectivistic societies, honor is given to all.

For ten years I trained Amoco employees for their overseas assignments. My colleague Dudley Woodberry, who holds a Ph.D. in Islamic

culture from Harvard University, helped these employees understand Muslim culture. He tells of one way collectivism works within Islam.[3] Many of the young Muslims have been trained in modern business and the technology of oil exploration. These well-trained professionals will still go to their fathers and grandfathers before making a business decision in spite of the fact that these elderly gentlemen know little or nothing about the technology of the decision. It is a matter of respect to bring the significant members of the community (extended family) into the decision making—not so they can affirm or question the decision but to show respect and assure that everyone is in solidarity. The elderly members, while not knowing the business or technological points, may raise issues of how this decision will affect the family, the community or the country. The younger professionals know the business, but the older ones who communicate from their traditions guard the important values and thus strengthen the bonds of the family and the community.

In Western societies we often speak of what we accomplished as though no one else contributed. A few years ago, I was fishing on Lake Michigan with a friend who had been doing this for years. Those on the boat took turns grabbing the poles at the sign of a fish being on. Soon it was my turn. The pole wiggled, I set the hook, and within thirty seconds everyone knew this was a big one—I mean it really was a big salmon. After about an hour I got it in the boat. I couldn't wait to brag about this one. We even got pictures to prove its size.

After getting back on land we were talking with some other charter boat captains, and I waited for my opportunity to blurt out, "You would not believe the size of the fish I caught today." My friend, the captain of the boat I was on, interrupted at the beginning of my wonderful story, which I was eager to embellish. He inserted a comment I will never forget: "Actually you didn't catch the fish. We all did. Some one had to drive the boat in such a way that the lines did not get tangled. Others pulled in the remaining lines so you had a better chance of landing the fish. Someone had to be skilled at netting the fish. Others helped with advice

and encouragement. We *all* caught the fish."

After I got over the feeling of deflation, I realized he was right. Everyone participated. It was a collective effort, and thinking of it as an individual effort was shortsighted and ungracious.

SHARING CHRIST ACROSS CULTURES

When we tell someone in the West about our faith in Christ, we assume the value of individualism is operating—we believe this person can make an independent decision apart from consulting family. However, when sharing Christ among Asian people, I was constantly told that they could not make a decision to follow Christ without asking a parent, uncle, aunt or all three. These people ranged anywhere from eighteen to thirty years in age! I thought it was an excuse not to make a decision. But in collectivistic cultures, people do not make major decisions without talking it over with the proper authority figures in their extended family.

As young people move to the city and to university, they also become less attached to the family and move a little toward independence. If they come to the West to study, they may become quite independent and make major decisions without checking for the proper approval. When this happens, there is a sense of sadness and loss among the family members.

Do we now only share with groups? Do we stop sharing with individuals? Of course not. You never know when the Holy Spirit has been working in the heart of a person and all that is needed is someone to help the person respond in faith to Christ. Younger people around the world are not so committed to collectivistic values and find themselves making up their own mind. Since you do not know, you take the opportunity God gives you. But if someone says, "I cannot make this decision without asking an elder," you know that the person is adhering to cultural traditions.

But is that the end of it? Not necessarily. If you have the time, you might say, "Great, can I go with you? I would enjoy meeting your relatives. We can all talk together." If this works out, I would be hesitant to

ask the family members for permission so that the person you have witnessed to can become a Christian. Almost certainly the answer will be negative, and perhaps they will forbid the person to see you again. It might be wiser to use the time to build trust with the extended family members. A culture that is collectivistic will probably also be relational. If you approach this in a task-orientation manner, it is unlikely that you will be successful.

In collectivistic societies, there are often group conversions—a whole village, having heard of Christ's love for them, will confess their faith in Christ as a collective unit. Usually this happens after months, sometimes years, of witness. In the individualistic West this sounds very foreign, even unbiblical. Yet, many of the conversions recorded in the book of Acts were group conversions (Acts 10:2; 11:14; 16:15; 16:31; 18:8). In a collectivistic society, the members talk about important issues. They may talk over a long period of time but slowly discover the heavenly Father moving them to give their lives to Jesus Christ as Lord. Missionaries have reported group conversions—a sign of a highly collectivistic culture. God works in individualistic cultures and in collectivistic cultures. Knowing the difference allows us to work more effectively.

MIXED MARRIAGES AND COLLECTIVISM

For a number of years I taught at a Christian liberal arts college. Several of my undergraduate students were American-born Koreans. Inevitably, a few fell in love with a person of different ethnicity and decided to get married. A parent, usually the father of the Korean student, would become very upset and bring pressure to bear on the son or daughter to stop the relationship. He would threaten to boycott the wedding, never to see her (usually it was a female), cut off her allowance and other privileges. Eventually the father would bring her childhood friends, hoping peer pressure would change her mind. Uncles, aunts, grandparents and anyone who might have influence would prevail on her to "come to her senses."

On one occasion the father came to the window of the house where she lived and began shouting his disappointment loudly enough for all to hear, pointing out her stubbornness and mistakes, and repeating threats made in the past. This last-ditch effort to shame her into changing her mind failed. The girl had grown so strong in her independence and individualism that the pressures of family and friends were not persuasive enough. The father, of course, was quite frustrated because these tactics would normally have worked back in South Korea. In the United States they proved fruitless.

Often the Korean American woman and the man of different ethnicity would come to me to try to figure out what was happening and what they could do. I would explain to them the differing cultural values of individualism and collectivism. This gave them insight into themselves and their parents and extended family who were still deeply rooted in collectivism. We also talked about the shame that the parents may have felt because their daughter was not marrying according to their expectations. (See chapter eighteen for more on shame.) In every situation I know, the parents slowly began to accept the daughter's decision, and by the wedding, all had joyfully reconciled.

The more young people are marrying across ethnicities and nationalities, the more everyone concerned must understand these values. Furthermore, as the two young people marry, they will discover cultural roots that have carried over from their homes. Failure to understand the differences in their respective cultural heritages will cause stress and conflict in the marriage that could be avoided or minimized with these insights.

Feeling strong bonds and obligations to one's family and peers often conflicts with the more individualistic lifestyle of Westerners. Whether in marriage, business, school, church, youth group or home, these values will surface, creating tension and, potentially, conflict. Worst-case scenarios can be avoided if everyone understands that we are dealing with cultural differences, not absolute rights and wrongs.

Respond to each point on the following individualism/collectivism continuum.

Individualism   1   2   3   4   5   6   7   8   9   10   Collectivism

1. Put an X indicating where you fall on the individualism versus collectivism continuum.

2. Put a P indicating where you think your parents are.

3. Put a C for whether your church is more individualistic or collectivistic in its time orientation.

4. Use any further symbols that are meaningful to you: S for spouse, F for friends, B for boss.

5. Use NC (new culture) to indicate where you think the people of the new culture will be on the continuum. How much distance is there between X (you) and NC?

D I S C U S S I O N   Q U E S T I O N S

---

1. How much do you think you will need to adjust on the individualism/collectivism scale as you enter another culture?

2. As you think of your present relationships, do you have difficulties with people who are different from you on this matter? How difficult will it be for you to adjust?

3. Do you think of individualism/collectivism in terms of right/wrong? What difficulties could this cause you in your new culture?

4. What practical steps can you take to adjust to differences in task and relationship?

5. How have your views been shaped by your family and upbringing?

16

Categorical and Holistic Thinking

*Human beings draw close to each other by their
common nature, but habits and customs keep them apart.*

CONFUCIUS

WESTERNERS TEND TO VIEW LIFE AND ARRIVE AT DECISIONS differently than
many in the Two-Thirds World. Westerners tend to approach a decision
in a categorical way, while Two-Thirds World people are more holistic.
Knowing the difference will save us some confusion, while understanding ourselves and others will reduce judgmentalism.

LIFE AS A TIMELINE: CATEGORICAL THINKING

Many who live in Western cultures see life as rather black and white.
They often think in a two-dimensional perspective such as we and they,
good and bad, moral and immoral, right and wrong, me and you, church
and state, or secular and sacred. Even the proverb "Do you see the glass
half full or half empty?" represents a two-dimensional or dichotomistic
way of seeing life.

Specialization fits this view of reality. Everyone has a niche. When two
people meet each other, the first question after getting the name is, "So,
what do you do?" It sounds innocent enough, but often that information
allows us to place the person in a category. It is a way of organizing our
lives and placing the person in a category or box. We have places where
we put things and categories where we put people. If I can place you in
a category, I know where you fit into the scheme of things. From that I
derive a sense of order and security. I know how to relate to you.

When categorical or two-dimensional people are asked to draw something that represents their life, they usually draw a timeline that has ups and downs in it—peaks and valleys—resembling a graph. Usually this line of ups and downs has a general upward direction indicating things generally get better over time. The peaks, of course, represent significant positive times and the valleys the difficult times. Most have a horizontal line intersecting the time line to indicate the point at which they became Christians. For non-Christians the horizontal line might represent marriage or some significant point in their lives. They see things in time segments, as positive and negative, good and bad, as relatively unrelated incidents. Specific segments of life are analyzed and remembered independently of other segments. In fact, we tend to suppress the valleys or low times.

LIFE IS A TAPESTRY: HOLISTIC THINKING

By contrast, many Two-Thirds World cultures tend to be more holistic in their view of life. They see life not so much as a timeline but as a tapestry where one sees threads and colors touching, overlapping and reinforcing each other, forming a whole that has its own beauty and integrity. The metaphor of a glass half full or half empty does not work for holistic people. They prefer the metaphor of an onion that gets peeled, layer upon layer. Life is unfolding; each layer is connected to the former and must be understood in relation to the whole and, indeed, part of the whole.

Peeling off a part of life and examining it apart from the whole does not make sense for the holistic person. For example, some years ago, the Olympic committee invited South Africa to participate in the Olympics. At that time, South Africa was under the apartheid system—the separation of races with a highly complex set of laws that kept all people of color out of power and economically deprived. Most other African nations rose up in protest saying they would withdraw from the Olympics rather than participate with South Africa present.

The mostly Western Olympic committee were confused and countered that sports were sports and politics were politics—they should be kept separate and treated separately—a categorical perspective. However, the majority of African nations saw it differently. "Sports is politics and politics is sports"[1] was their emphatic response. The two cannot be separated. Life cannot be compartmentalized and treated as though the pieces are unrelated.

The war in Afghanistan provides a more recent example. President George W. Bush said that the United States was attacking only Osama bin Laden and the Al Qaeda terrorist network, not Muslims or Arabs in general. Westerners understand this because we easily differentiate "me" from "you." But much of the world thinks more holistically—as "us," as solidarity, as one. So it should not be surprising to see protests against the United States or other symbols that show support of Osama bin Laden. News reports tell of Muslims having studied in the United States speaking of Osama bin Laden as their hero and of most of the babies born in Muslim Northern Nigeria during this war being given the name Osama.

A Middle-Eastern proverb contributes to our understanding of how Muslims think.

> Me against my brother;
> My brother and I against our cousin;
> My brother, my cousin and I against the boy from the next village.[2]

In other words, anyone outside the Muslim world who attacks a Muslim, for whatever reason, could become the enemy of the Muslim world. Of course, economics and politics always factor into these situations. But the proverb expresses the spirit of holism: we stand as one if we have a common enemy.

Holism is manifest in other ways. A Western newspaper reporter asked Mahatma Gandhi, "Mr. Gandhi, would you please tell us in one short sentence what your message is?"[3] This is a categorical question

because it intends to reduce something very complex into its simplest form or category so one can either accept or reject it. Mr. Gandhi gave a very holistic response, "My life is my message." In effect, he said, "I am a whole being, and if you have watched my life you know my message." That strikes me as a challenge for the Christian.

My own witness as a Westerner is quite categorical. I rely on words. Witness is a verbal activity for many of us. Yet perhaps the majority of the world looks at our lives as the primary witness. I wonder, do the people watching us get the distinct sense that we are followers of Christ?

I remember talking with a Christian from a Two-Thirds World country. I asked him what he thought of the Western couple who had arrived about six months ago to minister in this person's country. "Oh, it is too early to tell how they will fit in. It is best to observe them in many situations: ministering in the church, connecting with their neighbors, relating to each other as a couple, raising their children and handling problems and setbacks. Six months is too early to tell much." I confess to being shocked. I have the unhealthy habit of sizing people up and drawing conclusions in far less time. This person refused to draw conclusions even after six months. I liked the wisdom this holistic person demonstrated.

Westerners tend to categorize time between work time and personal time. They are rather clean categories for most of us. Drive or commute time becomes the buffer between the two worlds. On the way to work the commute time is when we set our personal life behind us. On the commute home, we set the work world behind us and reenter personal/family time. In much of the world the distinction between work and personal time is blurred. They seem to embrace both worlds as an intertwined whole. Work and personal time, like the threads of a tapestry, cannot be seen in isolation. Their relationship often fuses.

The same happens in business meetings. Before the meeting there may be a brief social time of small talk and getting acquainted. Westerners see this as social time—nonwork time. Many in the Two-Thirds

World do not differentiate between social and work time. Small talk is getting to know one another, sensing whether the "vibes" are good for business. Business should be conducted with people you know and trust. What better way to accomplish this than at social events when people are relaxed?

YOURS, MINE AND OURS

When my sons began using language, it seemed the most common word uttered was *mine*. A sense of ownership starts early on—what belongs to me versus what belongs to you. These categories permeate much of life: titles, deeds, licenses, property lines, certificates, bills of sale and a host of symbols that signal mine or not mine.

In much of the world and more so in rural regions, this sense of mine and yours does not exist so strongly. Things are freely shared or given away. In fact, if you have more of something than you need, you look around for someone who has need and share. People also feel free to ask of the one who has more. Categorical lines of "yours" and "mine" are not firmly drawn. This causes Westerners frustration.

For example, Westerners living in the Two-Thirds World often have more material possessions than local people. Local people may ask for favors, money or objects not being used, for example, items not being used in the garage or kept in storage. Westerners, when giving to people who ask, think of these as loans especially if the local person says, "May I borrow . . ." But borrowing usually has a permanent quality about it. Thus, when a loan does not get repaid or an object returned, disappointment and resentment may fester and disrupt the relationship. Westerners find such behavior very irresponsible.

The local person, however, has a different perspective on possessions. Possessions, especially more than you can reasonably use, are meant for sharing. If you see someone in need and you can help, it is immoral not to share. The category of yours and mine is not nearly so strong as the category of "ours." Here is one way it plays out. Several times I would

notice a younger child living not with their parents but with an uncle and aunt. When I inquired, I would sometimes get an evasive answer, which I will tell you about in a moment. But a few times I was told that the parents were poor and could not afford school fees and other things. So the parents would send the child off to a relative, and when the school fees were paid, teeth fixed and some new clothes purchased, the child would eventually be sent back to the parents. The uncle and aunt who were economically better off understood exactly what was happening and happily shared their resources.

But sometimes when I asked they were evasive, because to tell me the parents could not properly care for the children would cause the parents shame. This was especially true if I happened to know the parents. This "welfare system" worked wonderfully within the extended family because they thought of their possessions as "ours" rather than "yours" and "mine."

While it may seem unusual for Westerners to think in terms of "ours," it was not that unusual for people from the Middle East. Remember the story of the good Samaritan recorded in Luke 10:25-37? I want to focus on the three parties that had contact with the man who fell among thieves. Each displayed a different philosophy of possessions:

- The robbers: What is yours is mine if I can take it from you.
- A priest and Levite: What is mine is mine, and I have a right to keep it.
- The Samaritan: What is mine is yours if you have need of it.

I wonder which philosophy of possessions most closely matches yours? With shame, I confess that more often mine is like that of the priest and Levite. I earned my money by working hard, and I have a right to spend it or share it as I please. At least, that runs through my mind until I read this story and then I realize that everything I have belongs to God and he has loaned it to me so that I may do with it as *he* pleases. Categorical thinking such as "mine" and "yours" may not lead us to "lov[ing] your neighbor as yourself" (Luke 10:27).

JIGSAW PUZZLES

I grew up putting puzzles together during the long winter nights. One thing was predictable: whoever started the puzzle would separate all the pieces with straight edges and then choose the corners. Starting with the corners, we would then work on the outside pieces, the frame. It was the most logical thing in the world. Surely everyone did it that way.

A few years ago, I discovered that many non-Westerners began with colors. Ignoring the straight edges, they would gather the pieces that shared a common color and work from there. It made perfect sense to them. They were as convinced of their way as I was of mine. Our minds operated differently. Was one superior? What do you think? Do both have advantages? Disadvantages? It seemed to me that my way of putting the puzzle together was some reflection of my culture. Others who put puzzles together differently were reflecting something in their cultural heritage. Not right or wrong—just different.

F O R   R E F L E C T I O N

Respond to each point in the following categorical/holistic continuum.

Categorical 1 2 3 4 5 6 7 8 9 10 **Holistic**

1. Put an X indicating where you fall on the categorical versus holistic continuum.

2. Put a P indicating where you think your parents are.

3. Put a C for whether your church is more categorical or holistic in its time orientation.

4. Use any further symbols that are meaningful to you: S for spouse, F for friends, B for boss.

5. Use NC (new culture) to indicate where you think the people of the

new culture will be on the continuum. How much distance is there between X (you) and NC?

D I S C U S S I O N   Q U E S T I O N S

---

1. Does your culture have a clean separation of work life and personal life? How does that work? How might it look if such categories were blurred so that there wasn't a strong distinction between work life and personal life?

2. How much do you think you will need to adjust on the categorical/ holistic scale as you enter another culture?

3. As you think of your present relationships, do you have difficulties with people who are different from you on this matter? Explain.

4. Do you think of categorical/holistic in terms of right/wrong? What difficulties could this cause you in your new culture?

5. What practical steps can you take to adjust to the difference between you and the people of the new culture?

6. How have your views been shaped by your family and upbringing? Were your mother and father different on this scale? Discuss.

17
Logic: Straight or Curved

*You do not know a man until you have eaten
forty pounds of salt with him.*

RUSSIAN PROVERB

THIS CHAPTER ATTEMPTS TO EXPLAIN how people from various cultures reason differently. Thought patterns and ways of arriving at a decision vary greatly around the world. How does the mind work in defining an issue, solving a problem, making a point or coming to a conclusion? I was schooled in linear thought where one works in a straight line to the conclusion or decision. Linear logic was the format for my public speaking and sermon preparation classes. It was efficient, direct and precise. Everyone could follow the main points and would, therefore, arrive at the same conclusion—assuming my preparation was good and there were no weak links in this straight-line, chain-link logic.

When living in other countries, I tried to interpret the thought patterns of others through my linear frame of reference. It usually ended in confusion because most did not use a linear form of reasoning. I concluded two things: these people had not prepared well and they were very illogical. Because someone did something that confused me or that did not fit my frame of reference, I judged them negatively. (Remember negative attribution?) Once again I failed to see a cultural expression as different. I saw it as wrong. If it is wrong I can feel free to judge it and try to correct it.

DANIEL'S PROBLEM
Daniel had been one of my students as an undergraduate and a graduate.

He was Korean, though all his education had been in the United States. When he was my teaching assistant for several years we formed a wonderful bond. He later did a second graduate degree at Yale Divinity School. Since I often taught for a week each year near Yale, Daniel and I would meet a few times for some delicious Korean food.

On one occasion he asked if I wanted to take a drive up to the bluff overlooking the bay. Since I had come from the flatlands of Illinois, new scenery seemed a great idea. As we drove slowly to the destination, Daniel began to talk, vaguely and, from my perspective, without a clear point. It started out with his church, moved on to his ministry with the college group, what he was doing, who was attending and what was happening or not happening.

About forty minutes later and at the top of the bluff overlooking Long Island Sound, I got the first clue of what this was all about. Daniel said, "Do you think it is appropriate for someone in a pastoral position to date someone in the church?" In my get-to-the-point way I said, "Daniel, you are the college pastor. Are you interested in dating someone in your college group?" My bluntness caused him to falter for a moment, but then he agreed that was the issue. With that we both broke into laughter followed by a lengthy conversation about this topic that was presently consuming him.

Two metaphors come to mind to help the Western mind understand Daniel.

Onion. First, the metaphor of the onion—Daniel peeled off the outer layers one at a time, checking to see if I was listening, understanding and properly responsive. At any point where he felt uncomfortable with my response, he might safely stop, not having exposed the sensitive, core concern. Little-by-little, the layers came off and eventually we got to the middle of the onion—the heart of the issue. Daniel, so handsome and possessing an exceptionally beautiful personality, gave most of his energies to ministry and schoolwork. Dating, while it happened, did not preoccupy his life. But now, he was feeling the need to think about marriage

and the future. Thus, talking about dating, especially with a seriousness that might lead to marriage, was very sensitive, requiring every caution. Thus, he entered a more Korean mode as he talked with me.

Spiral. The second metaphor is one of a spiral[1] moving inward toward the center. Note in figure 17.1 that the spiral starts from the outside and slowly winds its way around until it comes to an end in the center. Daniel started with the more distant talk about his church, continued toward the center of the spiral when he evolved into talk about his college group, then the people attending and finally a girl.

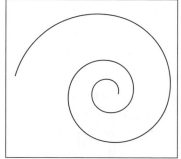

Figure 17.1

Daniel could be more direct, but when the concern was close to his heart and so sensitive, he reverted to the Korean way of thinking about it and explaining it. It was different from the logic I use, but it was effective for him and, in reality, it seems to possess some distinct advantages. First, he could test my interest and commitment as we went along. Was our trust strong enough for him to show me his heart on this tender matter? Second, by peeling the onion or slowly circling toward the center of the spiral, he was providing me with valuable history and information, which I would need if I were to offer any help. Third, Daniel, probably without realizing it, was telling me who he was. When it came to matters of the heart, he was deeply Korean in how he would handle it. For the years he was my student, he would accommodate to me, to my Western ways. Now that we were both professionals and I was on his turf, he would invite me into his world the way he lived it. It was my turn to accommodate. I needed to experience that. Too quickly I can believe that I am the norm and expect others to adjust to my ways.

Our friendship grew stronger that day. Later, Daniel spent a year in

South Korea, where he found a lovely young lady. He brought her back to the States and introduced me to her. I was honored to coofficiate with a Korean pastor at their wedding.

EASTERN AND WESTERN LOGIC

Miscommunication often happens because people from different traditions think in different cultural patterns. The sequential, linear logic of the West, sometimes likened to the links of a chain because of its connectedness, allows for more direct communication. Thus, Westerners get to the point and want you to give it to them straight without beating around the bush. The spiral logic, often used by Asians, allows for more indirect communication, important for protecting people's face and not causing shame.

Okabe offers this comparison:

> American logic and rhetoric value "step-by-step, "chain-like" organization, as frequently observed in the "problem-solution" pattern or in the "cause-to-effect" or "effect-to-cause" pattern of organization. . . . By contrast, Japanese logic and rhetoric emphasize the importance of a "dotted," "point-like" method of structuring a discourse. No sense of rigidity . . . is required in the Japanese-speaking society, where there is instead a sense of leisurely throwing a ball back and forth and carefully observing each other's response.[2]

It is possible to understand the words the other person is speaking and still not understand the message. The indirect and often imprecise language used in Asia tends to confuse Westerners who prefer clear, defined steps to the point, the conclusion or the solution. The directness of Westerners, often perceived as aggressiveness, may be offensive and even humiliating to the Asian. The confusion from such misunderstanding often leads each party to think suspiciously about the other. Thus, business contracts, learning and relationships are hindered, even disrupted.

Gudykunst and Young Yun Kim give the following account of how styles of logic can affect business. They discuss the topic within the category of worldview.

> Consider, for example, a business delegation from North America meeting with strangers from the East to decide whether or not their two companies should work together on a joint venture. Based only on their differing world views, it might be expected that misunderstandings will occur. The North Americans would analyze all of the "facts" and would develop a direct argument as to whether or not the two companies should do business together. The strangers, in contrast, would base their decision on a synthesis of all the data and on their intuition as to whether or not the idea is a good one and, in addition, would discuss the issues in an indirect rather than a direct method. Obviously, if one of the groups does not understand the other's world view and adapt their communication accordingly, misunderstanding is going to occur.[3]

Lustig and Koester quote Ishii's comment on the matter:

> The rules for language use in Japan demand that the speaker not tell the listener the specific point being conveyed; to do so is considered rude and inappropriate. Rather, the Japanese delicately circle a topic in order to imply its domain. The U.S. English concepts of thesis statements and paragraph topic sentences have no real equivalent in Japanese.
>
> Imagine the consequences of an intercultural interaction between a Japanese and a U.S. American. What might happen if one of them is able to speak in the other's language and is sufficiently skilled to convey meaning linguistically but is not adept at the logic of the language? The Japanese person is likely to think that the U.S. American is rude and aggressive. Conversely, the U.S. American is likely to think that the Japanese is confusing and imprecise. Both people in this intercultural interaction are likely to feel dissatisfied, confused and uncomfortable.[4]

Incidentally, one of the reasons Western teachers have difficulty understanding the papers written by students from the Two-Thirds

World is that the students often use a different logic in writing, especially if they are new to Western education. They tend not to start with a thesis statement, do not highlight main points and offer unclear supporting subpoints which do not lead to a firm conclusion. They are understandably confused when their paper gets a low mark accompanied by comments such as "Couldn't follow your reasoning," "Clarify your point" or "ambiguous conclusion."

One can also see the implications for sharing one's faith. Many Westerners are taught to share their faith in Christ in a Western linear logic that does not fit comfortably into the minds and hearts of people who use different logic. Also, as I said earlier, our witness is one of words whereas much of the world places emphasis on relationship before the words become important.

African Thought Patterns

My experience in sub-Saharan Africa reveals yet a different kind of logic with some similarities to Asia. I have heard hundreds of sermons and speeches of various sorts while living and traveling on that continent. I confess to a wide variety of responses but most not favorable, until I discovered the logic behind the words. Since I was critiquing everything through Western lenses, I judged most sermons inferior (more negative attribution) because they did not follow the linear logic of my homiletics and public speaking classes. In fact, I taught both subjects to my students in South Africa thinking that by straightening them out we might see some "good" pulpit ministry in the future.

After I had done a couple years of damage, I began to decipher the logic of my African brothers and sisters. The metaphor I use to describe their kind of logic is that of a flower—a daisy in particular. One thinks of the many petals surrounding and being attached to the center (see figure 17.2). Let me explain.

In Africa many speakers would begin with a point, which I would

represent as the center of the flower. The point would be the topic or issue that the speaker was going to address. Then, the speaker would use a Bible verse or illustration and, as it were, expand out into one of the petals. Then the speaker would return to the point or topic again. Then the speaker would go off in another direction, into another petal and return again to repeat, now for the second time, the main point or topic. Off the speaker would go into yet another petal soon to reiterate the point once again. By now the Western listener is thinking about how circular the reasoning is (not a positive thing in the West) and how repetitious this was getting. Such thoughts usually precede frustration and tuning out.

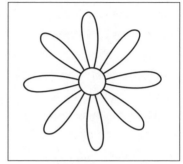

Figure 17.2

Yet there is something amazingly effective about this speaking style. It took me a long time to appreciate it, but once I did, I benefited more from this circular, flower petal style than from many of the linear sermons. For this reason, I much enjoy watching some of the African-American preachers on TV or visiting an African-American church.

A SERMON NOT FORGOTTEN

When I was teaching cross-cultural communications in the Detroit area, we would usually send our participants, all predeparture missionary appointees and usually an all-Caucasian group, to Greater Grace Temple for Sunday worship. Greater Grace was a mostly African American congregation where our group was always warmly received and given unconditional acceptance. On Mondays we would debrief their experience at Greater Grace. One time a person blurted out that it was a waste of time after the first five minutes. He went on to explain that the pastor simply repeated the same point again and again and again—maybe seven to eight times during the forty-minute sermon. I asked him what

the point was. He noted that it was two Scripture verses: "Surely I am with you always" (Matthew 28:20) and "Never will I leave you; / never will I forsake you" (Hebrews 13:5). And then he noted again with frustration in his voice, "I got that point in the first five minutes. He could have moved on, but he just kept going over it."

Nearly five years later this person came back from his assignment overseas and attended one of our furlough programs. Upon seeing me he came charging toward me with a force that bordered on frightening. He demanded, "Do you remember me? I was here almost five years ago." I acknowledged that I did indeed remember. "Do you remember my reaction to Greater Grace Temple?" I said that I did. Then he made a most remarkable comment, "I don't think I have gone more than two to three days during my entire time overseas without thinking about that sermon. I am convinced I would not have lasted if I had not heard it. It was the greatest sermon I have ever heard and certainly the only one that I remember in this way. Don't ever stop sending people to Greater Grace."

The pastor's topic and preaching style—so repetitive, frustrating and seemingly a waste of time for this young missionary—turned out to be the enduring truth that stabilized him for four years in another culture.

HISPANIC THOUGHT PATTERNS

Samovar and Porter summarize the differences between the Western style of negotiating and debate with that of Mexicans and, in a more general way, to Latinos.

> The American is persuaded by expert opinion and supporting hard evidence and uses such in presenting a position in negotiations. Mexicans, however, are less likely to be equally impressed. They generally prefer a *deductive* approach as opposed to the American inclination toward the *inductive*. Like other Latin Americans and other nationalities as well . . . the emphasis is placed on starting with the most general aspects by defining issues, categorizing them, and deciding on the main principle. Once this

is done, then logic follows along to the conclusion with less attention to supporting evidence. Or new evidence may be interpreted in the light of the main principle already determined.

This contrast in approach is sometimes found in UN debate. Americans become irritated with the time taken in argument over which principle applies, to which UN committee an issue falls, or the exact wording of a title to be assigned to a new issue. The Americans want to concentrate on the facts available, to look for cause and effect, and to get on to problem-solving.

Tentatively, Mexican reasoning may also be more complex because it incorporates some of the Spanish tradition of placing more emphasis on contemplation and intuition. . . . Emotion, drama, and feeling play a larger part as contrasted to American considerations of efficiency, scientific method, and practical application of the colder logic and reasoning of the French.[5]

WHAT DOES IT ALL MEAN?

1. People use different types of logic in different parts of the world. We must resist thinking of it as illogical or confusing and try to see how the mind works differently.

2. No form of reasoning is better or worse than another. We might prefer one style but others prefer another. It is to our advantage to learn several styles to be effective in this global village.

3. Listen and analyze the structure behind the words. It has been helpful for me to try to diagram a conversation, sermon or speech—not in my linear way but in the way that seemed to reflect the speaker's mind.

4. Just as there are variations on how people use linear logic in the United States, so there will be variations in other cultures. I hope the pointers in this chapter will give you an ability to suspend judgment until you can understand the local situation.

D I S C U S S I O N   Q U E S T I O N S

1. Have you ever experienced a logic different from what you are accustomed to? Explain, as best you can, what it was like. How did you feel during the experience?

2. Describe how you tend to handle situations that confuse you.

3. What can you do to prepare yourself for encountering different reasoning styles? For example, are there people you can connect with who represent a different culture? Perhaps you could read them parts of this chapter and ask them how they respond.

4. Do the writers of Scripture employ different kinds of logic or reasoning? Do the writings of Paul have a different style than John's, for example? What style seems more prominent in the Old Testament?

18

Achieved Status and Ascribed Status

Life requires a series of adaptations.

GUDYKUNST AND KIM

THIS CHAPTER CONTINUES TO EXPLAIN some of the differences that confuse or frustrate those who transition cultures. In the United States we think of status[1] as something anyone can achieve through diligence and hard work. In many parts of the world, one's status has nothing to do with hard work but with birth order, parentage and even gender. For example, in recent years, and especially with the Afghanistan war, the world has seen how differently women are treated in various parts of the world. For many women in other cultures, status is ascribed at birth, and it will not change outside of some intervention that disrupts the status quo. The caste system is another example. While officially outlawed in India, it maintains a functional grip on the masses. People of low caste (status) find themselves locked into that position while those of high caste protect their high status. How are we to understand this, and how is the Christian to respond to it?

North Americans support equality, having anchored the concept in the U.S. Declaration of Independence. One sees it in employment ads—"an equal opportunity employer"—a more diverse workforce, the growth of sensitivity training seminars and a multitude of efforts to treat people more equally. This appreciation of equality also means that people can move from rags to riches. Anyone can be president of a corporation or a company or, presumably, of the nation. A person of low status can achieve lofty goals and great accomplishments. For example, Jimmy

Carter was a peanut farmer before eventually becoming governor of Georgia and then president of the United States. He did not become the leader of the country because he was part of a monarchy or bloodline—ascribed status—but because he worked hard to get to the top—achieved status.

One U.S. employer was sending company shirts to all his Mexican employees in Mexico. Word came back that the plant manager in Mexico would not accept a shirt that matched the ones received by the other employees. A person of higher status deserved something distinctive, befitting his status. The U.S. employer, wanting to accommodate but still maintain some sense of equality, sent the plant manager a different kind of shirt but one costing the same as the others. A creative solution.

GREETINGS

The American teenager greets the grandparent with a simple "Hi, how ya doin'?" In much of Asia, the teenager will bow deeply when greeting an elder and will not speak until spoken to first. The older the person the more deeply the younger person will bow to show proper respect for the person of age. The teenager uses a special set of terms that convey honor and respect to the elder person. One uses different language for greeting a senior person than for greeting one's peers. The same holds true in conversation. The person's ascribed status, in this case younger person and older person, dictates language and behaviors.

BUSINESS CARDS

In status-ascribed cultures, people are treated differently depending upon their status. Status is determined by age, by rank in a company, by education, family of origin, title (doctor, surgeon, professor), possibly wealth and, as noted above, even by the caste one is born into, as in India. One's respect comes not so much from what you have done but who you are. Thus, business cards may be exchanged early in the meet-

ing of two businesspeople so that those from the status-ascribed culture know how to treat those they are meeting. Western businesspeople often miss the point of exchanging business cards. To receive a business card from another requires a careful read to determine the status of the person followed by signs of respect fitting to the status of the other person. Then the card should be placed in front of you not only to remind you of the status of the other person but as a sign of respect. To glance at another's business card and casually put it in a pocket or wallet would send the wrong signals.

STATUS AND PROTOCOL

People who are considered middle management would not receive the degree of honor that a president or senior vice president might receive. Thus, before doing business with someone in a formal way, one should know the appropriate symbols of respect to be shown for people at various status levels.

U.S. companies often err on this point in their global business interactions. The U.S. company may send lower level, more functional staff to one of their customers or joint-venture partners in another country. They are sent because they are best equipped to discuss the product, technology or financials. But the level of the people sent from the United States is often lower in status than the level of the group sent by the overseas customer or joint-venture partner. The overseas person feels devalued because it is rude and inconsiderate of the other party to require someone to do business with someone of lower status. Thus, negotiations often begin on a sour note usually without the Westerners realizing what has happened. One can argue against status or thinking in status terms, but the fact remains that is the way it is and it is unlikely to change anytime soon.

A similar situation occurred recently when U.S. Christian groups were sending late highschoolers and collegians into Eastern Europe to do training for adults and, in some cases, university professors. For peo-

ple of lower status to be sent to train people of higher status is an affront to their dignity. It did not work out well until changes were made. For this reason, when I did my conferences with several university faculties in Russia, Ukraine and other former Soviet Union countries, I always took Christians who were full professors from major North American universities.

An interesting note on these conferences came in the use of titles. I was never called Dr. Elmer but always Professor Elmer. I found this curious because in the United States, the title "doctor" is considered the highest honor. However, in Eastern Europe, to be called "professor" is the highest honor. Thus, by being paid the highest honor, I was on equal footing with (or of higher status than) others at the conference. This gave my colleagues and me credibility as we spoke.

Christians need to keep the status issue in mind as they conduct their affairs regardless of their vocation. To ignore it is to discredit yourself and jeopardize your purpose in being there. At the same time, one must think about not showing partiality, a matter we will take up later.

In education, the student or recent graduate would be treated very differently than the doctorate holder who teaches at a major university. I have taught at the university level most of my life. One student whose parents came to the United States from South Korea had been my student and teacher's assistant for much of his undergraduate and graduate programs. While I see Daniel (who I discussed in the last chapter) as a friend, he has never been able to address me by my first name even though he is now thirty-four years old and well into his doctoral program. I once asked him why, in spite of my repeated efforts, he could not relate to me on a first name basis. His answer was crisp: "Because in my culture to call someone of your status by their first name would be very disrespectful and I could never do that." That helped me understand. Forcing him to change would be asking him to betray his culture.

Shortly after New Year's day, about four years ago, Daniel walked into my office. I was going to hug him (not appropriate in some cultures)

after not seeing him for over a year, but he said, "Wait." He then proceeded to drop to his knees and bow deeply before me. I was stunned and a little chagrined, not knowing what to make of this display. Daniel immediately explained that around this time every year, younger Koreans would bow to those they most deeply respected. While it was usually reserved for parents, it was appropriate to do it to others. I was deeply honored.

Knowing that often when honor is given, there are ways that honor should be returned. Not knowing the custom, but wanting to respect the tradition, I said to Daniel, "Thank you for that wonderful expression of honor given to me. Is there something I should do in return that would respect this cultural tradition?" In a rather unusual display of frankness, Daniel said, "Yes, you should give me money." Both his bluntness and statement caught me off guard, and I began to laugh and he quickly joined me. Then Daniel explained that it was usually the parents or an uncle who would send a cash gift with the child as he was departing the home to return to job or school. Daniel paid me the same honor as he did his parents because he saw me somewhat as his parent away from home as well as his professor—both positions of high status.

EMBARRASSING QUESTIONS

If you do not have a high position and your status is unknown, you might get questions that relate to your family, your father's vocation or even something about the financial status of your family. In this way, a status-conscious person gets some idea of how to treat you. Most Westerners feel embarrassed at such questions and offended that people are treated differently according to status rather than treating everyone with equal respect. After all, everyone is a human being, worthy of dignity and possessing value. Handling such situations calls for wisdom so one neither violates the scriptural teaching that all people have equal value in the eyes of God nor violates culture in unnecessary ways.

Case Study

A few years ago I was the featured speaker at a Christian conference in a status-conscious country. After my first address, an interpreter ushered me to the door so I could greet the people as they left the room. As the people paraded by, the interpreter quietly gave me the pedigree of everyone he knew. These tidbits of information clued me on how deeply to bow, how many times and the kinds of honorific terms to use. "President of a big company," whispered the interpreter, "student," "professor at prominent university," "wealthy businessman," "pastor," "respected grandfather" and so the labeling went. When the interpreter said nothing, I took that to mean that the person was of low status and would not need the same degree of respect as others of higher status.

This posed a moral dilemma for me. How could I knowingly treat people so differently on this matter of respect when I was taught to respect everyone equally? Some people would take a strong stance and proclaim that they treat all people alike, so they do not need any information about status. Thus, the president and the pupil would be given the same honor. Some Bible texts suggest that this would be the right way to view people and to treat them.[2] Yet other texts seem to call for greater honor to some, such as parents (Exodus 20:12; repeated numerous times throughout Scripture), the aged (Leviticus 19:32: "Rise in the aged, show respect for the elderly") and the humble (Proverbs 22:4), while others are not to receive honor (the fool of Proverbs 26:1). I was also keenly aware of my guest status in their culture. If I trampled their values, I would be disrespectful. Furthermore, I would be seen as an arrogant American trying to tell the world how to conduct their lives. I found myself between a rock and a hard place: trying to uphold biblical values while not being seen as arrogant and paternalistic. So what was I to do?

Here is what I did, though I cannot say it is the right response for everyone. Having traveled and observed Asian cultures, I had some

sense of how to give different degrees of honor. But my preference and conviction was to treat them with equal respect. In fact, if I err in giving honor, I err on giving more to those who receive little from their society. Jesus' treatment of the poor and marginalized seemed to support this.

Even though I bowed more deeply to some than others, I tried to give each the respect and honor each deserved as human beings (1 Peter 2:17). Thus, those of high status got what they were expecting, and those of lower status got more than what they were expecting (perhaps Paul's idea in 1 Corinthians 12:23 and Romans 12:10). My attempt was to treat everyone with respect but in ways that did not crudely tear at the fabric of the culture.

My approach was modeled after that of Don Douglas, who told me a similar story many years ago. While living overseas he was invited to a large social event. Being a foreigner, he was given the status of a dignitary. The high-status people milled around the center of the room with their drinks and finger food while those of low status squatted at the perimeter of the room. None of the dignitaries would even acknowledge any of the squatters. Don's discomfort with this pushed him to ponder how he might build trust with the low-status people while not breaking trust with the high-status people. He refused to ignore the squatters as though they were invisible or unworthy. Yet to give them undue attention would certainly alienate him from those who invited him and whose relationship he wished to maintain. Several times during the evening he would slip away from the crowd to greet one or two of the squatters that he knew. After acknowledging them, which they appreciated immensely, he would slip back into the crowd. Later he would repeat this excursion into the squatter world. The plan was not complicated, but it did take intentional thought and in so doing, he managed to honor his values and theirs. He also maintained trust with both groups.

LOSS OF STATUS

In one of my overseas stints, I was the president of a Bible school. Work-

ing late on a Friday, I noticed the grass had not been cut. The church used our buildings on Sunday, and I was feeling a bit ashamed to have them come to a ragged-looking place. Everyone else had gone home, so I got out the lawn mower and cut the grass myself in my shirt and tie. The school was located on the border between a largely Indian community and another that was mostly mulatto or colored (mixed race). Being late in the afternoon, hundreds of people saw me laboring away. I must confess, I felt rather positive about the fact that I was modeling out humility before all these observing people. Surely my esteem would go up as this example of someone who did not consider himself above the menial.

The following Monday morning the students came to me confessing that they had forgotten their job and wondering how the grass got cut. I proudly announced that I did it, hoping that they too, would see my humility. Noticing the glances of consternation they exchanged among themselves, I asked if anything was wrong. One of the senior students politely and gingerly announced that I had lost status before the entire community. "How can that be?" I fired back. "They saw you cutting the grass and believed that you had lost all authority in the school. You were not able to get any students to do it or any of your faculty or even your secretary." Furthermore, the school also lost credibility (remember collectivism?), because who can respect a place where everything is in chaos? After the shock wore off, I resolved to restore my status in the community and that of the school. For the next several months, I stood outside looking regal and authoritative while the students did their work.

In a different incident, a man was carrying a propane tank from the store to his house. The fact that he did not get his servant, spouse or older child to do it communicated to those around he had lost his authority in the house and could get no one else to do even the small things. From that point on the local merchants negotiated with the wife, who obviously had the status and power in the house. The husband had lost status.

MAKING A STATEMENT

I have tried to honor women in cultures where they possess little or no status, often being treated as low status servants of the males. By asking them about their children, extending courtesies, praising them for the wonderful meal they have prepared, thanking them for the gracious hospitality and warmth of their home, I hope to say to all watching, "They are people made in the image of God and worthy of respect and honor as much as anyone else." Does the message always get through? I am not sure, but that is not entirely my concern. My concern is to make some kind of statement that disturbs the status quo but without coming across as the ugly American who thinks his way is superior to every other way.

Keep in mind that if you insist on imposing your cultural values and even your biblical values on the rest of the world in way that others perceive as crude or harsh, you will not get a hearing for the gospel. As I noted earlier, the message of the cross is offensive, but that does not give us the right to be offensive! Respect among people is an important value to me. Furthermore, I believe it to be a biblical value based on the fact that God has endowed every human being with dignity, loves everyone, does not show partiality and exhorts us not to do so either. Attempting to live out that truth may mean expressing it differently depending on the culture we are in. One size (one way) may not fit all.

I do not believe I have the right to wantonly ignore the values that have been practiced for hundreds if not thousands of years—that would be rude, disrespectful and constitute a lose-lose situation. Rather, find a way, if possible, where you can uphold the cultural values while bringing your own biblical values to bear on the situation in a sensitive way—a win-win situation. Keep in mind that if you associate with the poor and oppressed, you are making a public statement that you, a high-status person, are identifying with low-status people. I wonder, is this what Jesus was doing when he identified himself with sinful humanity? with the outcasts? with women?

F O R   R E F L E C T I O N

Respond to each point in the following ascribed status/achieved status continuum.

Achieved status   **Ascribed status**

1	2	3	4	5	6	7	8	9	10

1. Put an X indicating where you fall on the status achieved versus status ascribed continuum.

2. Put a P indicating where you think your parents are.

3. Put a C for whether your church is more status achieved or status ascribed in its orientation.

4. Use any further symbols that are meaningful to you: S for spouse; F for friends, B for boss.

5. Use NC (new culture) to indicate where you think the people of the new culture will be on the continuum. How much distance is there between X (you) and NC?

D I S C U S S I O N   Q U E S T I O N S

---

1. Did you agree with the author on how he handled the moral dilemmas? Would you do anything differently?

2. Do you think of achieved status and ascribed status in terms of right/wrong? What difficulties could this cause you in your new culture if this is practiced?

3. Read James 2:1-13. How does this influence your thinking about status?

4. Read Matthew 20:25-28 (note context) and Matthew 23:1-12. What insights from these passages help us think about our own conduct in relationships?

5. If you differ with the new culture on status, how should you deal with it so that you stay true to Scripture and still show proper respect to the people? How do you determine your rights to try to change things in a new culture? Or, do we have any right to try to change things? Does Jesus' life provide any guidelines?

Guilt and Shame

Effective interaction means giving of yourself—trying to see the world of others and respect their life ways. It means not forcing your ways on them. Yet, at the same time, it means being true to yourself and your ways. To be really effective, interaction must be a two-way street or, of course, it is not interaction at all. That is, all interacting individuals should be doing so from a basis of awareness, understanding, and knowledge.

CLARENCE C. CHAFFEE

MOST NORTH AMERICANS ARE FAMILIAR WITH GUILT. Often we associate it with our conscience telling us we have done something wrong. Many cultures think more in terms of shame. While the lines between guilt and shame are not easily or strictly drawn, it might be helpful to make some distinctions to sensitize us and help us adjust our behaviors. Because we can inadvertently injure a relationship, this chapter will alert us to a danger many overlook.

GUILT AND SHAME CULTURES

In my attempt to clarify and simplify, I run a danger of becoming simplistic and losing accuracy. Guilt and shame are two of the more difficult concepts to explain without getting mired in unnecessary detail. Many experts, though not all, find it helpful to think of societies as either guilt based or shame based. I am going to share their insights, blend them with my own and hopefully help us use this important information for

building and sustaining strong relationships with people who are different from us.

John Condon and Fathi Yousef state that in shame cultures "pressures to conform to the norms of the society are explicit and exerted
from without, while in guilt cultures, there is an internalized sense of
'wrong' so that one who feels guilty punishes himself."[1] Similarly, David
Augsburger says:

> In a culture shaped predominantly by shame controls, the expectations,
> sanctions, and restraints of the significant others in a person's world be-
> come the agents of behavior control. The shame incorporates the basic
> anxiety and shapes the guilt through the promises of acceptance or threats
> of rejection. . . .
>
>   In a culture controlled predominantly by guilt, controls are expected to
> be internal, within the conscience. The guilt is focused on the violation of
> specific prescribed behavior and the anxiety and shame tend to be re-
> pressed or denied and the energies redirected.[2]

Augsburger quotes Pitamber in supplying an example: "In a shame-
culture, approval of 'parents' is more important than the actual performance of a deed."[3] There is a curious side to this:

> Shame is not aroused in a person if he [she] feels that his [her] acts have
> been approved by those considered significant. When a person performs
> any act in the interest of the community, he [she] is not concerned about
> the wrongness or rightness of the acts, but only with the approval of the
> self. . . . If a shame-prone person commits violence which is considered
> valid (in the community of significant people) then such a person has no
> reason to feel shame.[4]

By way of summary, it is important to note that shame and guilt
are complex concepts. It appears that some societies are more dominated by shame where external forces such as people and circumstances exert more influence on one's thinking, believing and
behaving. Other cultures are more dominated by guilt where internal

forces exert a more dominant influence on one's thinking, believing and behaving. Both shame and guilt are present in every society, according to the experts, but it is a matter of knowing which tends to be emphasized.

GUILT

Generally speaking, Western—individualistic—societies are more guilt based while Two-Thirds World—collectivistic—societies tend to be more shame based. In a guilt-based society, people feel guilty for what they have done. An act, perhaps a lie or a violation of some rule, triggers the conscience that a wrong has been committed. In this society, people are careful to separate the bad act from the person. So the person might be punished for the bad act, but there is assurance that the person is not bad.

A guilt-based society responds to the external laws of the land, rules of the institution, morals of the church and code of the home. It is hoped that these become internalized in the person. It is further hoped that when the individual is tempted to break a rule or actually does, that it will trigger the conscience, causing a sense of guilt and prompt the individual to stop. Just as one is driven to avoid certain behaviors by an internal mechanism, like the conscience, so one is also driven to achieve, not so much to please others, but to fulfill an inner drive to accomplish a goal. Certainly, one wants to honor one's family and country, but these are usually not the strongest driving forces.

SHAME

In shame-based societies, the critical factor is not to bring shame upon oneself, upon one's family, one's tribe or even one's country. One strives to succeed, driven by the desire to uphold family, school, company or national honor. Living up to the expectations of one's significant others tends to be the dominant value even to the point where morality, ethics and right/wrong are defined by one's dominant

group, or in-group. One feels shame when disappointing important others or not living up to expectations of family, supervisor or company. Thus, motivation comes more from the people who surround you at different points in life and in different situations. Failure is defined in terms of one's inability to meet the standards or expectations of important others.

For example, Asian students may go to special classes on Saturdays for several years in order to gain entrance into the most desired university. If successful, the entire family is honored (that is, not shamed). If not, the entire family is dishonored. In extreme cases students have been known to commit suicide to restore family honor.

In an attempt to control littering in Malaysia, a fine of $400 (U.S.) would be levied to any offender caught. In addition, the culprit would be forced to sweep the streets in a T-shirt with the words "I am a litterbug" printed on it. The government minister, Ting Chew Peh, said he "hoped public shaming would deter others."[5]

GUILT, SHAME AND THE BIBLE

Does the Bible speak to shame and guilt? Actually, the occurrences of shame are considerably more than those of guilt. However, the Western church has emphasized the guilt more because it fits most comfortably into our cultural values. The apostle Paul uses guilt (Romans 3:19) when speaking to the Romans, a Western guilt-based society, but switches to shame (Romans 9:33; 10:11) when he addresses the Jewish Christians in Rome. The writer of the book of Hebrews uses shame, not guilt, as the forceful thought that hopefully would keep the believers committed to following Christ (Hebrews 2:11; 11:16; 12:2).

SHAME, FACE AND HONOR

Shame, face and *honor* are powerful words in much of the Two-Thirds World, though not talked about much in North America. We can make some serious mistakes if we do not understand these concepts and their

significant role in many societies. Though the three words differ slightly in meaning, I will treat them as essentially the same. Thus, maintaining one's honor in Japan and much of Latin America is not very different from "saving face" in Thailand and much of Africa or "not causing another to feel shame" in the Philippines.

The Thai word for losing face means, literally, "to tear someone's face off so they appear ugly before their friends and community." The word among the Shona in Zimbabwe means, literally, "to stomp your feet on my name" or "to wipe your feet on my name." In many societies (the Middle East, for example) the dirtiest part of the person is the bottom of the shoe. Thus, the act of wiping your shoes on someone's name is a grievous offense and humiliation. It is a direct attack on them and their character. In the Middle East, taking one's shoe off and waving the sole at someone is the worst insult. For this reason, in most Arab countries, one does not sit in such a way as to expose the bottom of one's shoe/sandal to another person. It shows serious disrespect.

Western concepts that carry similar impact include disgrace, severe public humiliation or intense embarrassment. There are two important differences, however. In the Two-Thirds World, nothing worse could happen to you. To cause someone else shame strains, if not breaks, the relationship. Not so in the Western mind. The difference is partially explained by the fact that many of the Two-Thirds World people think holistically—they do not differentiate between criticism of an idea and criticism of a person. To criticize my thought is to criticize me and that causes me shame or loss of face. The Westerner will often put the criticism of an idea in one category and separate that from the category of self or criticism of self. Thus, criticism of an idea is not taken personally or not taken as personally.

The other difference is that in the Two-Thirds World if you cause someone else shame, you also shame the entire family or school or office or nation depending upon the status of the person and their net-

work of relationships. This is not as true for the Western mind. Again, one sees the influence of holistic thinking. What happens to one happens to all or, at least, affects all. This is not foreign to Scripture. (See 1 Corinthians 12, especially verse 26.) What may be worse is causing shame without even knowing it. The reason? Westerners are not sensitive to these issues because they are not a part of the fabric of the other culture. So we must learn about them and, hopefully, avoid the mistakes.

CAUSES OF SHAME

In my book *Cross-Cultural Conflict* I write:

> Shame, loss of face and dishonor may occur in a variety of ways. One may dishonor oneself by not living up to certain goals. For example, the Japanese student who was denied entry into the preferred university; the businessperson who does not get the contract; the leader who makes a serious mistake. Or, one might be shamed by the actions of a family member. In Arab society, especially Muslim, to become a Christian is to shame the family and the Islamic religion. The shamed family tries to restore honor and face by excommunicating the Christian convert and treating the person as though she/he were dead or never existed. If the family wishes to restore itself from extreme shame, it may physically punish the departed member, sometimes threatening or even taking the person's life.[6]

What follows are some ways in which we may unintentionally cause people to lose face or feel shame. I then provide an alternative response that is less likely to cause shame.

Blame. Stating or implying the other person is to blame for something. Rather, hold your tongue and be known for your wise silence. Westerners tend to separate the person from the act—we have categories for each—but most cultures believe that blame from someone is an attack on their person. For example, a Westerner might say, "Don't take this personally but . . . " People from the Two-Thirds World usually can

take it only one way: personally. They think holistically and do not separate themselves from their acts or words.

Shortcomings. Pointing out a shortcoming, especially if anyone else is present. Rather, don't point out shortcomings or failures at all. If you must, do it in private with statements about how much you value the relationship and want to preserve it.

Error. Suggesting they have made an error whether it be in thinking, speaking, logic, grammar, behavior and so on. Rather, let these things go. We do not need to correct everything; we are building relationships not giving a test.

Requests. Asking of them something that would be difficult, costly or impossible to do. Rather, make indirect requests —"It would be nice if . . ." or "Someday I would like to . . ." or "I have heard that . . ." They can respond to such requests if they can, but not cause you to lose face if they disappoint you.

Comparisons. Comparing how things are done in your country versus this country, especially if you think your country is better. Rather, don't compare. If people ask you to compare, praise their country for its strengths (and there will be many if you look) and be modest about the strengths of your own country. Criticism of one's own country is generally not well received so go easy on that.

Refusals. Saying no to a request they make of you. Rather, say, "I would like to help you out, but right now I do not think I can. If things change, I will let you know."

Remember, you are a guest in their culture.

COMMUNICATING CHRIST

As you go about your activities with the hope that some will become followers of Christ, you are, by implication, suggesting that their traditional beliefs are not as good, but defective or even misleading. This causes them to feel loss of face, dishonor and shame. You have pointed out something that is wrong with their life, and they have a response that is

very natural in their culture. The extended family may then get involved because if one member is thinking about changing to become a follower of Christ, they would all feel the shame and loss of face. Any place of honor they had in the community would be gone and everyone would see them as failures.[7] Thus, they rally to protect their "family face" and "family honor" by trying to persuade the person not to leave the family religious tradition to become a follower of Christ.

The convicting work of the Holy Spirit often overcomes the family pressures, but not always. However, sometimes we present the gospel in a way that is offensive to the listeners in their cultural context. Because of their sensitivity to shame, loss of face and dishonor, they may hear our cultural insensitivity and not the message. So how can we communicate the love of Christ so that they hear with open ears and not feel the negative impact?

First, share your testimony including the sin that separated you from God. In this way, you put yourself in position of shame by not being pleasing to God. Second, rather than saying to the others that they too are sinners, try using collective language: God says we are all sinners— our sin has caused God shame—everyone stands in need of a Savior. Third, explain that just as Adam and Eve caused God to feel shame when they sinned, so all of us have caused God shame by not obeying his commands and refusing the gift of his son, Jesus. Fourth, the ultimate shame is in putting one's trust in the wrong place. God promises that if we put our trust in Jesus, we "will never be put to shame" (Romans 10:11; note verses 9, 10; see also Romans 9:30-33 and 1 Peter 2:6). Fifth, God has wonderfully taken care of our shame. Jesus bore our shame on the cross (Hebrews 12:2) so that he may call us brothers, family (Hebrews 2:11).

Remember that we want to share Jesus in a way that will be heard by their mind and heart, not in a way that seems foreign, even confusing. Following are some other cultural differences that may confuse us unless we get some advance insight.

LEARNING MORE FROM EUNICE

I would like to return to the story of Eunice (pp. 58-65), because there is more to the story. Eunice spoke some English, but her heart, mind and actions reflected Zulu values. Let's analyze this story further from the perspective of shame. Notice that I implied that Eunice had done something wrong, which caused her to feel shame. I did not intend to, but Eunice understood it like most people of the world would. In her discomfort she still answered calmly. To save face, or avoid shame, she insisted that the "dish fell from her hand and is dead." It was her way of saying clearly that it was an accident—a statement of truth from her cultural perspective.

Eunice came from an animistic culture. In animism, outside forces control nearly everything, so one does not take personal responsibility for something that lies outside of one's control or so the belief goes. Thus, the use of the passive and stative voices simply acknowledges that other forces are active, including evil spirits and good spirits.

One last point: notice my expectation. Since Eunice spoke English, I expected her to respond in keeping with my cultural heritage. When she didn't, I placed blame rather than seeking understanding. In my confusion I made some negative judgments; I blamed Eunice for my confusion. Beneath the negative judgments (see lower track on the cultural adjustment map, p. 72), "I was wishing Eunice would be more Western, more like me, so I would not be forced outside of my comfort zone. If I could change her, I could avoid the awkwardness of changing myself."[8] In other words, I wanted to retain my squareness. While hoping to make her more square, I was resisting becoming more round, like Eunice.

I revisited this incident to demonstrate that a number of factors are often at work in explaining a particular situation. It is not important that you try to analyze everything from all angles. It is important that you are aware of how easy it is to cause someone to lose face, feel shame or be dishonored and that you avoid such activity.

DIFFERENCES AND HUMAN NATURE

Differences are not the problem when working cross-culturally. The way these differences are expressed is the problem. For example, everyone values and uses time. However, the confusion arises when some cultures demonstrate their use of time differently. Everyone wants and deserves respect (status), but some cultures display it differently. If you show me respect in a way I am not accustomed to or not expecting, I will consider you disrespectful. The misunderstanding comes not from the value itself but in how it is demonstrated in day-to-day living. Thus, we must try to separate the value from its expression. Our ability to do this will help us respond in culturally appropriate ways rather than simply react out of our cultural frame of reference.

It is important, therefore, to realize that as human beings we often desire the same thing, but fail to realize it. We focus on the way a value is lived rather than on the value itself. Seeing the value unites us in our humanity. Seeing only the difference in expression moves us toward divisiveness.

FOR   REFLECTION

Respond to each point on the following guilt/shame continuum.

Guilt	1	2	3	4	5	6	7	8	9	10	Shame

1. Put an X indicating where you fall on the guilt versus shame continuum.
2. Put a P indicating where you think your parents are.
3. Put a C for whether your church is more guilt or shame oriented.
4. Use any further symbols that are meaningful to you: S for spouse; F for friends, B for boss.
5. Use NC (new culture) to indicate where you think the people of the

new culture will be on the continuum. How much distance is there between X (you) and NC?

D I S C U S S I O N   Q U E S T I O N S

1. Do you respond more out of an internalized guilt feeling or more out of how other people are going to see you and think about you?

2. As you think of your present relationships, do you have difficulties with people who are different from you on this matter? How difficult will it be for you to adjust?

3. Does the guilt-shame difference raise any questions for you?

4. How were your concepts of guilt and shame shaped by your family and upbringing?

20

Worship Expression: From Low to High

You worship God with your head.
We worship God with our whole being.

ZIMBABWEAN PASTOR

THIS CHAPTER ATTEMPTS TO DESCRIBE the differences we find in worship. The past fifteen years or more have found many congregations in the United States either moving from traditional worship styles to contemporary or adding a contemporary worship service to the traditional one. This transition has caused considerable stress as people have tried to look at it from a theological and a cultural perspective.

DIFFERENCES IN WORSHIP STYLES

While we use the word *contemporary*[1] in the United States, other groups stateside and around the world have utilized contemporary forms of worship for decades if not centuries. If you enjoy a very traditional form of worship, you may be confronted with a very contemporary form in your cross-cultural journey. Or you may worship best in a contemporary style, but find yourself in a deeply traditional worship style, as I was recently in Haiti. In either case, I am hoping this chapter will help clarify these two expressions of worship as different, allowing you to accept that which is not part of your tradition. In fact, I hope you will be able to appreciate and affirm that which is not like you but is acceptable to the Lord.

Considerable controversy surrounds the way people worship. Everyone has a preference and tends to believe that their way is the best way to worship God. Quickly deciding that one form is right and the other wrong should be avoided. We might rather say, "It is the best way *for me* to worship God." Not everyone approaches God the same way. We do it in a way that allows us to most meaningfully express our adoration and devotion.

CONTEMPORARY WORSHIP

Many churches in North America have struggled with the issue of a contemporary worship service. Contemporary worship usually means the music is more modern or contemporary. It may mean the addition of drama. Often it includes a more relaxed form of dress and seems to appeal to the younger generations. There are other differences too. In much of the contemporary worship there is a higher level of participation among the worshipers. For example, one often sees hands being held up, stretched out or slowly waving during the singing. Some express their whole being freely in worship with hand clapping, body swaying and other body movements. Responding verbally to the speaker, standing while most sit and even individual dancing in the aisle are acceptable worship expressions in many churches.

Emotions are evident in the form of joyful smiles, celebration, singing with feeling and volume, tears, hugging, faces pointing upward with eyes closed and other signs of deep feelings of worship to God. Frequent shouts of "praise the Lord," "hallelujah," "amen" and other verbal encouragements usually show that people are actively engaged in the event—high expression, high participation. The pastor may use considerable voice range, volume, physical movement across the platform and forms of drama in preaching the Word. People sitting behind the pastor and choir members may alternatively stand and sit depending on the point the pastor is making and the emotional response they want to make. Sometimes people may twirl their bodies or dance, not unlike

King David in the Old Testament (2 Samuel 6:14; Psalm 149:3).

Because one does not put a time limit on God or how he moves on people in worship, services may go longer than an hour. In some parts of the world they may last three hours or more. Time, being on schedule or keeping things moving are quite irrelevant in this style of worship. Concern is for the quality of worship, meeting with God, feeling his presence and expressing one's being in worship to him.

THE ISSUE

At the end of each chapter on differences we may encounter in another culture, I have placed a continuum from 1-10. That continuum suggests one may place oneself anywhere between 1 and 10. Keep in mind that I am suggesting there is a range between high and low expression in worship. Many people and churches have chosen the degree of expression they are comfortable with in worship, while others are still undecided. Often people choose or reject a church depending upon how it fits their own preference. Of the expressions I have noted above, you may practice few or many. That is not the issue. The issue is to know where you place yourself on the continuum and how you respond to others who place themselves at a different point on the continuum. Since these are differences, we can accept those who place themselves at different points along the continuum rather than stand in judgment of them.

TRADITIONAL WORSHIP

In traditional worship, at least among the Caucasian traditions I am familiar with, the worship participants express limited participation. That is, they stand/sit, sing/remain silent, read responsively/remain silent. Sometimes there may be testimonies, but for the most part the worshipers have limited participation in worship.

People preferring worship with less expression usually appreciate more planning, direction, uniformity, order and schedule. Services usually start and finish at specified times. Advance planning has gone into

the service, and the plan is given to each attendee in the form of a church bulletin. The pastor and song leader direct the service telling people when they are to sing, stand, greet others and sit. Congregational activity beyond that which is directed by a leader is generally infrequent and discouraged. A rather solemn but dignified mood characterizes the service. During the sermon people remain quite motionless and voiceless in recognition that the Word is being preached and one must be attentive. Any response is a response of the mind and heart and kept within oneself. This group would cite 1 Corinthians 14:40, "But everything should be done in a fitting and orderly way," believing this text supports this style of worship.

Both Legitimate

I want to be careful I do not imply that one group worships God better or more effectively or that one group is more pleasing to God in their worship. That is not the case at all. What I am saying is that people can worship differently while still being genuine, meaningful and pleasing to God. Ultimately, worship is the soul reaching out to God in praise and adoration. You may do that differently than I do, but God, who sees the heart, may be equally pleased.

Responses to Worship Changes

Some churches have split believing any change violates some biblical mandate. I always grieve when the body of Christ splinters. Others have gone to two services with one being traditional and one contemporary. This keeps the body together but often separates families and generations. The third option is some form of mixed worship combining both traditional and contemporary. Even though I am from the older generation, I prefer a mixed style of worship because I enjoy being around the emerging generations. We have opportunity to learn from each other and grow together. We need each other. Something important is lost if we do not struggle together to discern what God is saying and doing.

WHAT TIME DOES GOD COME TO CHURCH?

Before we look at worship in the Two-Thirds World, I want to illustrate how culture has formed aspects of North American worship. Only a short time ago, virtually everyone arrived for church at 11:00 Sunday morning. Why? Most of us did not know why this particular time was so sacred. Some churches that dared to have a 9:00 morning service were severely criticized. A few who had Saturday evening worship were considered scandalous. What made 11:00 Sunday morning the sacred, biblical time, so to speak? Quite simply, it was the earliest time that the farmers could get to church in the early days when most people were farmers. Every morning the cows had to be milked and chores done followed by bathing and getting the horses hitched for the trip to church. The time was a matter of convenience, not a biblical principle. The biblical principle was to worship, but the time was flexible. Would it also be fair to say that the biblical principle is worship, and the style should be flexible? It all depends on one's culture and preference? I am inclined to think so though I know not everyone agrees with me.

MISSIONS AND WORSHIP

As missionaries took the story of Jesus into other cultures, they took their worship styles with them. Churches around the world reflect those styles today. However, sometimes worship styles were established that did not reflect the preferences of the local culture. Missionaries who believed their own preferences were the most biblical, instituted those in the local culture. Today we are realizing that worship style is not a matter of right and wrong but a matter of difference, of preference. In many places, styles are changing. In Latin America, those churches which adopted the more traditional worship styles are changing to fit the natural expression of Latino life. The greatest church growth in Latin America is among the churches where there is high expression in worship.

Yet in Haiti, where my wife and I just returned from a seminar with

medical workers, it is mixed. Our host, a medical doctor, was preaching in one of the largest evangelical churches the Sunday we were there. It was very traditional with organ music and hymns. We talked about it afterward, and our host said that he and many others simply could not worship in a more contemporary way. It was too close to the voodoo experiences of his childhood. But I couldn't help wondering if his children, who did not experience the voodoo activities, will continue to appreciate the traditional worship.

Harare, the capital city of Zimbabwe, had a church planted by missionaries in a strategic location. The church struggled but saw little success until the missionaries went home on leave and then it died. For a couple years the padlocks were on the doors until a Bible school graduate caught a vision for that location. He opened the church, cleaned it up and started services. When we visited, it was one of the prospering churches in the country.

What made the difference? I had visited the church during both eras. In my opinion the difference can be explained simply: the missionaries were less expressive, and that became the style of worship. The new Zimbabwean pastor was more expressive, as was the culture, and developed a style of worship that embraced cultural forms. Let me explain by telling you about the last service I attended.

While my wife and I arrived on time, about 35 to 40 percent of the congregation did not. Yet, the music began only a few minutes late. The music was lively with seven song leaders in the front, but they did not start any of the songs. They arose spontaneously from different audience members. As someone began a song we all chimed in as did the finger drummer on our right, the guitarist in the front row, somebody with tambourines behind us and a bass drummer off to the left. These scattered instrumentalists blended in and quickly set the pace while the song leaders sang, clapped, dipped at the knees and swayed to the beat.

As the latecomers arrived and found a place, people smiled, reached out to touch them and verbally welcomed them all while the congrega-

tional singing continued. The musical celebration inspired joy in everyone; some responded with their own dance to God while others stretched their arms out to God and others just sang with eyes closed. The evidence suggested that each was meeting God and God was meeting with them.

About ninety minutes later, after two sermons from two people, attendees began a line and marched outside where each person out the door greeted each who had gone before. All the while people were singing and clapping hands. My guess is that we sang that chorus about thirty times and my hands were beginning to feel numb. No one else seemed to notice. Eventually we were all outside, had greeted everyone else and formed a circle, holding hands. The pastor led us in closing prayer as the heavy pedestrian traffic walked by and took note.

The two-hour service was over, but no one was in a hurry to leave. Visitors were swamped with greetings and good wishes. Everyone was talking, laughing, praying and encouraging. It was a wonderful worship experience and people wanted to linger in its significance. The church that was dead for two years had been resurrected to bear witness to God's grace in a culturally appropriate way.

A CLOSING THOUGHT

Worship styles around the world are as varied as they are in North America. But with each year, the trend seems to be more and more toward the more expressive style of worship described above. Most cultures of the world are more expressive in their cultural celebrations, and they are bringing those elements into the church in a way that makes worship more meaningful to them. Yes, there are dangers. But there are dangers of worshiping God in traditional style, especially if it is stilted and mechanical.

Most of us have a preferred style of worship. In earlier years, the traditional style of worship in North America was based largely on cultural preference. That style, however, was taken around the world and established as *the* way to worship God. It still dominates in some sectors of

North American culture today. Possibly, some of you have rejected, or at least had difficulty with, the worship style of your parents or the church you have attended. If you are younger, my guess is that you prefer a more contemporary style. If you are older, the contemporary style may not be so meaningful for you, and you may have a little more discomfort in some countries where the worship style is quite expressive.

I am hopeful that as a result of reading this, we will be less judgmental about other worship styles. In fact, I hope that we may be more open to it, bless those who prefer it and never let it disturb our unity. After all, we worship the same God through Christ and by the power of the Holy Spirit. I hope that if the worship style is different in the new culture you will sense the presence of God anyway and be able to join the others in ascribing worth to our heavenly Father.

FINAL NOTE

This chapter, as with the others in this section on cultural differences, is intended to get you launched in a new culture with some pegs to hang your experiences on. These pegs are a way of naming your experience so you have a way of understanding a situation rather than falling into confusion, which often brings a judgmental attitude. As you spend time in a culture, you will discover more specifics than I could ever begin to name in this book. But, it is my hope that these chapters on cultural differences will be a good starting point as you navigate the new culture.

FOR REFLECTION

Respond to each point on the following lower/higher expression in worship continuum.

Lower expression in worship					Higher expression in worship				
1	2	3	4	5	6	7	8	9	10

1. Put an X indicating where you fall on the continuum.

2. Put a P indicating where you think your parents are.

3. Put a C for whether your church is lower or higher in its expression in worship.

4. Use any further symbols that are meaningful to you: S for spouse; F for friends, B for boss.

5. Use NC (new culture) to indicate where you think the people of the new culture will be on the continuum. How much distance is there between X (you) and NC?

DISCUSSION QUESTIONS

---

1. Describe the ways in which your worship service is lower or higher in expression.

2. If you could, how would you change your worship experience?

3. Is it difficult for you to enjoy worship different from your preferences? Explain.

4. What are the dangers of extremes in lower expression worship and higher expression worship?

RETURNING
HOME

21
Re-Entry:
You Are Never the Same

The Lord will watch over your coming and going
[your entry and re-entry]
both now and forever.

Psalm 121:8

Psalm 121 has been called the pilgrim's song. The people of Israel sang it as they ascended to Jerusalem to celebrate feasts and holy days. Christian pilgrims through the centuries have echoed its words as they have gone throughout the world talking about the Jesus of Scripture. As we think about being a sojourner, let's remember that the Lord himself is watching over us in our cross-cultural entries and re-entries.

SQUARE HEADS RETURNING FROM ROUND CULTURE

Remember the square heads and round heads (see p. 66)? Once you leave square culture and live for awhile in round culture, you tend to change; you become less and less square and more and more round. Of course you do not lose all your squareness, but you do change to fit the culture you have been living in. Because cultural immersion is a high impact experience, even people who have been gone only a week often claim significant change. These changes usually create a little disturbance when you get back with your friends and relatives. They have not changed because they have not had your experience.

REVERSE CULTURE SHOCK

It seems strange to think that re-entering your home culture would cause culture shock, but it does. And, sometimes it is worse than the culture shock you experience when you enter that new culture. The reason? When you leave your home culture for a new one, you expect things to be different. When you leave the foreign culture to return to your home culture, you expect things to be the same. In one case you are expecting the shock of differences but in the other situation you are expecting that everything will be just as you left it. This seems to be true for international students as well, who, after extended study in the West, find it difficult to fit in again in their home culture.

There are several reasons why you may experience reverse culture shock. Change is the underlying factor beneath the reasons.

You. You have changed. You are not the same person who left for an assignment in another culture. Your contact with other worldviews, life styles and values has left its mark on you. People remember you as you were before you left. They don't know how to relate to the new you. In some ways you may seem like a stranger to them. When one woman returned from Pakistan after living in a place where water was severely rationed, she was aghast at how extravagant we are in water usage and waste. Another person, returning from Beirut, Lebanon, where food was so scarce during the war years, could not enjoy Thanksgiving because it was "too much food." You will change.

Home culture. Your home culture has changed. Life in North America changes quickly. New TV shows, slang, styles, technology, business practices and medical breakthroughs emerge quickly, and you were left behind.

Family and friends. Your family, friends and colleagues have changed. Life has not been standing still for the people that were part of your life before. When you left they filled the vacancy with other people and activities. Plus, their lives were impacted by weddings, births, ill-

nesses, deaths, graduations, job changes and geographical moves. The people you left are not the same either. Everyone has changed, and change means readjustment.

The re-entry and readjustment into home culture may or may not be traumatic depending upon how long you were gone and how deeply you identified with the host culture—how much squareness you lost and how much roundness you took on. Let's look at some issues you might experience depending upon your time away and the amount of change that occurred.

RE-ENTRY ISSUES

I am going to look at the re-entry issues from four different time frames according to the amount of time you have been away. I am assuming that you have made sincere efforts to learn some/much of the local language and build meaningful relationships with the people of the host culture. I am also assuming that you have had a largely positive experience with the people of the round culture.

Short-term stay. If your time in another culture has been short, say one week to a month, you might expect the following:

1. People will ask you about your trip and politely listen for about three to five minutes and then want to move on to a topic they are more interested in.

2. You or the group may be given ten minutes to share during a church service.

3. You will have had some major things impact your mind and heart, and they will be hard to put into words, especially in a few minutes.

4. You will see your square culture in a new way. Its materialism, self-absorption, lack of world awareness, insensitivity to social issues such as poverty and perhaps shallow spirituality are largely unseen, though now you see them. You feel people should not overlook these matters that have recently become important to you.

5. You find mild disappointment in your home culture, but in a couple weeks the busyness of life consumes you and many of your feelings and thoughts become submerged in being square again.

Medium-term stay. If your time in another culture has been longer, say two to six months, then the following might be true when you return to your home culture:

1. You will probably have learned some of the local language and built deeper relationships. The changes will have been deeper, more significant and some you have resolved to incorporate into your life because you think it will be a qualitative improvement. In fact, you think it would be beneficial if everyone in square culture would do the same.

2. You experience the first five points mentioned in the short-term stay, but with two differences. First, you are able to verbalize more clearly what has happened to you. Second, when people's interest in your experiences is brief, you get more frustrated, even a bit angry. *They don't get it, and they don't care that they don't get it* goes through your head.

3. You find others who have had experiences like yours and spend your time with them. They understand you and actually help you process your cross-cultural experience.

Long-term stay. People who spend six to twenty-four months in another culture generally find the following true when returning to their home culture:

1. Life has been reshaped in significant ways. You had begun to feel and talk about life as the local people did using more and more of the local language. While the home culture does not seem strange, it has changed—actually you have changed—and you realize that fitting back in will not be quick nor easy. Life has gone on in square culture,

and you have been left behind.

2. You realize how much of your squareness has left you, and you are quite comfortable with the roundness you have taken on. You find the relationships in the new culture were more meaningful than those you have returned to in square culture. You find yourself with some longing to return to round culture.

3. While disappointed that others do not want to hear your story in more detail, you realize that they have no context for understanding what happened to you. Their view of the world comes through the newspapers and the evening world news. They operate with a very basic world awareness limited to thirty-second news bytes. They expect you can condense your story in the same way. But, you realize such brevity only promotes stereotypes and yet, you are usually given no choice. Accept it since nothing negative is usually intended. Yet, you will do well to find someone who listens and debriefs your experiences. Telling your story brings a clarity and settledness to your time in the other culture.

4. You would love to instruct your organization (business, church, corporation) that sent you and help them understand how they could change for the better if they would only listen. Generally they are pleased for the positive impact on your life but are content to let it remain only your experience.

Very long term. People who spend more than two years in another culture generally find the following true when returning to home culture:

1. You will discover that most of what has been said above is true for you.

2. Additionally, you are neither square nor round, but some combination. More accurately, you are partially square and partially round, but it is hard to know which is which. You do not fully belong in

either culture. The experts call you a bicultural person. It helps to have a name for what you are but it does little to explain what it means. Most missionary kids are bicultural.

3. You struggle to determine if you have returned home (to square culture) or whether you have left home (round culture). The longer you have been in round culture, the more it will feel like you have left home, and coming into square culture will seem like a foreign experience.

4. You can fit back into square culture, but only partially and with some reluctance. You are surprised at how round you have become, especially mentally and emotionally. Much of your conversation goes back to life in round culture, the place of comfort where you had learned the rules and knew how to play the game of life rather effectively. Now the rules have changed, and you must start over again, or so it feels.

5. Criticism of square culture comes easy even though it was once your comfortable home culture. You really don't fit in square culture anymore. You don't like the way things have changed while you have been gone, and adjustment is hard. You spend a lot of time figuring out how things are done now on the job, in church, in school, in the community, everywhere. You have been left in the dust, so to speak, and that brings confusion, discomfort and criticism.

6. Even though you have lots of acquaintances that you maintained while in round culture, you have no close friends. Your close friends have filled their lives with other relationships as soon as you left. Furthermore, you build close friends when you share common ground, and you have little common ground with the square people.

DEALING WITH REVERSE CULTURE SHOCK

The longer you have been in round culture and the more round you have become, the more you are likely to experience reverse culture shock. I

prefer to think of it as a good problem. It is good because you have incorporated some wonderful new insights and values into your life. You are a much richer person now. But, the problem part remains. You must deal with re-entering your home (square) culture, and that will take some intentional effort. Consider the following insights on re-entry and things you can do to readjust.

Euphoria. This is your first response to being home. That first feeling has caused many to kiss the ground when they first step on North American soil again. The joyous reunion with acquaintances and celebrations make this a grand experience.

So what do you do? Enjoy your celebrity status but realize it is momentary.

Disappointment. You are likely to feel disappointed for reasons noted above and also because most people have a short attention span when it comes to listening to you tell your story. They may even interrupt you to turn the conversation back to their life experiences, which may seem quite boring compared to what you experienced. The pictures you show them are whisked through without any desire for explanation except for the occasional exotic one that captures their attention.

So what do you do?

• Build realistic expectations.

• Know that many people will simply want the five-minute version and go with that.

• Show only a select fifteen to twenty photographs with one-sentence explanations. Give more detail only when asked.

• Look for one or two people that will listen longer, ask questions and meaningfully enter into the world of your cross-cultural experience. This will probably be your mother or a friend or relative who has traveled extensively and knows how valuable it is to have someone listen.

• Be patient with the others. They have no way of even beginning to understand what you experienced and how you have changed. They have probably lived their whole lives in square culture and have nothing

with which to compare your sojourn in another culture.

• Periodically insert bits of insights and changes as relationships continue. Let people know you see things a little differently than before. This does not make you superior but a little different.

• Resist being overbearing in talking about all that happened to you. This will make you appear superior and, perhaps, arrogant.

Negative emotions. Frustration, anger and sometimes depression are emotions people frequently experience during the re-entry process. These reactions can have a variety of sources:

• not being heard

• sensing people do not care

• getting back into a fast pace without time to "decompress," to come to terms with what the cross-cultural experience means

• meeting other people's expectations as though nothing has changed

• having to perform as though you are up-to-date on everything

• a general sense that coming home was not what you were expecting

So what do you do?

• Give yourself some space, more than you think you might need. You can always accelerate, but it is usually hard to slow down once you have re-entered the fast pace of life. You were probably not expecting to change so much when you left and thought the readjustment process would be quick and smooth.

• Tell a few trusted people that you need time with them just to listen to you. They might be people at work, in the family or friends. Tell them this would be a special ministry they can have toward you. Or, in the case of a non-Christian, say that this would be a special favor they could do for you.

• Some people find journaling a good way to deal with stressful emotions. Writing about your thoughts and emotions can be very therapeutic.

• Avoid self-pity. You are richer for having had the experience in the new culture. You are the blessed one, not the victim. It is quite normal

for those who have not had a similar experience not to fully appreciate what has happened to you. Accept it. Don't get angry because they can't enter into something they have never experienced except possibly on a cruise ship or one-week tour of all Europe.

Move on. After some space to process your experiences in round culture and now in square culture, resolve to get into the flow of life. Choose to set aside any negative emotions and move on.

So what do you do?

• Identify the most significant ways you have changed and what those will mean in your job, church, home and community. Keep these in mind as you re-enter life in square culture.

• Take it one day at a time. There's no need to be embarrassed if you lack some knowledge. Simply say, "I was out of the country when that happened. Can you brief me?" Most people will be happy to help you and not think less of you. Some people suggest you watch a little more TV than you normally might to catch up on slang and the things people are talking about. However, you don't have to violate your values in what you watch.

• When your cross-cultural experience can contribute to the conversation, let it happen. That is part of who you are now. But watch for signals that you might be overdoing it. No one likes a show-off.

• If you struggle with some negative emotions, look for the good things in the people and the culture. It is akin to counting your blessings.

• Get involved in causes, in square or round culture, that extend compassion to those less fortunate. This will keep alive some of the sensitivities and changes God worked in you while in round culture.

A GIFT FROM GOD

Your experience in another culture was a gift from God to you. Hopefully, you were also God's gift to the people in round culture. Be thankful for what God has done in you. Use the growth from that gift to benefit others. It would be a shame to waste the good that has been accomplished when God intended to bear more fruit through your experience.

DISCUSSION QUESTIONS

1. How can you prepare ahead of time for re-entry into your home culture? How can you stay connected while away?

2. How do you think a cross-cultural experience will change you?

3. What creative ways can you use to tell people about your experience?

4. What difference might/will your time in another culture make in how you live your life?

Epilogue

CRITICAL TO SUCCESS IN ANOTHER CULTURE are the right attitudes and the right skills applied in a timely manner. If one expects to think and act in another culture the way one did in one's home culture, it would be best to stay home. The rules of life are different in other cultures and you have to be ready to learn and play by the rules of the local people. To ignore them would be, at best, naïvely uninformed or, at worst, arrogantly rude. In either case, such behavior would contribute to perpetuating the ugly American image.

In my opinion, most of us do not set out to be ugly Americans as we enter another culture. We simply do what comes naturally to us, not realizing how we may be tearing the fabric of the local culture and inadvertently stomping on local values. So most of our problem grows out of being naïve and well motivated but uninformed . . . like the monkey. Fortunately, we have a choice. We can avoid being the monkey, and we can change the image of the ugly American.

Why is this important? Any action or attitude that makes us look like the ugly American also reflects on our Christianity. Most of us entering another culture desire to represent Christ in our presence there. Let's make every effort to prepare well for our time in that other culture so that they may see the beauty of Jesus in us and be drawn to a relationship with him. I know of no greater motivation to prepare diligently and well for that wonderful opportunity to live among people that God loves in another part of the world.

"The Lord will watch over your coming and going both now and forever" (Psalm 121:8).

Appendix

REFLECTING ON YOUR CROSS-CULTURAL EXPERIENCE

This appendix is intended to be read after you complete your venture into that new culture. Reflecting on what has happened is beneficial for a number of reasons. First, it helps us summarize our experience and what it means. We look back and see the pieces as well as the whole and ask what impact it had on us. Second, reflection allows us to review what happened and ask if we could have done something different. Third, reflection helps us consolidate what we have learned. We usually experience considerable positive growth from our cross-cultural experience. Yet, we may lose that benefit if we do not intentionally think about it and own it.

Jesus wanted to know what his disciples had learned from their excursion into ministry (Luke 10:1-20). He listened to their rehearsal of some of the marvelous things that happened and then responded in a way that might adjust some errant perspectives to make sure that they learned what he had intended.

GENERAL REFLECTIONS

Please respond to the following questions. They are designed to help you pull your reflections together and give words to your memories.

1. What things stand out as you look back? Think of people, events, situations and so on.

2. What was the best part of the journey and why?

3. What was the most important thing you believe you accomplished?

4. What did you learn about
• God?

• missions?

• cross-cultural ministry?

• people in the new culture?

• people from your own culture?

PERSONAL REFLECTIONS

1. In what ways did you change? Which change was most significant?

2. What did you learn about yourself?

3. What would you do differently if you had the chance to do it over again?

4. What advice would you give someone who would like to do what you have done?

Notes

Chapter 1: Monkeys, Mission and Us
[1]Ann Templeton Brownlee, I am told, has originated the story of the monkey and the fish. However, I have not seen it nor was I able to locate the source. The version in the text is my own, and the degree this story overlaps with that of Ms. Brownlee's is unknown.

Chapter 2: Your Part of God's Story
[1]"2001 World Population Data Sheet," Population Reference Bureau 2001 <www.prb.org>.
[2]David B. Barrett, and Todd M. Johnson, "Status of Global Mission, 2001, in Context of 20th and 21st Centuries," *International Bulletin of Missionary Research* (January 2001): 25.

Chapter 4: Culture Is Everywhere, and It Sneaks Up on You
[1]L. Robert Kohls, *Survival Kit for Overseas Living,* 2nd ed. (Yarmouth, Maine: Intercultural Press, 1984), pp. 47-50.

Chapter 5: Culture Shocks
[1]Paul Hiebert, *Anthropological Insights for Missionaries* (Grand Rapids, Mich.: Baker, 1985), p. 66.
[2]Kalervo Oberg, "Culture Shock: Adjustment to New Cultural Environments," *Practical Anthropology* 7, no. 4 (1967): 177.
[3]Dwight Gradin, story told frequently during programs in language acquisition techniques, Missionary Internship, Farmington, Michigan.
[4]Analogy often used by Dr. Muriel Elmer in various teaching situations. Short-termers usually have people on site who structure their living situation, transport them around and define the day's activities so the relationship issues are minimal and not addressed.
[5]Statement often made by Dwight Gradin when teaching language learners to persevere in learning difficult language sounds.
[6]Cindy Shabaz, conversation with author, Holland, Michigan, October 2001.

Chapter 6: Identifying Expectations
[1]Eunice's story is told in my book *Cross-Cultural Conflict: Building Relationships for Effective Ministry* (Downers Grove, Ill.: InterVarsity Press, 1993), pp. 52-56.
[2]I know we talked about suspending judgment earlier. Yet it is so critical at different points in our cultural transition, I would rather risk overstating than have it considered unimportant and forgotten.

Chapter 7: Square Heads and Round Heads
[1]Dwight Gradin, "Square Heads, Round Heads" (Farmington, Mich.: Missionary Internship, 1973). He has freely shared the diagram in his class presentations as public domain.
[2]Cindy Shabaz, e-mail conversation with author, January 2002.
[3]Wayne Shabaz, conversation with the author, Holland, Michigan, October 26, 2001.

Chapter 8: Cultural Adjustment Map

[1]Faculty of Missionary Internship, "The Cultural Adjustment Map," Farmington, Mich.: Missionary Internship, 1975. This classroom presentation is freely shared with anyone who wants to use it as public domain. I was on that faculty at the time and have made modifications to the design.

[2]I am adopting Paul Hiebert's definition of "Two-Thirds World" as broadly encompassing Asia, Africa and Latin America. Some people use the term "Third World," but that has negative connotations, and I prefer the demographic definition of "Two-Thirds." See Paul G. Hiebert, *Anthropological Insights for Missionaries* (Grand Rapids, Mich.: Baker, 1985), p. 9.

Chapter 11: Trust: How to Build Strong Relationships

[1]The concept of a prior question of trust belongs to Marvin K. Mayers, *Christianity Confronts Culture* (Grand Rapids, Mich.: Zondervan, 1974).

Chapter 13: Time and Event

[1]Sherwood G. Lingenfelter and Marvin K. Mayers, *Ministering Cross-Culturally* (Grand Rapids, Mich.: Baker, 1986), pp. 37-51.

[2]Edward T. Hall, *The Dance of Life: The Other Dimension of Time* (New York: Anchor, 1983), pp. 44-57. See also Fred E. Jandt, *Intercultural Communication,* 3rd ed. (Thousand Oaks, Calif.: Sage, 2001), p. 270.

[3]I am indebted to insights from *Ministering Cross-Culturally* by Sherwood G. Lingenfelter and Marvin K. Mayers for much of chapters ten through eighteen.

Chapter 14: Task and Relationship

[1]Wayne Shabaz, conversation with author, Holland, Michigan, October 26, 2001.

[2]James Kelly, "East Meets Reagan," *Time,* April 30, 1984, p. 24.

[3]Ibid., p. 25.

[4]Wayne Shabaz, conversation with author, Holland, Michigan, September 3, 2001.

Chapter 15: Individualism and Collectivism

[1]Robert N. Bellah, Richard Madsen, William M. Sullivan and Steven M. Tipton, *Habits of the Heart* (Davis, Calif.: University of California Press, 1996), p. 142.

[2]Ibid., p. 143.

[3]I first heard Dr. Woodberry's story about Islamic collectivism at an Amoco workshop in Houston, Texas, April 1977.

Chapter 16: Categorical and Holistic Thinking

[1]Which of the following two statements comes closest to your own view? "Sports are sports and politics are politics," suggesting they should not be mixed; or "Sports are politics and politics are sports," suggesting they cannot be separated. Your answer indicates whether you lean more toward the dichotomistic side of the continuum or more toward the holistic side.

[2]J. Dudley Woodberry, phone conversation with author, January 2002.

[3]Source unknown.

Chapter 17: Logic: Straight or Curved
[1]Many people credit Robert Kaplan ("Cultural Thought Patterns in Inter-Cultural Education" in *Language Learning* 16 [1966]: 2) as the one who developed the idea of spiral logic or spiral reasoning.
[2]R. Okabe, "Cultural Assumptions of East and West: Japan and the United States," in *Intercultural Communication Theory,* ed. William Gudykunst (Beverly Hills, Calif.: Sage, 1983), pp. 29-30.
[3]William B. Gudykunst and Young Yun Kim. *Communicating with Strangers: An Approach to Intercultural Communication.* (Menlo Park, Calif.: Addison-Wesley, 1984), p. 42.
[4]Quoted from Myron W. Lustig and Jolene Koester, *Intercultural Competence: Interpersonal Communication Across Cultures* (New York: HarperCollins, 1993), pp. 219-20. Lustig and Koester are summarizing the ideas of Satoshi Ishii, "Thought Patterns as Modes of Rhetoric: The United States and Japan," *Intercultural Communication: A Reader,* ed. Larry A. Samovar and Richard E. Porter, 4th ed. (Belmont, Calif.: Wadsworth, 1985), pp. 97-102.
[5]Samovar and Porter; *Intercultural Communication,* p. 199.

Chapter 18: Achieved Status and Ascribed Status
[1]Geert Hofstede has developed a similar idea called "power distance." It is well researched and worth reading if you want to pursue the topic of status more thoroughly. See his *Cultures and Organizations* (London: McGraw-Hill, 1991).
[2]See Leviticus 19:15; Deuteronomy 1:17; Proverbs 24:23; Acts 10:34-35; Romans 2:11; Ephesians 6:9; and James 2:1-11.

Chapter 19: Guilt and Shame
[1]John C. Condon, and Fathi Yousef, *An Introduction to Intercultural Communication* (New York: Bobbs-Merrill, 1975), p. 116.
[2]As quoted in David W. Augsburger, *Pastoral Counseling Across Cultures* (Philadelphia: Westminster Press, 1986), p. 123.
[3]Dayanand Pitamber, "Psychosocial Enquiry into the Phenomenon of Physical Violence Against Harijans," unpublished paper, Bangalore, India, 1982. Quoted in David W. Augsburger, *Pastoral Counseling Across Cultures* (Philadelphia: Westminster Press, 1986), p. 129.
[4]Ibid., p. 130.
[5]*USA Today,* August 6, 1997, p. A4.
[6]Duane H. Elmer, *Cross-Cultural Conflict: Building Relationships for Effective Ministry* (Downers Grove, Ill.: InterVarsity Press, 1993), p. 55.
[7]Remember the chapter on collectivism and individualism? In collectivism, when one member decides to make a life decision, it affects everyone, and everyone not only takes it seriously but wants to be included in the decision-making process.
[8]Elmer, *Cross-Cultural Conflict,* p. 53.

Chapter 20: Worship Expression: From Low to High
[1]I do not prefer the words *contemporary* and *traditional,* but since they are commonly used, I have chosen to stay with the common usage.

Selected Bibliography

"2001 World Population Data Sheet." Population Reference Bureau 2001 <www.prb.org>.

Augsburger, David W. *Pastoral Counseling Across Cultures*. Philadelphia: Westminster Press, 1986.

Barrett, David B., and Todd M. Johnson. "Status of Global Mission 2001 in Context of 20th and 21st Centuries." *International Bulletin of Missionary Research*, January, 2001.

Bellah, Robert N., Richard Madsen, William T. Sullivan and Steven M. Tipton. *Habits of the Heart*. Davis, Calif.: University of California Press, 1996.

Chaffee, Clarence C. *Problems in Effective Intercultural Interaction*. Columbus, Ohio: Battelle Memorial Institute, 1971.

Chandler, Paul-Gordon. *God's Global Mosaic: What We Can Learn from Christians Around the World*. Downers Grove, Ill.: InterVarsity Press, 2000.

Condon, John C., and Fathi Yousef. *An Introduction to Intercultural Communication*. New York: Bobbs-Merrill, 1975.

Dalton, Maxine, Christopher T. Ernst, Jennifer J. Deal and Jean B. Leslie. *Success for the New Global Manager: How to Work Across Distances, Countries and Cultures*. San Francisco: Jossey-Bass, 2002.

Depree, Gladis. *The Spring Wind*. New York: Harper & Row, 1970.

Depree, Gordon, and Gladis Depree. *Faces of God*. New York: Harper & Row, 1974.

Dodd, Carley H. *Dynamics of Intercultural Communication*. 5th ed. Boston: McGraw Hill, 1998.

Elmer, Duane H. *Cross-Cultural Conflict: Building Relationships for Effective Ministry*. Downers Grove, Ill.: InterVarsity Press, 1993.

Elmer, Duane H., and Lois McKinney, eds. *With an Eye on the Future: Church and Development in the Twenty-First Century*. Monrovia, Calif.: MARC Publishers, 1996.

Fowler, Sandra M., and Monica G. Mumford, eds. *Intercultural Sourcebook:*

Cross-Cultural Training Methods. Volumes 1 and 2. Yarmouth, Maine: Intercultural, 1995.

Grunlan, Stephen A., and Marvin K. Mayers. *Cultural Anthropology.* Grand Rapids, Mich.: Zondervan, 1979.

Gudykunst, William B. *Bridging Differences: Effective Intergroup Communication.* 2nd ed. Thousand Oaks, Calif.: Sage, 1994.

Gudykunst, William B., ed. *Intercultural Communication Theory.* Thousand Oaks, Calif.: Sage, 1983.

Gudykunst, William B., and Young Yun Kim. *Communicating with Strangers.* Menlo Park, Calif.: Addison-Wesley, 1984.

Hall, Edward T. *Beyond Culture.* New York: Doubleday, 1976.

————. *The Dance of Life: The Other Dimension of Time.* New York: Doubleday, 1983.

————. *The Silent Language.* New York: Doubleday, 1959.

Hesselgrave, David J. *Communicating Christ Cross-Culturally: An Introduction to Missionary Communication.* Grand Rapids, Mich.: Zondervan, 1978.

Hiebert, Paul. *Anthropological Insights for Missionaries.* Grand Rapids, Mich.: Baker, 1985.

Hofstede, Geert. *Cultures and Organizations.* London: McGraw-Hill, 1991.

Jandt, Fred E. *Intercultural Communication.* 3rd ed. Thousand Oaks, Calif.: Sage, 2001.

Kealey, Daniel J. *Cross-Cultural Effectiveness: A Study of Canadian Technical Advisors Overseas.* Hull, Canada: Canadian International Briefing Agency, 1990.

Kelly, James. "East Meets Reagan." *Time,* April 30, 1984. p. 24.

Kohls, L. Robert. *Survival Kit for Overseas Living: For Americans Planning to Live and Work Abroad.* 2nd ed. Yarmouth, Maine: Intercultural Press, 1984.

Kohls, L. Robert, and Herbert L. Brussow. *Training Know-How for Cross Cultural and Diversity Trainers.* Duncanville, Tex.: Adult Learning Systems, 1995.

Kohls, L. Robert, and John M. Knight. *Developing Intercultural Awareness: A Cross-Cultural Training Handbook.* 2nd ed. Yarmouth, Maine: Intercultural Press, 1994.

Lanier, Sarah A. *Foreign to Familiar.* Hagerstown, Md.: McDougal, 2000.

Lingenfelter, Sherwood. *Agents of Transformation: A Guide for Effective Cross-Cultural Ministry.* Grand Rapids, Mich.: Baker, 1996.

Lingenfelter, Sherwood G., and Marvin K. Mayers. *Ministering Cross-Culturally: An Incarnational Model for Personal Relationships.* Grand Rapids, Mich.: Baker, 1996.

Mayers, Marvin K. *Christianity Confronts Culture.* Grand Rapids, Mich.: Zondervan, 1974.

Oberg, Kalevero. "Culture Shock: Adjustment to New Cultural Environments." *Practical Anthropology* 7, no. 4 (1967): 177.

Plueddemann, Jim, and Carol Plueddemann. *Witness to All the World: God's Heart for the Nations.* Wheaton, Ill.: Harold Shaw, 1996.

Seelye, H. Ned, ed. *Experiential Activities for Intercultural Learning.* Volume 1. Yarmouth, Maine: Intercultural Press, 1996.

Shabaz, Wayne, and Cindy Shabaz. The Corporate Genome CDawnLearning. <www.cdawnlearning.com >.

St. Kilda, Martin. *Near the Far Bamboo.* Camp Hill, Penn.: Christian Publications, 1993.

Stafford, Tim. *The Friendship Gap: Reaching Out Across Cultures.* Downers Grove, Ill.: InterVarsity Press, 1984.

Stewart, Edward C., and Milton J. Bennett. *American Cultural Patterns: A Cross-Cultural Perspective.* Yarmouth, Maine: Intercultural Press, 1991.

Storti, Craig. *The Art of Coming Home.* Yarmouth, Maine: Intercultural Press, 1997.

―――. *The Art of Crossing Cultures.* Yarmouth, Maine: Intercultural Press, 1995.

―――. *Cross-Cultural Dialogues: 74 Brief Encounters with Cultural Difference.* Yarmouth, Maine: Intercultural Press, 1994.

Triandis, Harry C. *Individualism and Collectivism.* San Francisco: Westview, 1995.

Trompenaars, Fons, and Charles Hampden-Turner. *Riding the Waves of Culture: Understanding Cultural Diversity in Global Business.* 2nd ed. New York: McGraw-Hill, 1998.

Ward, Ted. *Living Overseas: A Book of Preparations.* New York: Free Press, 1984.

Weeks, William H., Paul B. Pedersen and Richard W. Brislin, eds. *A Manual of Structured Experiences for Cross-Cultural Learning.* Yarmouth, Maine: Intercultural Press, 1986.

CPSIA information can be obtained
at www.ICGtesting.com
Printed in the USA
LVHW051224190219
608010LV00017B/318